Contemporary China

Contemporary States and Societies Series

This series provides lively and accessible introductions to key countries and regions of the world, conceived and designed to meet the needs of today's students. The authors are all experts with specialist knowledge of the country or region concerned and have been chosen also for their ability to communicate clearly to a non-specialist readership. Each text has been specially commissioned for the series and is structured according to a common format.

Published

Contemporary India
Katharine Adeney and Andrew Wyatt

Contemporary Russia (3rd edition)
Edwin Bacon

Contemporary China (2nd edition)
Kerry Brown

Contemporary South Africa (2nd edition)
Anthony Butler

Contemporary France
Helen Drake

Contemporary America (4th edition)
Russell Duncan and Joseph Goddard

Contemporary Japan (3rd edition)
Duncan McCargo

Contemporary Britain (3rd edition)
John McCormick

Contemporary Latin America (3rd edition)
Ronaldo Munck

Contemporary Ireland
Eoin O'Malley

Forthcoming

Contemporary Spain
Paul Kennedy

Contemporary Asia
John McKay

Also planned

Contemporary Africa
Contemporary Europe
Contemporary Germany

Contemporary States and Societies
Series Standing Order ISBN 978–0–333–75402–3 hardcover
Series Standing Order ISBN 978–0–333–80319–6 paperback
(*outside North America only*)

You can receive future titles in this series as they are published by placing a standing order. Please contact your bookseller or, in the case of difficulty, write to us at the address below with your name and address, the title of the series and one of the ISBNs quoted above.

Customer Services Department, Macmillan Distribution Ltd, Houndmills, Basingstoke, Hampshire, RG21 6XS, UK.

Contemporary China

Second Edition

Kerry Brown

First edition 2013
Second edition 2015

Published by
PALGRAVE

Palgrave in the UK is an imprint of Macmillan Publishers Limited, registered in England, company number 785998, of 4 Crinan Street, London, N1 9XW.

Palgrave Macmillan in the US is a division of St Martin's Press LLC, 175 Fifth Avenue, New York, NY 10010.

Palgrave is the global imprint of the above companies and is represented throughout the world.

Palgrave® and Macmillan® are registered trademarks in the United States, the United Kingdom, Europe and other countries.

ISBN 978–1–137–51010–5 hardback
ISBN 978–1–137–51009–9 paperback

This book is printed on paper suitable for recycling and made from fully managed and sustained forest sources. Logging, pulping and manufacturing processes are expected to conform to the environmental regulations of the country of origin.

A catalogue record for this book is available from the British Library.

A catalog record for this book is available from the Library of Congress.

Typeset by Cambrian Typesetters, Camberley, Surrey, England, UK.

Printed and bound in the United States of America

To my mother, Jacqueline Howe

Contents

List of Illustrative Material

Map

Illustrations

Figures

Tables

Boxes

List of Abbreviations

CCP	Chinese Communist Party
CCTV	Chinese Central Television
CDIC	Central Discipline and Inspection Commission
CIC	Chinese Investment Corporation
CMC	Central Military Commission
CNOOC	China National Overseas Oil Corporation
CPPCC	Chinese People's Political Consultative Conference
DPP	Democratic Progressive Party
DRC	Development Research Council
DPRK	Democratic People's Republic of Korea
EEC	European Economic Community
EU	European Union
FOCAC	Forum on China Africa Cooperation
IMF	International Monetary Fund
IPR	Intellectual Property Rights
NDRC	National Development and Reform Commission
NPC	National People's Congress
OECD	Organisation for Economic Co-operation and Development
PLA	People's Liberation Army
PRC	People's Republic of China
SARS	Severe Acute Respiratory Syndrome
SASEC	State-owned Assets Supervision and Administration Commission
SEZ	Special Economic Zones
SOE	State Owned Enterprises
WTO	World Trade Organization

Acknowledgements

I would like to express my thanks in this new edition for the help of Steven Kennedy, before his retirement from Palgrave, for his help in initiating and providing feedback on the first drafts, and I also thank Stephen Wenham for taking up the baton on Steven's retirement. I am also grateful to Keith Povey for his editorial help.

KERRY BROWN

The author and publishers would like to thank the following who have kindly given permission for the use of copyright material: David Goodman for photographs used in Illustrations 1.1, 1.2, 1.4, 2.1, 5.1, 6.1, 7.1 and C.1; and Gail Tverberg for Figure 5.3.

China's Provinces and Major Cities

Brief Facts about China

Official name:	People's Republic of China
Capital:	Beijing
Area:	9,598,088 sq km
Population:	1,339,700,000 (2010)
Official Language:	Mandarin Chinese
Political System:	One-Party Republic
Head of State:	President Xi Jinping (since March 2013)
Ruling Party:	Chinese Communist Party (CCP)
Party Leader:	Xi Jinping (since 2012)
CCP Political Standing Committee Members:	Xi Jinping, Li Keqiang, Zhang Gaoili, Yu Zhenghsheng, Zhang Dejiang, Wang Qishan, Liu Yunshan
Hong Kong SAR	
Capital:	Victoria Area: 1,092 sq km
Population:	7,061,200 (2010)
Status:	Special Administrative Region (SAR) of People's Republic of China (since 1 July 1997)
Chief Executive:	Leung Chun-Ying (since June 2012)
Administrative Secretary:	Carrie Lam (since June 2012)
Taiwan	
Capital:	Taipei Area: 35,980 sq km
Population:	23,061,689 (Sept 2011, Taiwan government figures)
Official Language:	Chinese
Political System:	Multiparty Republic
Head of State and Government:	President Ma Ying-jeou (KMT) (since May 2008)
Ruling Party:	Kuomintang (KMT)
Premier:	Mao Chi-kuo (KMT) (since November 2014)

Preface to the Second Edition

In contemporary China it has almost become a truism that nothing stays the same for even a few months, let along the three years since the first edition of this book appeared. Over that time, the new leaders I covered briefly in the original edition have settled into their positions and become more dominant than many expected. The era of the former leaders, under Hi Jintao, seems more remote by the day. An extensive anti-corruption campaign has exposed some of the most important figures of the previous leadership and the networks around them. Underlying all of this, however, is a country that, having produced amazing growth levels for much of the last three decades, is now acclimatizing itself to an era of more modest growth. For a political leadership that has consistently staked so much on its economic prowess being the key to its right to govern, this is significant, and frames much of the discussion of not just China's economy but also its internal political dynamics and the way in which it engages with the rest of the world.

The context in which to read this book (which has been substantially revised and updated from the first edition) is to bear in mind, as the introduction and first two chapters endeavour to show, that China is both an *old* and a *new* country – culturally very ancient but politically only existing in its current form since 1949. This mixture of callowness and wisdom comes across in much of its artistic, political and economic discourses. For many of the citizens of the People's Republic in the second decade of the twenty-first century, no matter what personal opinions they hold about their government, culture or the environment, there is a great deal of evidence of a general pride in what China has achieved in its great project of modernization (particularly since 1978, when reforms began in earnest). But even the fact that the country remains mostly unified and relatively stable is also a source of pride, and put to good use in government and party-state propaganda.

This book attempts to take many of these emotions and aspirations of Chinese people seriously, and to describe the country of dazzling statistics and overwhelming numbers on a more human scale, through some of the experiences and words of those who currently live, work and think about China within its borders. This is a bold enterprise. Getting to really know what the thoughts and dreams of Chinese people are has proved a tough task – even for the country's leaders. So at many times in this book, particularly at a transition point like this where it is clear the government is trying to take China in a new direction, it is good to refer directly to the experiences of Chinese people themselves and what they say about the events that are happening in their own country.

This is a book primarily intended for those with no previous experience of China, though I hope it can be also read with profit by others who have more knowledge. I have assumed no *prior* knowledge and have explained whatever specialist terms or vocabulary occur in the text the first time they appear. There are suggestions for selected reading at the end for those who wish to pursue particular issues in more depth.

KERRY BROWN

Introduction: Why Does China Matter?

If for no other reason, the People's Republic of China (PRC), founded in 1949, is special because of its size, both geographically (the world's third-largest country) and in terms of its population (currently the most populous). This vastness, married to its long and complex history and internal diversity, means that it is hard to come up with a single, all-embracing framework within which to see the country. As this book will seek to show, there are many different aspects of modern China (from here on, 'China' will be used as a shorthand term for the People's Republic of China, while Hong Kong will refer to the Hong Kong Special Administrative Region of the People's Republic, and Taiwan to the Republic of China on Taiwan island), and many ways of viewing the country. Often, the greatest challenge is to forget preconceptions and try to look hard at what the country actually is in itself. There are many ways, as I shall argue later, in which it resembles a continent more than a country, with all the diversity and complexity that involves, and this has become especially so in an era in which its 31 provinces and autonomous regions have economies that often equate in size to those of major European economies.

In terms of raw statistics, China matters simply because of where it ranks. It has become the world's second-largest economy in the three decades since 1978, and the largest importer and exporter. As of 2014, it holds almost US$4.5 trillion in foreign reserves, the largest in the world – money that has accrued through its exports to the outside world. It has pushed itself up the tables of most economic indicators. But it is also a country of stark contrasts, with over 150 dollar billionaires in 2014, but 150 million people living on less than US$2 a day – the World Bank standard of poverty – and as many as 24 million who are malnourished (Yang, 2012).

China is also different because of its political model. The modern country was founded, and is still run, by one of the world's last surviving Communist parties enjoying a monopoly on power. This makes dealing with China a highly politicized issue. Often, people's comments about the country are analysed in terms of what they reveal about whether the writer or speaker supports or opposes the ruling Chinese Communist

Party (CCP). Attempts at neutrality are difficult. Historically, at least in Europe and the USA, being friendly towards China in the years of its relative isolation between 1949 and 1972 were taken as indicative of one's own political position. Only those with relatively benign views of the country's political elite and its systems were able to visit the country. For the rest of the world, it was a place of mystery and isolation.

The politicization of China as a subject may have continued, but the inaccessibility of the country has long gone. In 2013, more than 97 million Chinese people travelled abroad, and about the same number of foreign tourists entered the PRC. From the time of the Great Financial Crisis of 2008, Chinese tourists became the largest credit card users on London's Oxford Street (Osborne, 2011) and amongst the highest spending in other European capitals. There have been over a million and a half Chinese overseas students since the reforms began in 1978, with many staying on in the West to pursue academic or business careers. China became the world's largest market for cars from 2008, about the same time as it became the world's largest polluter. In 2014, a grim statistic proved that it emitted more per capita than the EU. In the auction houses of London, modern and classical art from the PRC is fetching record prices. But Chinese consumers are also leaving their mark on the art world, with one Qing Dynasty vase worth millions of pounds being bought (controversially, by a businessman from the PRC who subsequently failed to pay the auction house for his purchase) in 2011. From 2013, Chinese went to Australia and bought up so much vintage wine that special ships had to be chartered to export it to customers in China. And Australia was uniquely able to withstand the recessions which inflicted other major developed economies because of the continuing hunger from 2008 for its resources by Chinese manufacturers and companies.

In the early 1980s, the average Chinese person lived in a world where foreign travel was a remote dream, and while income levels were reasonably equal (everyone was relatively poor), the most that people dreamed of was to own their own bicycle, their own radio, to have a fridge, and perhaps have access to a television. By the 1990s, they were dreaming of videos, freezers and a holiday within China, but by 2014, the Chinese were among the world's biggest users of Bentley cars, and the world's largest Louis Vuitton shop had opened in the sometimes smoggy city of Taiyuan in Shanxi province, servicing the new wealthy who had made untold fortunes from the plentiful coal found there. Chinese were buying real estate in London, Paris, Sydney and New York, and Chinese investors putting their hard-earned money into brands like Weetabix or Volvo, seeking better returns than at home.

The China that confronts observers now puzzles because it fits no easy narrative. It is the result of long, complex historical forces and influences, some of which will be discussed in this book, and many of which were contradictory, from adherence to Buddhism imported via the Tibetan plateau in the seventh century to Marxism which came probably via Japan in the early twentieth century. The China that presents itself to us today is actually more like an amalgam of diverse influences and forces, a composite which has emerged from these, forged over many centuries and in many different ways.

Because of this complex history and its continuing influence on the identity of China and its people today, understanding its past to illuminate its present and plot where it might go in the future are important. From 1949 to 1978, in particular, it experienced a specific version of Marxism in which the figure of Mao Zedong (1893–1976) came to dominate the life of the nation. Mass campaigns were waged in waves from 1952 onwards, to achieve utopian goals, and bring about a perfect socialist society. But the ideals of the leaders were to end all too often in tragedy. China's economy did grow during this period. The Maoist era saw a rise in its gross domestic product (GDP) – the sum of all goods and services produced in an economy – of 5–6 per cent a year. Life expectancy increased dramatically. The PRC was a healthier, wealthier place by the time of Mao's death in 1976. It had also started to reconnect with a world which it had been at odds with for much of the post-1949 period –. China's struggle with modernity has been epic, profoundly painful and often carried a high price. This battle goes on to this day.

As this book will show, perhaps the most important date in modern Chinese history after 1949 was not 1978, but the moment in 1969 when, after a scuffle with the Union of Soviet Socialist Republics (USSR) that led to hundreds of casualties on the country's northern border, the Chinese leadership around Mao was forced to rethink their nation's global position. This process confirmed their view that the USSR, ostensibly their Communist political ally, was in fact their greatest threat, not the capitalist USA. It was the re-engagement between China and the USA, culminating in the historic visit by President Nixon to the PRC in 1972, that marked a fundamental shift, the consequences of which can still be felt to this day. Not least of the results of this visit was the ways in which it made the opening up and reform process of seven years later possible. This marked the rise of pragmatic politics in China – a pragmatism that still dominates the country despite the rhetorical commitment to Marxism-Leninism to this day.

The year 1978, however, figures in most histories as the watershed moment when the centre of gravity in the country shifted fundamentally. Two years after the death of Mao, it saw the start of the second great phase of modern PRC development, when, in a military hotel in Beijing (still off-limits to non-Chinese visitors), at one of the regular Plenum meetings of the Party Central Committee, a decision was made to engage with a new generation of reforms and a new, much more Western-orientated concept of modernity. These will be described in this book. The key thing to note here is that one result of the reforms is that they created a divide in the narrative of historic development of the PRC. On the one hand, its early Maoist history links it to a movement of revolutionary struggle against colonial oppression and Western domination, a movement in which society domestically was convulsed by great internal conflicts between different classes and social forces. On the other hand, there is the Dengist modernizing China from 1978 which has accepted the very forces of modernization and Westernization that it had once seemed to set its face against, embracing things which were anathema prior to 1978 – foreign capital, a domestic market and private enterprise. For those inside and outside China, trying to marrying these two eras with their stark differences is increasingly challenging.

Looking out on the great coastal cities of the PRC which have resulted from this reform process visitors can sit in their plush five-star hotel rooms, and be deceived by the brash modernity of what looks like capitalism in China. Cyclists are now almost a protected species in the capital, Beijing, where cars rule as much as they do in the West. The Metro rapid transit system, built in the space of a few years in Shanghai, puts the more ancient versions in European or American cities to shame. The energy and pace of development of urban China is overwhelming, with many avant-garde Western architects finding their most open-minded clients and their best business in the country (despite President Xi Jinping's complaints in 2014 about 'weird' buildings being no longer in favour). Almost inevitably, China has been vying to build the world's tallest skyscraper. Shanghai now has to accept the tallest structure in Asia as a consolation prize since Dubai stole pole position in 2010. The southern city of Shenzhen's rapid development in the 1980s, when it was designated a special growth zone, meant that so many buildings were erected so quickly that more than 30 per cent collapsed because of shoddy construction (Koolhass and Leong, 2001). Videos of 'tofu buildings' collapsing (so called because of the softness of the building materials) have become hits on Youku (the Chinese version of You Tube) and other internet websites. The breathtaking activity of contemporary China is something first-time visitors are warned of, but few can easily take in their stride. Some embrace what they see, enjoying its dynamism, while others feel threatened and alienated by it. The contemporary PRC leaves very few bored or cold. The dominant emotion after reasonably lengthy exposure is in fact more akin to exhaustion.

Finding the continuities in what China has been through during its long and often fragmented history proves more demanding. Often, the PRC of today seems adrift from its past, alienated from itself. People who live on the contested island of Taiwan off the southern coast of the PRC are fond of boasting that they have preserved a truer 'Chinese culture' than is found in the PRC, which has been through so much trauma and change. But there are tortured questions about what, in fact, is 'true' Chinese culture. The debates about China's physical, ethnic and cultural composition will be covered in this book. But the question 'What is China?' proves harder to answer the longer one dwells on it.

As the PRC has grown more prominent economically, so it has aroused increasingly complex responses in the outside world. Debates rage about how the Chinese are becoming the new colonial masters of Africa because of the increase in investments that Chinese companies are placing there, predominantly to obtain resources. Excited reports of the Chinese buying up the rest of the world are headlined across newspapers and magazines in Europe, Australia and the USA. News reports tell authoritatively of China directing a massive cyber-espionage campaign. The unpleasant stain from this history of demonizing what China is and what it intends sometimes remains, however faintly. Claims that the Chinese are creeping insidiously into 'our space', and trying to 'overwhelm 'us' through these tales of investment or cyberspace warfare draw on this fear of what China is doing and how it is different from 'us'. Yet finding hard evidence for the Chinese manipulation of investment or other instruments of influence proves more challenging. There may be valid reasons for the world to worry about China – but, as will also be argued in this book, there are plenty of reasons why people in China worry about the world outside, and about themselves. Worrying about China has great cultural roots (Davies, 2009). Engagement with China is not for the relaxed or complacent. It is a country that, even as it changes, develops and evolves, it is hard to remain complacent about, often forcing a response or reaction as it becomes increasingly a part of our established economic, cultural and intellectual space.

Part of the function of this book is to provide at least a few ways in which to question, engage and understand China in more complex, and sometimes contradictory, ways. China, like any country, shares many attributes with other places, but has some features that belong to it uniquely. Its size, of course, magnifies these. But it would be a pity to fall into extolling the exceptional nature or uniqueness of China. There are many things the country has that have been borrowed from the USSR, from the developed West, and from neighbouring countries in the region. There are also aspects of its history that help to explain the surprising things that are happening today. It is best not to approach China as some mystery that keeps its meanings hidden behind an inscrutable exterior. The explosions of protests that occur every day in the modern country show that the narrative of a passive, incomprehensible people is a stereotype. There is plenty of energetic expression of feeling and ideas in modern China, something that is attested to by the huge debates that occur amongst China's estimated one billion users of social media.

Fitting modern China into a more interesting and nuanced framework – one that can accommodate the many aspects of the country in a way that does justice to a place which, in the space of only three decades, has increased the size of its economy almost sixfold, reformulated its own international role, and, to some degree, reshaped its identity – is one of the key ambitions of this book. This is accompanied by an attempt to show this epic story through the lives of Chinese people themselves, and their huge diversity now. Bringing the story of China from its epic trope down to human, individual scale is important.

That China does matter in the contemporary world is shown through its role in the global supply chains that are fundamental to the modern global economy, through its hosting of events such as the 2008 Olympics in Beijing, highlighting its importance as a major global and a regional leader, through its impact on global emissions and the world's environment. The issue is no longer solely about whether China matters to the world, but also how the world matters to China. I hope this introduction to contemporary China will help at least to convey a more complicated and nuanced view of where this remarkable country now stands, where it has come from, and what its future impact might be.

1

What Is China?

The People's Republic of China (PRC) is the world's third-largest country in land area, and has the largest number of people. It is a country dominated by the Han people, who make up more than 91 per cent of its population, but there are also 55 other officially recognized ethnic groups. The country is split into 22 provinces, five autonomous regions (Tibet, Xinjiang, Ningxia, Inner Mongolia and Guanxi), four cities directly under the central government (the capital Beijing, Tianjin, Shanghai and Chongqing), and two special administrative regions (Hong Kong and Macau). Taiwan has a special status and will be covered below. The provinces vary in size from ones such as Sichuan and Henan, with populations of around 100 million, to those such as Qinghai with barely five million. The PRC covers an area of 9.6 million square kilometres (3.7 million square miles), with an eastern coast bordering the South China Sea, Bohai Sea, Korea Bay and the East China Sea, and land borders with 14 countries, ranging from its longest, with Russia, to its shortest (with Afghanistan). The PRC's current borders were settled after 1949, though many of them were established centuries before, in periods of expansion during the Qing Dynasty (see Chapter 2). The traditional area of Chinese culture in which farmers settled was around the base of the two major rivers, the Yellow River and the Yangtze. These supplied the fertile plains on which earlier dynasties established vast irrigation projects, and as early as the thirteenth century CE during the Yuan Dynasty were able to support a population of over 20 million. The contrast between this settled area, with its particular model of governance, state formation and tax payments, and the vast nomadic areas of inner Asia to the north and north-west has been one of the great elemental contrasts in the development of China as a culture, and a nation. While the current state, the PRC, has settled its borders with all but one of its land neighbours (the outstanding dispute being with India), the previous entities known as China have varied dramatically over the centuries, and claims to a history of 5,000 years of continuity often need to be highly qualified, especially since archaeologists in China are now dating the earliest coherent state to only 1700 BCE. In its 1982 constitution, the PRC declares that it is a 'multi-ethnic' country. Others have claimed it resembles an empire or a civilization rather than a traditional nation state (Jacques, 2008). That the current PRC is the successor state to entities that had complex, interlinked and sometimes divergent histories is clear, as is the fact that the PRC itself is a complex terrain, in terms of populations, ethnicities and languages as a result of this varied and rich history.

The Geography of China

The historic complexity of China is captured in its geography. Fundamentally, the current PRC divides into a number of contrasting zones. One of the most striking includes the vast mountains to the west of the country, starting from the Tibetan plateau and running eastwards towards the middle regions in a huge continuous slope. Here the world's highest mountain range, the Himalayas, dominates the western borders, with Everest being partly claimed by the PRC. In Tibet itself, the region's capital Lhasa is the world's highest city, some 3,650 metres (12,000 feet) above sea level. The landscape is arid, sparsely populated and dominated mainly by nomads. In the eastern areas, around the confluence of the two great rivers, the Yangtze and the Yellow River, the population density is among the highest in the world, the climate is temperate, with long, hot summers and mild winters, and the land, when irrigated, is fertile and perfect for rice plantations. In the south-western provinces of Yunnan and Sichuan, there are remnants of jungles, the climate is semi-tropical, and the fauna and wildlife – were it not for the devastating impact of dense human habitation in recent decades – rich and varied. In central China, with cold winters and dry summers, crops range from maize to wheat. In the north, winter temperatures can fall to as low as minus 40 degrees C. Inner Mongolia, a vast region that abuts the northern border with the Mongolian People's Republic and the Russian Federation, has immense grasslands, some of which have been overgrazed in the last century since the start of intense Han settlement in the late Qing era, creating a major desertification problem. The Gobi Desert lies in the west of the province, along with a swathe of different grasslands where much of China's mutton and wool are sourced. These regions only began to be settled during the twentieth century.

The PRC's territory covers more than 5,000 kilometres (3,000 miles) from west to east, and despite the fact that the country is now run on one time zone settled in Beijing, it is clear there are three real time zones across the whole country. In terms of diet, lifestyle and culture, therefore, while many Chinese assert strongly that there is unity, in fact what strikes most visitors who spend time in the country is the diversity of the people and their lifestyles. The modern PRC embraces semi-nomadic Mongolian and Tibetan herdsman practising Yellow Sect Buddhism, and family-shrine-worshipping rice farmers in the south-east, many of whom have been working their land for generations. It runs from the Turkic-looking, Islam-practising Uyghur group in the Xinjiang region in the north-west, to the highly assimilated Manchus from the area historically called Manchuria in the north-east, whose script and language now largely only figure on imperial monuments in Beijing, a reminder of their status as rulers during the Qing Dynasty (1644–1911). While those living in Guangzhou or Fujian may never see snow, in the Harbin area of Heilongjiang the winters are sufficiently cold to hold a three-month-long ice festival with building-sized replicas of famous monuments sculpted in ice out in the open. Diet ranges from meat eating and bread consuming in the north, to sea food and rice in the coastal areas. The diversity of China's food is world renowned, with some areas (Hunan and Sichuan) famous for spicy food and the heavy use of chili, and others (the north-east and Beijing) for meat-filled dumplings. The Guangzhou diet, with its fondness for exotic seafood and meat contrasts with tofu and vegetarian dishes in areas such as Zhejiang, despite their being neighbouring provinces.

The Creation of Chinese Identity and History

While we can talk about the unity of the Chinese language, and about the creation of a geographical entity that is now Greater China (a term which embraces the People's Republic, Hong Kong and Macau, and Taiwan – see section on the latter below) there is the issue of whether we can find a common historic narrative on which to make sense of what China is now. Chinese history until 1911 and the collapse of the Qing is divided into dynastic periods – dynasties being the equivalent of the reigns of particular family groups, usually derived from a founding figure through bloodline succession until the collapse or overthrow of the line. The kinds of territories these dynasties presided over physically, and indeed the unity they actually had, varied widely. But some key 'high points' remain powerful even in today's memory. The most striking of these are the Han Dynasty, the Tang Dynasty, the Song Dynasty, the Yuan and the Ming (see Chapter 2). There were a number of other dynasties sandwiched between these, of varying importance and cohesiveness, but these constitute the backbone of Chinese dynastic history after the unification of parts of Chinese territory under the Qin in the third century BCE.

The Han Dynasty (206 BCE to 220 CE), as successor to the short-lived Qin, was almost simultaneous with the high period of Roman imperial rule in the West (Scheidel, 2009). It is now celebrated as a time in which the Chinese nation started to gain some of its cultural and social coherence, with celebrated scientific discoveries, the flowering of art, and the adoption of Confucianism as a state ideology. The Han period saw the first production of systematic historical writing through figures such as the great Sima Qian, author of *Record of the Grand Historian*, a vast account of the biographies of key historic figures from political, cultural and religious fields, in the first century BCE.

The dynasty that eventually succeeded the Han (though with lengthy interludes under the Jin (265–420) and Sui (580–618) periods was the great Tang, three centuries from 618 in which, from the capital of Chang'an (modern Xian) the empire enjoyed stability, was able to create rich trade links via various routes with the outside world, and experienced

Box 1.1 Sima Qian, China's master historian

If anyone can be said to have created the template for the narrative of Chinese history, then it would be Sima Qian. Born in 139 BCE, and dying in 86 BCE, his vast *Record of the Grand Historian* (Shi Ji) is one of the supreme masterpieces of literary and historic culture, and it is thanks to this one work more than any other that we have such a detailed knowledge of the early period of Chinese civilization. Initially a palace attendant, and then successor to his father as court astrologer, he was also an advisor to the Emperor Wu on more broad political and strategic issues. It was in this role that he earned disapproval, speaking up for the disgraced general Li Ling who was defeated by a band of Xiongnu tribespeople. His reward for this was to choose either death or castration. Because of his belief in the importance of his mission to write the grand history he had been planning, he endured the pain and humiliation of the latter.

His history was compiled over the coming decade till his death, and is a core source to the present age of Chinese development. Like Herodotus in Greek literature, or the great historians of Rome, Sima Qian created a sense of historical continuity and a story of cultural and state mission. He covers figures as diverse as Confucius and the first emperor, painting powerful and often surprisingly modern accounts of their psychology and motivations.

a number of capable rulers, perhaps the most celebrated being the sole female ruler in China's dynastic history, Wu Zetian. This was an era of unparalleled literary creativity, with the great poets Li Bo and Du Fu producing works that remain celebrated to this day. It was also an era of true cosmopolitanism, with a China linked to the outside world and trading with it in ways which are still being discovered by archaeologists, some of whom have discovered Tang products in shipwrecks deep in the Pacific and Indian Oceans.

A period of instability from 907 to 980 saw divisions within the territory that had been dominated by Tang political control. From 980 to 1271, the Song Dynasty ran in parallel with the Liao Dynasty. As a sign of the fractures of the empire over this period, Song is divided almost equally into a period in which the capital was in modern-day Kaifeng, and then, after losses of most of its northern territories, when it was forced to relocate to modern Hangzhou. The tragic figure of the emperor Huizong best represents this era, a man remembered now as one of Chinese history's most cultivated rulers, someone well versed in the three arts of calligraphy, painting and poetry, but who presided over a spectacular collapse of authority, ceded the throne to his son, and then watched helplessly as the empire was brought to its knees by invading Jurchen tribesmen. Huizong was to die in 1135 in captivity in Northern China, a symbol for successive generations of disinterested and therefore ineffective and remote imperial rule (Ebray, 2014).

The traumatic collapse of the early Song and the Jin Dynasties was matched by the Mongolian conquests up to 1271 which created a dynasty in which Han were under subjugation by non-Han. This set a precedent for the coming millennium (the Qing too was to be run by Manchus, not Han). The violence of the Mongolian attacks, and the vast, unwieldy empires they created, have left a profound memory trace, with shadowy deserted cities simply obliterated by the attacking Mongolian armies existing to this day in the western regions of China. That Genghis Khan's grandson, Kublai Khan, and his successors were able to create a functioning centralized state which lasted for more than a century is largely forgotten. The acquisition of many of the marks of Chinese civilization by the new overlords was also noteworthy. The Mongolians, coming to power through a campaign which considered genocide for southern Chinese, reverted to a traditional state model, where citizens were taxed, the bureaucracy reconfigured and at least some semblance of order and artistic achievements restored. The Mongolians left their mark in this era on more than just China, reaching across central Asia as far as the Danube in Europe, where they were poised to launch attacks into the European heartland before being recalled because of leadership succession issues. The Mongolian memory trace remains in the modern English language, with the loan word 'horde' (Brook, 2010).

The collapse of the Yuan through disunity and internecine arguments in 1368 led to the establishment of the Ming Dynasty under a former beggar, Zhu Yuanzhang, who became the founding emperor. The Ming's almost three centuries of stable rule saw the first tentative steps to influence not just as a land power, but also as a sea one, with the brief but extremely successful voyages of the celebrated eunuch admiral, Zheng He, in the fifteenth century. These adventures were eventually deemed to be too expensive, and were abandoned. The collapse of the Ming in 1642–4 was the result of internal rebellion and division. The most noted emperors of this period were Yongle (1360–1424) who usurped a sitting emperor in 1402 and instigated one of the most devastating purges of his bureaucracy in order to eradicate all traces of loyalty to his predecessor, Wan Li (1563–1620), whose infatuation with a concubine and the inactivity it consigned him to caused the whole governance system to grind to a halt (Huang, 1982).

The recurrence of division and then unity throughout more than two millennia of dynastic history is striking. Perhaps it is this recurrence of disorder after periods of stable rule that lies at the heart of the modern Chinese central government's fears of instability and the sense that even

Table 1.1 Key Chinese dynasties

Name	*Date*
Xia	2070–1600 BCE
Shang	1600–1029 BCE
Western Zhou	1029–771 BC
Eastern Zhou	770–256 BCE
Qin	221–206 BCE
Han	206 BCE–220 CE
Jin	265–420 CE
Sui	580–618 CE
Tang	618–907 CE
Five Dynasties and Ten Kingdoms	907–980 CE
Song	980–1271 CE
Liao	907–1125 CE
Yuan	1271–1368 CE
Ming	1368–1644 CE
Qing	1644–1911 CE

modern leaders give of feeling they are both weak and strong at the same time – brought together by a rich, diverse and long history, but also with plenty of examples of collapse, decline and discord in the past. Not for nothing has history in China sometimes been called a prison (Jenner, 1992). In one of the great classical novels from the Ming period, *Romance of the Three Kingdoms* by Luo Guanzhong, the famous first words are: 'The world under heaven, after a long period of division, tends to unite; after a long period of union, tends to divide. This has been so since antiquity.' The swaying between periods of centralization and stability and then division and anarchy are mapped through the great dynasties and the eras in between of unrest and decline (see Table 1.1).

Hong Kong, Taiwan and Macau

An additional issue when trying to understand what China is today is recognizing that there are contesting territories all saying they are in fact, the one true 'China'. This is the final issue left over from the colonial era. After 1949, there were two parts of the Chinese mainland (the geographical part of the country on the main Asian landmass) which remained under foreign sovereignty – Macau and Hong Kong, and one large offshore area over which the PRC claimed ownership but which was ruled by the competing regime of the Republic of China on Taiwan, under the Nationalists. Resolving these became important political and diplomatic challenges from 1949, though in each case the issues were different.

For Hong Kong and Macau at least there were some timeframes within which the government of the PRC could work. The most important lease, by which parts of Hong Kong were ceded to the British under various treaties in the late nineteenth century, was set to expire in 1997, and Macau was due to revert from Portuguese to Chinese control in 1999. Under Mao Zedong, these issues were largely left alone. In the Cultural Revolution between 1966 and 1976, explosions of protests in Hong Kong against British colonialism caused the British administration of the territory to become nervous and wonder whether the more bellicose-sounding Beijing government was about to make military repossession moves. In fact, during the period of China's maximum isolation (in 1967, for example, the PRC only had one full ambassador posted abroad in Egypt, all the others having been summoned back to Beijing) Hong Kong was a hugely useful conduit for badly needed goods and revenue, so it would have been counter-productive for the PRC to close this off. With the arrival of the more liberal leadership under Deng Xiaoping in the late 1970s into the

1980s, however, the issue came up more urgently, because of the expiry of the lease for the main territory apart from Hong Kong Island in 1997. Preliminary British approaches were framed in terms of an extension, but it soon became clear this was not feasible. Hong Kong Island's viability on its own (the lease on this was in perpetuity) was impossible because of lack of water, energy and other resources. By 1984, therefore, the British government, under Prime Minister Margaret Thatcher, started negotiations in earnest to hand back the area to the Chinese, largely through a mechanism supposedly devised by Deng Xiaoping for Taiwan of 'one country, two systems'. The outcome of this was the 1984 Framework Agreement between both parties which agreed a timetable and a broad understanding for how reversion of sovereignty of the territory to the PRC would be achieved. Under this, Hong Kong was able to maintain its strong legal system, and its independence in all areas except defence and foreign affairs. It would maintain its currency, be able to set its own budgets and taxes, and have, in the words of the agreement, 'a high degree of autonomy', being labelled a 'special administrative region'. The Basic Law which grew from this, hammered out over the next few years between the British and Chinese, was to serve as a de facto constitution. Despite the shock of the 1989 Tiananmen Square uprising, the British were able to finalize the reversion of sovereignty deals with the PRC so that, in July 1997, a ceremony marked the end of 150 years of British involvement there and the start of 50 years of special status under PRC sovereignty until full reversion to PRC control in 2047. The 'one country, two systems' rubric for Hong Kong served as the model for the reversion of Macau to China two years later – though in this case, the smaller size of the area and population meant that the negotiations were far less contentious. The large-scale protests in Hong Kong from August 2014 onwards over announcements that made clear that there would not, as had originally been believed, be universal suffrage for the election of a Chief Executive to run the region from 2017, was a sign once more of how distinctive Hong Kong is as a part of modern China.

Taiwan offers far greater challenges, and these remain unresolved. The island, formerly called Formosa, and its nearby satellites, were originally occupied by people of Polynesian ethnicity (remarkably, they are related to the Maoris of New Zealand, but not to the Aborigines of Australia) but successively colonized by migrants from the southern part of the main landmass of China. The islands were under Japanese control from the late Qing era in 1895 to 1946, when they became part of the Republic of China. With the collapse of the Republic on the mainland after the Civil War with the Communists from 1946 to 1949, over a million Nationalists fled to the island, setting up an alternative government. The bloody suppression of indigenous revolt on the island over this period and the brutal suppression of opposition is a subject which has only been openly discussed in Taiwan since democratization in the 1980s and 1990s. It was here that Chiang Kai-shek, leader of the Nationalist Kuomintang (KMT), established his seat of government, claiming sovereignty over the whole of the rest of the mainland, and occupying the Chinese seat at the UN until 1971. Rapprochement between the US under Richard Nixon and the PRC in 1971–72 was part of the reason why the Republic of China on Taiwan was replaced by the PRC at the UN. In 1979, under President Carter, the USA transferred its formal recognition of diplomatic status from Taiwan to the PRC. Taiwan was, from this point, dealt with by most major powers under the 'One China' policy, where it was recognized that there was only one China, and Taiwan was part of China.

Taiwan's rapid economic expansion in the 1960s and 1970s meant that, by the 1980s, it enjoyed one of the highest per capita GDP levels in Asia, and had built up a well educated population, with many engaged in the hi-tech and knowledge economies, and with some of the highest living standards in the world. The political impact of this was that martial law was finally lifted by Chiang Ching-kuo, Chiang Kai-shek's son and successor, in 1987, and a raft of reforms were introduced recognizing unions, allowing a free press, and tolerating the establishment of political opposition groups. By 1996, Taiwan was in a position to hold its first fully democratic elections for president. The response of the PRC to this was to undertake military operations around the island, only calmed by the dispatch by the US Pacific Command of two aircraft carriers to the region.

Taiwan's evolution as a democracy over the following two decades has been dramatic, with power passing in 2000 from the ruling Nationalist Party, which had dominated the island's politics for the previous 50 years, to the opposition Democratic Progressive Party (DPP) under Chen Shui-bian. Chen was re-elected in 2004, though the Nationalists under Ma Ying-jeou returned in 2008. Ma was re-elected for his second term in 2012, but, as in the US system, must leave office in 2016. Taiwan's greatest challenge today is finding ways of conducting relations with an increasingly powerful and assertive PRC, one with which Taiwan is deeply economically interlinked but which refuses it any proper recognition of its autonomy, asserting that the island is part of mainland Chinese territory. Extensive protests across Taiwan in April 2014, dubbed the Sunflower Movement, by students and others objecting

Table 1.2 China's municipalities, provinces and autonomous regions

Name	*Capital*	*Population (as of 2010)*	*Area (sq. kilometres)*
Beijing	Beijing	19,612,368	16,800
Tianjin	Tianjin	12,938,224	11,305
Hebei	Shijiazhuang	71,854,202	187,700
Shanxi	Taiyuan	35,712,111	156,300
Inner Mongolia Autonomous Region	Hohhot	24,706,321	1,183,00
Liaoning	Shenyang	43,746,323	145,900
Jilin	Changchun	27,462,297	187,400
Heilongjiang	Harbin	38,312,224	454,000
Shanghai	Shanghai	23,019,148	6,341
Jiangsu	Nanjing	78,659,903	102,600
Zhejiang	Hangzhou	54,426,891	102,000
Anhui	Hefei	59,500,510	139,700
Fujian	Fuzhou	38,894,216	121,300
Jiangxi	Nanchang	44,567,475	167,000
Shandong	Jinan	95,793,065	153,800
Henan	Zhengzhou	94,023,567	167,000
Hubei	Wuhan	57,237,740	185,900
Hunan	Changsha	65,683,722	210,000
Guangdong	Guangzhou	104,303,132	180,000
Guangxi Zhuang Autonomous Region	Nanning	46,026,629	236,000
Hainan	Haikou	8,671,518	34,000
Chongqing Municipality	Chongqing	28,846,170	83,300
Sichuan	Chengdu	80,418,200	485,000
Guizhou	Guiyang	34,746,468	176,000
Yunnan	Kunming	45,966,239	394,000
Tibet Autonomous Region	Lhasa	3,002,166	1,228,400
Shaanxi	Xian	37,327,378	205,600
Gansu	Lanzhou	25,575,254	454,300
Qinghai	Xining	5,626,722	721,200
Ningxia Hui Autonomous Region	Yinchuan	6,301,350	66,400
Xinjiang Uyghur Autonomous Region	Urumqi	21,813,334	1,660,400
Hong Kong Special Administrative Region	Hong Kong	7,061,200	1,104
Macau Special Administrative Region	Macau	552,300	29
Taiwan	Taipei	23,140,000	35,581

to over-close relations with a predatory Mainland underlined just how contentious this issue remains, with most surveys showing that people regard themselves as either Chinese Taiwanese or Taiwanese, and very few claiming to be Chinese alone, as a mark of their distinctive identity.

The Unifying Element: Chinese Language

Through their long dynastic history, the predecessor states before the PRC underwent radical change and transformation. Historians in the PRC are fond of referring to the unification of the country from among a group of warring states by the first emperor, Qin Shi Huangdi, in 221 BCE. The Qin emperor created a unified money system and a road network throughout the territory he had conquered and these stand today as powerful symbols of the earliest unifying moment in Chinese ancient history. But the drain of his grandiose plans on state coffers led to the rapid collapse of his empire after his death in 210 BCE as a result of bankruptcy, with the more enduring Han Dynasty replacing it, spanning the four and a half centuries from 206 BCE to 220 CE. One particular monument associated with the Qin emperor is the Great Wall of China, which continues to accrue myths to this day (see Box 1.2).

When faced with this geographical, historical and cultural diversity, it is immediately challenging to try to work out where these strong modern assertions of Chinese national identity in fact arise. The strongest tangible bond is written language. The current PRC is a country with a wide array of dialects, some of them mutually incomprehensible, ranging from the local language used in Shanghai to the wholly different tonal structure of Cantonese spoken by around 100 million people in the south of the country. But at least in terms of the written script there is a striking unity (despite the array of different writing systems used by Tibetans, Mongolians and Uighurs on the border areas). The Chinese language, made up of some 2,000 characters used in daily communication and as many as 10,000 in the most comprehensive dictionaries (the most adept scholars usually claim facility in up to 8,000) remains at the heart of Chinese identity, something that is used consistently across the whole territory of the PRC, and among the 60 million Chinese diaspora spread throughout the world.

The dialect now used on national broadcasts and in official communication in Beijing, Mandarin Chinese (Putonghua, or 'standard speech') is, in fact, relatively recent. The four tones (falling, rising, high and neutral) impact directly on the meaning of the many thousands of

Box 1.2 The Great Walls of China

Sweeping over thousands of kilometres, the Great Wall of China, along with Tiananmen Gate in Beijing, has become one of the central symbols of contemporary China. But perceptions of the monument are enveloped in historical inaccuracy and mythmaking.

The first problem is that there is not one but several different walls. The most popular ones that tourists visit close to Beijing, at places such as Badaling and Mutianyu, are heavily restored, and date only from the Ming Dynasty (1368–1644). Badaling, in particular, with its classically rolling hills atop which the Wall perches, was heavily renovated in readiness to receive President Nixon in 1972. When presented with the view of the Wall, he famously reportedly told his guests, 'That is a great wall', though he proceeded to say the somewhat more meaningful 'And it was built by a great people'. Other, much older, parts of the Wall exist to the west, as far as Xinjiang. In Gansu, the old Qin dynasty era mud and earth wall still dots the landscape sporadically, though it has been worn down in some places to non-existence or just a faint vein on the landscape.

The second problem is, in fact, working out why these walls were built. Far from being effective defensive structures, it seems they failed almost every challenge thrown at them. The epic Mongolian onslaught in the thirteenth century, in which the armies of the great Khans conquered most of southern China, was barely held up by the walls. And in any case, for much of its length the Wall is no such thing but rather a low raised road, as along the Gansu Corridor. Modern debate has centred on the Wall's demarcation of territory, and its use as a communication channel. What is less easy to explain is why the immense human cost that construction of the walls involved, whether in the second century BCE or in the Ming Dynasty, was considered worthwhile. The third problem is simply one of translation. As Julia Lovell has pointed out, while non-Chinese refer to the 'Great Wall', for Chinese people it is simply the far less grand 'Long Wall' (Chang Cheng) (Lovell, 2006). As a symbol, therefore, it has great ambiguity. For some it has been presented as typifying all that is great and stirring about traditional Chinese civilization but, for others, it simply shows introspectiveness, defensiveness, and outright tyranny.

one- and two-syllable phrases which constitute words in modern Chinese. Each of these is represented by a character, usually made up of a classifying radical (usually strokes at the left, right, top or bottom) and an identifying core component. The most ancient characters were discovered on bones used for divination dating back to the earliest semi-mythical Shang Dynasty over 4,000 years ago. Many of these were similar to

Illustration 1.1 The Great Wall in western China

Illustration 1.2 The Great Wall near Beijing

The Great Wall is one of the world's legendary structures, but its uniformity is overemphasized. It covers many thousands of kilometres, and was built in many different phases over two millennia.

Illustration 1.3 The Chinese character 'hu'

The Chinese character 'hu' (rising third tone) meaning 'lake'. The left-hand-side three strokes is the radical for 'water', with the middle and right-hand portion of the character together being pronounced 'hu'.

characters still used in modern China. Texts by the pre-Qin philosophers over 2,500 years ago were written in highly condensed classical Chinese, in terms of grammar at least. It was only with the 'Baihua' movement that started at the end of the nineteenth century that concerted attempts were made to modernize the way Chinese was written, and improve accessibility at a time when most people were simply unable to read or write because of the huge amount of time needed to master the written language. In the period after the First World War (1914–18) novels were produced in the new idiom, with reformed grammatical structures. The scholar Hu Shi was at the forefront of this. Language reform remained a constant throughout the twentieth century, with the Communists making their own distinctive contribution through the work of the remarkable Zhou Youguang (1906–) who simplified many characters, and produced the 'Pinyin' form of transliteration. (In 2014, at the age of 108, Zhou was firing off spirited criticisms of the current government for their lack of interest in culture and political reform.) To this day, while Hong Kong and Taiwan use traditional characters, in the PRC the simplified ones prevail, though in recent years there has been a reversion to traditional forms on the mainland, largely on aesthetic grounds.

What Do Chinese People Believe?

One of the puzzles for missionaries going to China in the seventeenth century, some of them to live there for the rest of their lives, was the question of what, in fact, Chinese people believed. Were they ancestor worshippers, as some appeared to be, or Confucianists, as the Imperial Court practised, or Buddhists? This question was never answered successfully. It is a question that remains alive to this day. While people might assert that China is a Communist country, or a capitalist one, or a Confucian one, or Buddhist (Buddhism has seen a major revival in recent years) in fact the ways in which either Catholic or Protestant Christianity became so dominant as a religious belief system in the USA or Europe has no easy equivalent either in Chinese history or the modern PRC, where depending on the dynasty and sometimes even the specific ruler there were wide differences.

Confucianism remains the ideology associated most closely with the Chinese state, at least since the Han. But while there might be agreement about the broad tenets of Confucianism – the need for hierarchy, for just rulers who understand the need to observe the correct state rites, and the idea of an ordered world under heaven – consensus on specific issues like the role of the ruler, the issue of justice and the rights of the people, remain highly contentious. As an historical figure, the Sage (as he has been called) is elusive, with parts of his collected sayings, *The Analects*, attributed to writers long after his time, and the corpus of his work as open to widely differing interpretations as the Gospels in the New Testament. That *The Analects* have been used with semi-religious canonical force many times in the last two millennia and have had remarkable longevity and impact even to today is undisputed. So too has been the ability of Confucianism and its followers to reinvent or reinvigorate the Master's appeal. Adoption of Confucianism as a state ideology in the Han period in the first century BCE was followed by a relative decline in the intervening dynasties till a renaissance under the neo-Confucianists in the eleventh century. Confucius's stock has risen and fallen in the last thousand years, but his influence has never been entirely eradicated. The most recent comeback is one of the more spectacular: Confucius was harangued as the brand carrier of everything old, feudal and reprehensible under Mao Zedong during the Cultural Revolution, and he was even used as a proxy in the famous 'Criticize Confucius, Criticize Lin' campaign against disgraced leader Lin Biao in 1973–74. But by the 2000s, institutes under the ancient philosopher's name started springing up across the world, supported by the central government and being used to promote Chinese culture. A statue of Master Kung (as he is known in China) even appeared briefly in the hallowed space of Tiananmen Square in Beijing before being unceremoniously removed in 2008. Perhaps most tellingly of all, during the opening ceremony of the 2008 Beijing Olympics, while Confucius made an appearance in the historic pageant portrayed at the start, Mao Zedong was nowhere to be seen (see Chapter 7).

While modern revisionists argue about the need to get back to the original Confucius (as though that were possible), there is little dispute now that his work, and those of the schools of contending ideas around him, such as those associated with other historical figures such as Mozi,

Mencius and Xunzi, do not offer the kind of grand metaphysical explanations found in Western religious texts. They are rooted in addressing practical questions such as understanding human behaviour, and the best modes of governance and human organization. In that sense, they serve as ethical or political philosophies. Confucius's celebrated statement in the *Analects* of the golden mean, 'Do not do to others what you would not have done to yourself', is also paralleled by the powerful articulation of the obligations of the central ruler over his people, and, in Mencius's case, of human goodness and the ways in which it can be protected in an imperfect world. That the pre-Qin philosophers set the boundaries of fundamental areas of enquiry and discussion, much as the Greek philosophers did in Europe, and had a profound impact on subsequent intellectual culture, is well understood (Yan, 2011). What is perhaps distinctive is the ways in which state bureaucracy and its political behaviour over the last two millenia have so often been closely shaped and directed by an elite deeply schooled in Confucianism and its associated scholarship, feeling that they were embodying its values and derived legitimacy from it. Confucianism as a religious practice, with temples, rites and a priesthood, however, is a different matter, and while contemporary China has some Confucian temples, they exist more as tourist locations than places of authentic worship.

Illustration 1.4 Monks in Beijing

China is led by a Communist Party that continues to subscribe to the eradication of religion, and yet its population practises diverse faiths.

Buddhism is one of the diverse faiths practised in China. In recent years there have been revivals of Buddhism in areas such as Inner Mongolia, and the renovation or building from scratch of large new temples in urban centres such as Shanghai and Guangzhou, much of it funded by Buddhist association branches in Taiwan, Hong Kong or among the overseas Chinese diaspora. Yellow Hat Sect Buddhism prevails in both Tibet and Inner Mongolia, though there are famous divisions between practices and leadership in both places. Buddhism's lasting appeal in China is another great paradox. Brought across the Tibetan plateau from its homeland in India in the Tang Dynasty, it was to achieve remarkable success, with the monk Xuanzeng (602–664 CE) undertaking a long journey to and from India in order to learn more about the faith and bring it back to his homeland. His journey became the basis for one of the great Chinese works of literature, the *Journey to the West* which remains popular to this day. At a time in which Buddhism has largely died out in its founding territory, therefore, China may well claim over 500 million adherents. Despite this historic common point, modern China and India have remarkably little sympathy or understanding of each other's cultures.

Contemporary China strikes many who visit as a materialist and money-driven place, one that has embraced the tenets of Western capitalism with great energy and lost its own values in the process. What people believe about the meaning of their lives, and what the ultimate purpose of their existence might be, is often brushed away in the excitement of day-to-day life in a country that is developing so quickly. One Westerner searching for a renowned hermit in central China was distressed to discover on finding him that he had a state-of-the-art mobile phone (Gifford, 2008)! This is compounded by the fact that the views of the Chinese government towards religion have been complicated. From 1949 until the early 1980s, under a Communist leadership subscribing to dialectic materialism and atheism, there was widespread persecution both of religious figures, and of practices and rites associated with them. Maoism arguably became a religion in its own right at its height in the 1960s and early 1970s, with daily recitations of the Chairman's statements and a semi-religious status imputed to almost every word that he uttered.

Since the early 1980s, a more liberal leadership in Beijing has at least allowed some relaxation of these draconian rules. Today, while it still subscribes to the phasing out of religion in the long term, in the short term the modern Communist Party tolerates the discreet practice of religion. This has allowed an explosion of numbers turning to Christianity as much a testament to the pressures of modern life in China as to what many, among them the Nobel Prize winner and dissident, Liu Xiaobo, have called the spiritual emptiness at the heart of life in China (Liu, 2012). Part of this emptiness can be laid at the door of the dizzying journey many middle-aged and older Chinese have had to make from a period when society subscribed to Maoist utopia to one where it seems that almost everything is monetarized and up for sale, and where on the whole there is widespread cynicism about politics and any social good.

Christianity is going through a remarkable emergence in China. Estimates of those practising some form of Christianity range from 60 million to 150 million (Gardam, 2011). However, even here there are issues. The status of the Catholic Church in the PRC is particularly problematic, not only because since 1949 it has been banned, but also because of the Vatican's continued recognition of Taiwan as the legitimate government of China rather than the PRC (it is one of 23 countries that do this). The need for Catholics to accept the infallibility of the Pope on matters of doctrine has also been something interpreted in Beijing as a direct challenge to the legitimacy of the CCP leadership. Beijing has established a Patriotic Chinese Catholic Church, and outlawed formal links to the Roman Catholic Church, which means that those who wish to maintain adherence to the Vatican have to practise their religion in secret. The greatest issue arising from this is the existence of non-approved bishops in China who are sanctioned by the Vatican, and the imposition of bishops from Beijing not recognized by Rome. In 2011, after a period of relative peace, Beijing once again insisted that its Patriotic Catholic Church approve a number of bishops, some of whom were opposed by Rome. Despite this, the Vatican continues to hold talks, in hopes that one day the Catholic Church will be allowed to operate in a country where so many are converting.

Many Protestants in China worship through so-called household churches – small, informal gatherings throughout the country, where the Bible is read, a lecture is given, and hymns are sung. These groups, despite their great number, are regarded with suspicion by both central and local governments, and there are frequent clampdowns. The issue is one of control. The CCP wants to ensure its claim on organizational life and regards the networking power of Christian groups with suspicion.

China does have an authentic tradition of popular folklore, and in almost every area of the country there are different versions, each with its own contours and content. As elsewhere, parts of the landscape are associated with specific spirits and gods, and there are local myths and superstitions, linked to historic events, or at least to their re-imaginings. Since

Box 1.3 Liu Yunshan, Defender of the Faith

One of the more surprising aspects of the new era of Chinese leadership under Xi Jinping from 2012 was the emphasis laid on thought management, on returning to traditional values of Party building, and stressing the importance of unified ideological commitment. At a time when so many other influences and forces were coming into China via the internet, or through the mobility of Chinese people as they travelled internationally, this seemed a puzzling trend.

One interpretation of this was that the Party felt in the Hu years it had grown lazy and over-lax in enforcing loyalty from its core membership. The man who had been intimately linked to ideological work since 2007, Liu Yunshan, was appointed in 2012 to be in charge of all ideological and propaganda business in the Standing Committee. Liu had an unusual background for such a position. Having grown up in the Inner Mongolia Autonomous Region, he had spent his first few years working as a journalist for the state Xinhua news agency, becoming their livestock and agricultural produce correspondent in the 1980s before catching the attention of the local leaders who supported his move to Beijing to work in the national propaganda bureau. It was here that he remained for the next decade, working on unifying the message of the Party to its members and the outside world. Liu was involved, amongst other things, with the new emphasis on soft power by the Hu leadership, the attempt to use the Olympics in 2008 to brand China globally and the management of such difficult news issues as the Wenchuan Earthquake in 2008 and the Tibet and Xinjiang uprisings in 2008 and 2009. Reportedly criticized for the management of the 2011 Wenzhou train crash, in which local officials inexplicably tried to buy a whole fast train carriage involved in the incident, Liu was a surprise member of the core leadership appointed in 2012. But his core quality was immense fidelity to orthodox Chinese Marxist ideology. In this, he managed to see the country's record on journalistic freedom fall to the world's fifth worst, according to the 2013 Reporters sans frontières assessment. But as an ally for President Xi in enforcing thought unity, Liu was a faithful servant.

1949, the central government has waged energetic campaigns against what it calls superstition and feudal belief forms. Though these often recur, ranging from attacks on shamans (people regarded as having the power to summon spirits and exorcise evil demons) in some areas of China, to using fortune-tellers or the burning of paper money for good luck in others, superstitions have persisted. Some have seeped out of

China and become very popular in the West, with Feng shui (geomancy) – attention to the layout of the landscape and the home and its link to good fortune – and shadow boxing (Taijiquan) being particularly heavily exported.

Falun Gong

Where the central government has become more hardline has been over more proselytizing and politicized forms of worship, most particularly the Falun Gong group, established in the early 1990s by a former soldier in Northern China. In the space of only a few years, it gained substantial numbers of followers, even within the ranks of the CCP. Falun Gong – in Chinese Falun Dafa (meaning 'the principle of the revolving wheel') – began innocuously enough with a practice centred on breathing exercises, much like other forms of meditation. It developed, however, into something with a more threatening social and political edge when almost 10,000 followers surrounded the central government compound in Beijing in 1999 after an academic had attacked the group earlier in the year in a government newspaper for its superstition and lack of scientific credibility. While the demonstrators dispersed peacefully, the government was shocked by how effectively and quickly the group had been mobilized, and immediately set out on an energetic campaign to stamp it out. In areas of the country where it was particularly strong, such as the north-east, there were heavy-handed campaigns to prosecute followers, with many accusations that security agents had tortured and sometimes killed adherents who refused to renounce their beliefs.

Observers were initially puzzled as to why the sect had shaken the government so much, and what had provoked the ferocious campaigns against it. In the end there seemed to be two strong reasons why Falun Gong had been interpreted as a major problem. The first was that it had acquired a following deep into the countryside, and among this constituency, which the CCP regarded as their natural power base and followers, there could be no move to change or challenge their thinking about the government. In addition, there were rumours that Falun Gong had also gained believers in the higher levels of the government. The more lurid stories implied that even within the Politburo there were followers, though this was unlikely. But certainly there was a following among some government officials. Again, the campaign against Falun Gong took on some of the shape and form of previous efforts to 'rectify the ranks' and purify thought, as had occurred earlier in the PRC's history.

Borrowing the words of the Russian philosopher Mikhail Bakhtin, writing about the USSR in the Stalinist era, Liu Xiaobo talks about contemporary China being like a 'carnival'. It has no dominant creed or thought-system, despite the fact that for the power elite the ideology of Marxism–Leninism at least suffices for the moment (Liu, 2012). For all the historical 'invasions' of different ideas and belief systems, what has been left is something of a vast empty shell. Outside the tiny minority of 'Marxist–Leninist' true believers, there is as much a market place for beliefs as there is for material goods. The diversity of ideals and convictions in China is reflected in the geographical richness of the country. The question that was posed over three centuries ago by visiting missionaries, therefore, of what it was exactly that the average Chinese believes, remains as tricky to answer today as it did back then.

Box 1.4 Daoism

Daoism is seen in classical Chinese philosophy and thought as the great alternative to Confucianism. Both traditions of thinking can be located in the Han period, in the third and fourth centuries BCE, and both were based on canonical texts – in the case of Daoism, the *Way of Dao*, reputedly written by Laozi, and the texts of Zhuangzi. The first was edited and arranged authoritatively from various fragments by Wang Bi in the third century CE. Both continue to have immense influence on the religious thinking of people, not just in modern China, but also elsewhere in the world.

Daoism in essence celebrates 'the way', a process of constant change which has to be embraced by human actors in order to engage with their existence, to not be defeated, and to become 'sages' – able to fit into the natural order of the world and live fully. Through elusive concepts such as 'wu wei' (non-being), Daoism was taken by many practitioners, including those who were leaders and statespeople, to be a prescription for meditation, living at one with the natural world, and practising regimes of self-mastery and control. Daoism's celebrated concepts of 'yin' and 'yang' are linked to positive and negative, feminine and masculine or other binary oppositional forces in the universe, and the seeking of a balance between them. The famous 'I Ching' (Book of Changes) sets out a number of hexagram shapes, which can help to mould and direct reality. Perhaps Daoism's greatest attraction was not its placing of unfathomable mystery at the heart of its practice and belief, but rather the setting out of practical modes for how to live a 'good' life and to progress. Belief in Daoism has even been imputed to Mao Zedong. Its influence therefore lives on.

The Issue of Ethnicity

One of the outcomes of the complexity of Chinese dynastic history and the territories that have become part of the country is China's present-day ethnic diversity. In the 1982 Chinese constitution, it is spelt out clearly that the country is a multi-ethnic state. But despite decades of using various means to forge harmony, achieving true unity within a country with this ethnic composition remains a vexed issue. As noted earlier, the population of the current PRC is composed of 56 separate groups. Everyone is reputed, at least in official state accounts, to live in happy harmony, with China in contemporary discourse described as a big and contented family.

Unsurprisingly, the reality is a little more complicated. The creation of a sense of modern, unified nationhood has been a long, hard one. In many ways, it is still incomplete. The history of ethnic classification in modern China has a long pedigree. Sun Yat-sen, in his works before and during the early years of the Republican Era (1911–49 – see Chapter 2) had talked of the Chinese population following five key religions – Buddhism, Islam, Daoism, Catholicism and Protestantism, and five key ethnic groups – the Han, the Hui, Mongolian, Uyghur and Tibetan. Sun's vision of the multi-ethnic state based on the three principles of the people was sometimes contaminated by social Darwinism, which had seeped into China at the end of the nineteenth century. Han Chauvinism was one of the key attack points for Mao Zedong, who accused the Republican Government of the Nationalists in 1935 of ignoring the rights of the ethnic minorities, and refusing to allow them greater autonomy in the regions in which they lived. He promised the Inner Mongolian area would be run as a fully autonomous quasi-state after the final victory of the CCP in 1935 – a promise the region is still waiting to be fulfilled, eight decades later (Bulag, 2002).

That the CCP was influenced by Soviet thinking on ethnicity was clear when it undertook the classification of ethnic minorities in the 1950s. A group in Beijing was mandated to scour the country, ensuring that everyone was able to put one of the prescribed ethnic identities on to their household registration card, a document that functioned like an internal passport and which still exists. It was at this point that 56 groups were recognized. In some provinces, such as Sichuan and Yunnan, there were great issues about how to adapt the framework supplied by the central government to the rich ethnic and cultural worlds that existed in these places. Often, classifications were arbitrary. In remote areas of the south-western provinces, it could be argued that there were perhaps hundreds, maybe thousands, of different ethnic groups with their associated language, kinship rituals, cultures and scripts. The issue was how ethnicity was defined.

For Stalin in the USSR, ethnicity had been connected with religion, diet, language and cultural practices. In China, there had been talk before 1949 of nationality carrying some of these markers of difference – but with the arrival of scientific Marxism, there needed to be something easier to define and tabulate. Language, a recognized culture and a homeland were to be the prescription in this case. So in this way ethnicity made its entry into PRC mainstream thought. How ethnicity and the recognition of ethnic forms of self-identity and social and political practices lived alongside the more centralizing, state-building and nationalistic elements of the CCP's overall programme was another matter. For a start, the state was reluctant to recognize the 400-plus ethnic groups that put themselves forward for separate status and identification. By the time of the Cultural Revolution, some ethnic minorities were targets of heavy attacks by zealous Red Guard groups, because of what was claimed to be their disloyalty to the Han-dominated central state and to its class-centred, rather than ethnic-centred ideology as a marker of identity. The political leadership were, after all, largely Han, with the exception of Ulanfu, the sole Mongolian on the central leadership team till his fall in 1967. The Han ethnic majority, in terms of government and Party position, became dominant, and the ethnic minorities were pushed increasingly into a position where they were judged as being undeveloped, backward, and needing help to modernize. This was seen most clearly in remote areas such as Tibet and Xinjiang, where there were influxes of Han Chinese to assist locals in modernizing and becoming scientifically and technologically advanced. This attitude persists at the time of writing, with central campaigns to open up the west of China from 1999, and reports issued by the central government producing blueprints to bring Tibet and Xinjiang into the twenty-first century being common.

In the last decade, even Han mainstream thinkers themselves have questioned the traditional ethnic rubric of the central government. Hu Angang, of Qinghua University in Beijing, and Ma Rong, of Beijing University, have developed what has been called the 'second generation of ethnic minority policies'. They have argued that the idea of autonomous regions where preferential policies are directed at minorities violates the egalitarian ethos of the Party and needs to be revised. They have also spoken about this being, indirectly, the source of intra-ethnic conflict, because it socially encodes inequality between Han and other ethnicities rather than aspiring to make them utterly equal. Behind this new argument hovers the Maoist idea of the fading away of ethnic differences and the assertion of a sort of transcendent social basis for what people think they are and how they act. In view of the ongoing unrest in Tibet, Xinjiang and elsewhere in China where ethnic resentment clearly plays a role, both Ma and Hu may well be accused of wishful thinking, and at least as of 2014 ethnic politics in China, despite much central leadership attention and talk of a new era of harmony, looks no closer to resolution.

Tibet and Xinjiang

Tibet and Xinjiang together constitute only a tiny proportion of China's population, but they occupy key strategic areas and account for over a third of China's current area. They are also key bases for resources.

Both areas have complex histories. The vast Tibetan plateau, which covers an area over twice as big as the current Tibetan Autonomous Region, was occupied by Tibetan ethnic groups from at least the Bronze Age. A kingdom was established in the seventh century CE, which adopted Buddhism and waged campaigns against some of the neighbouring kingdoms. Conquered in stages by the Mongolian armies in the middle of the thirteenth century, it became a part of Yuan administrative rule, but with the collapse of that dynasty it reverted to local rule until the Qing conquests in the middle of the eighteenth century. The collapse of the Qing and incursion by the British in the early twentieth century brought about a region with a high level of autonomy, but, despite efforts during the Chinese Republican era to receive recognition as a state at the United Nations, the creation of the People's Republic of China in 1949 led, in 1951 to partial annexation of the region, and, in 1959, to full political assimilation. The fourteenth Dalai Lama fled to India where he remains based to this day. Modern Tibet is 97 per cent inhabited by ethnic Tibetans, and according to some accounts largely reliant on central subsidies. In recent decades PRC propaganda has stressed how their development model has lifted Tibetans from feudal serfdom and an unenlightened theocracy into modernity. But the 100,000 Tibetans who have fled over the border since 1959, and the major uprisings in 1987, 1989 and then 2008, along with the tragic series of self-immolations since 2011 show that this is not a view shared by a significant number. At a very fundamental level, the world view of most Tibetans, cast in terms of Buddhism and reverence for the Dalai Lama as a living god, is in stark opposition to that of the current atheist leadership in Beijing (Ma, 2011).

In the case of Xinjiang, issues have been further complicated by the brief memory of part of the region being independent under Soviet

Box 1.5 The Chinese 2010 census

Like most countries, the PRC undertakes a nationwide census every decade. The 2010 census was an epic of organization and logistics, with many tens of thousands contracted to canvass returns across the country, and to analyse data and prepare statistics. The provisional results were issued in 2011. They showed that that the country was much more urbanized than in 2000, with an older and slightly larger population, but also a much better educated one. The key findings were:

- Mainland China's (excluding Hong Kong, Macau and Taiwan) total population was 1.34 billion, an increase of 5.84 per cent since 2000 – a sharply slower rate of growth than the 2000 census showed. China's 2000 census put the country's total population at 1.265 billion, a rise of 11.7 per cent over the 1990 figure.
- The annual population growth rate was 0.57 per cent in the decade to 2010, compared with 1.07 per cent in 1991–2000.
- In 2010, 16.60 per cent of the population was aged 14 or younger, a sharp decline from 22.89 per cent in 2000.
- In 2010, 8.87 per cent were 65 or older, compared with 6.96 per cent in 2000 and 5.57 per cent in 1990.
- China had 105.20 males for every 100 females, with females accounting for 48.73 per cent of the total.
- Nearly half of the population – 49.7 per cent – lives in urban areas, indicating a rapidly urbanizing country.
- In 2010, the number of people with a university education was 8,930 per 100,000, almost 2.5 times more than in 2000, when it stood at 3,611.

Source: Thomson Reuters: http://www.trust.org/alertnet/news/factbox-chinas2010-census/) accessed 13 May 2011.

influence from 1946 to 1949. Since the establishment of the autonomous region there, however, the region has been progressively settled by increasing numbers of, in particular, Han, and exploited for its mineral wealth. The 2009 unrest erupted after internet clips seemed to show Uyghur workers being beaten up in southern China after protesting at a factory. But in 2014, tensions escalated with an attack by Xinjiang separatist activists in Kunming Station, Yunan, that left over 30 dead through knife attacks. A suicide bomb attack in April in Beijing killed two, but occurred in one of the most sensitive places in the country, Tiananmen

Square. Two subsequent attacks at Urumqi station and with a van loaded with homemade bombs driven into a market in the capital of Xinjiang, in April and May 2014 respectively, resulted in over 30 deaths.

At central meetings in Beijing in June, the Xi Jinping leadership committed themselves to a policy based on three principles: ethnic harmony, national unity and economic development. But the more worrying aspect for them was the internationalization of the conflict, with evidence of links to extremist groups in the Middle East. As a sign of their increased nervousness, Dr Ilham Tohti, one of the most moderate Uyghur voices still active in China was detained in early 2014, and then given a life sentence in September.

2

The Making of Modern China

The two great overarching themes of Chinese history from the beginning of the nineteenth century to the present day are the country's efforts to modernize, and attempts over this period by the various states, academics, cultural figures and others to articulate a cohesive sense of Chinese national identity. These two phenomena, of modernity and identity, were connected by the fact that they both, to varying extents, involved China's relationship with the outside world. The first, because modernization had largely risen from Western processes of scientific enquiry and industrialization, and the second because Chinese intellectuals and politicians often located themselves in opposition to Western models, and posited a sense of 'Chineseness' which was in some way alternative or different from these – an aspiration to be like the West in some ways, but different to it in others. This exists to this day in forms of Chinese exceptionalism and notions like 'socialism with Chinese characteristics'.

Precursor to Modern China: The Qing

At the beginning of the nineteenth century, China was in the second century of Qing rule by the Manchus, members of an ethnic minority from an area which is now the north-eastern part of the PRC but which was, prior to the fifteenth century, outside the formal limits of predecessor Ming-dominated territory. The Manchus had occupied the imperial throne after their conquest of the Ming Dynasty during the years 1643–4. In this era, the borders of the country had been expanded to include the vast north-western New Territories (still called 'Xin Jiang' to this day, from 'xin' meaning 'new' and 'jiang' meaning 'boundary'), which were absorbed into the Chinese centralized state in the mid-seventeenth century during a period of military activity, and parts of what is now the Tibetan Autonomous Region, conquered in the eighteenth century.

Box 2.1 Key dates in China's history

1368	Fall of Mongol-led Yuan Dynasty; creation of Ming
1642–4	Collapse of Ming Dynasty; start of Qing
1661–1722	Reign of the Kangxi emperor; conquests of the Tibetan and Xinjiang regions
1722–35	Reign of the Yongzheng emperor
1735–96	Reign of the Qianlong emperor
1793	Lord Macartney's trade mission to China from Great Britain
1839–41	First Opium War with Great Britain, resulting in the signing of the Treaty of Nanjing ceding parts of Hong Kong
1859–61	Second Opium War
1850–64	Taiping Uprising
1893	Birth of Mao Zedong
1911–12	Collapse of the Qing; establishment of the Republic of China
1919	May Fourth protests in Beijing by students protesting the unfair settlements ceding territory to colonial powers at the end of the First World War
1921	Communist Party of China holds its first Congress in Shanghai
1925	Death of Sun Yat-sen; Chiang Kai-shek becomes leader of the Republic and the KMT
1931	The Marco Polo Bridge incident near Beijing between Japanese and Chinese troops is the first act that leads to all-out war later in the decade
1934–5	The Long March by Communists as they seek refuge from Nationalist attack
1937	Start of Japan–China War
1942	Mao Zedong becomes dominant leader of the Communist Party; works as part of a United Front with Nationalists to defeat the Japanese

→

Under the rule of the emperors Kangxi (1662–1722), Yongzheng (1723–35) and Qianlong (1735–95) Qing China enjoyed stability, remarkable cultural and intellectual growth, and a strong, centralized governance. The current entity we call the People's Republic of China (PRC) has its roots in the vast and ethnically diverse geographical terrain secured by the great Qing emperors. Their legacy lives into the twenty-first century through the borders of the PRC which largely follow the

→

1945	Defeat of Japan in the Second World War
1946–9	Civil War in China between Nationalists and Communists
1949	Victory of Communists in Civil War; foundation of the People's Republic of China
1950–3	The Korean War
1953	Introduction of first Five Year Plan
1957	The 'Hundred Flowers' campaign ends in a clampdown on intellectuals in China
1958–61	The 'Great Leap Forward' attempts to drive forward China's industrialization, but results in major famines and economic breakdown in most of the country
1966–76	The Great Cultural Revolution
1971	Death of Mao's successor, Lin Biao, while attempting to flee the country; the People's Republic of China rejoins the United Nations
1972	Visit of President Richard Nixon to China
1976	Death of Mao Zedong; fall of the Gang of Four
1978	Reform and Opening Up policy introduced by rehabilitated leader Deng Xiaoping
1980	Creation of first Special Economic Zones
1989	Tiananmen Square massacre; fall of Zhao Ziyang; Jiang Zemin becomes Party Secretary
1992	Deng Xiaoping's Southern Tour restarts economic liberalization process
1997	Death of Deng Xiaoping; return of Hong Kong to Chinese sovereignty
2001	China joins the World Trade Organization
2002	Hu Jintao replaces Jiang Zemin as Party Secretary
2008	China hosts the Olympic Games
2012	Xi Jinping replaces Hu Jintao as Communist Party Secretary, and, in 2013, country President

territory they defined, in some cases conquered, and then assimilated into the more ancient Chinese heartland territory.

Despite the illustriousness of high Qing rule, the empire that had been created contained some worrying fault lines. The world's largest economy until 1830, China began to slip rapidly as the West, and in particular Europe and North America, undertook dramatic industrialization, something that had arisen as a result of the practical application of scientific discoveries made over the previous century. Great Britain in particular introduced a number of innovations that revolutionized the way artifacts were produced, and how people lived, with the population undergoing rapid urbanization as a result of these changes. By 1839, China was largely isolated from these developments, linked into the global economy through its exports of silk, spices and tea, but taking very little in return, and still operating on a mercantilist, largely agricultural economy supplemented by small businesses. For missionaries who travelled through China at this time, the static sense of the country they witnessed which was composed of endless rural areas heavily populated by people who had lived this way for centuries was something that came across consistently from their various reports. One of the more famous, by the French missionary, the Abbé Huc, describes a tour from 1844 to 1846 through 'Tartary, Thibet and China' in which he and his companions witness a country which is largely bereft of well made roads, or any significant signs of the new urban cultures rising in the Western world of the time (Huc, 1859).

Qing China's initial encounter with Western modernity can be dated to the influx of missionaries, with their ideas and scientific instruments, over the era of the three great emperors from 1662 onwards. However, the first real diplomatic clash with one of the newly emerging major powers, Great Britain, came with the delegation led by the highly experienced diplomat, Lord Macartney, to Beijing in 1793. The visit remains famous both for the brusque way with which the Qianlong emperor dismissed the need to import any of the goods available from the West into the empire over which he ruled, and for the battles about the way the British presented themselves to the Qing court on terms of parity without bowing as vassals or subjects. Despite these problems, however, trade between China and the outside world slowly expanded into the 1830s. A more problematic issue soon arose, though, over the increasing imbalance in trade caused by Qing China exporting vast amounts of silks, spices and other goods to the rest of the world, but importing little back in its turn. The practical result of this was that the empire began to own most of the world's silver reserves, which foreigners used to pay for the goods they bought. This has haunting parallels with the PRC's trade disparities with much of the developed world in the early decades of the twenty-first century.

The Opium Wars

The response of European, and in particular British, merchants was to identify one product China did not have but which its people were willing to buy – opium, the drug processed from poppies. A new trade in the highly addictive powder appeared, and fast became the key business of exporting to China, but it also created huge problems of addiction and social misery in the country. An angry backlash in 1839 from the Qing court attempted to close down the business by military means. This proved unsuccessful. The heavily armed modern British ships reduced the more primitive Chinese navy, such as it was then, to an ungainly retreat, and allowed the British to level harsh reparations in the Treaty of Nanking in 1842, part of which was the ceding of Hong Kong island as a free port in British hands in perpetuity. A second Opium War (1856–60) only saw more concessions by the Qing court, including further parts of the Hong Kong area, and large openings for trade throughout the southern coast of the country. While the Opium Wars have been cited by the Communists since their takeover of China in 1949 as landmarks in the subjugation and humiliation of the country by external aggressors, for many Chinese intellectuals at the time they served as painful wake-up calls for the urgent need for their country to modernize. This became even more intense with the wholesale adoption of Western industrial processes in Japan after the Meiji Restoration in 1868 (Lovell, 2011).

While post-1949 historiography within the PRC frequently places immense symbolic importance on the Opium Wars and locates them in a distinctive narrative of victimhood and colonial bullying, in the mid-nineteenth century they were merely events in a larger tale of decay and internal conflict. This relates to China's battle since the nineteenth century to create a sense of national identity. The country created by the Qing conquests was simply too vast and diverse to rule easily, and even in its traditional heartlands there were frequent uprisings. The most devastating of these were the Taiping and Nian Rebellions. The Taiping (Chinese for 'great peace') Rebellion was the most deadly, convulsing the country from 1850 to 1864, and, on some estimates, leading to more than 20 million deaths. Started by a failed candidate for the provincial civil service exams, Hong Xiuquan, whose exposure to translated Christian literature had inspired him to declare himself the brother of Jesus Christ sent to China to usher in a new era, it reached deep into the rural areas, creating something close to civil war. Its threat to the stability of the Qing court was so great that only the deployment of the full resources of the Beijing government were able finally to quell it. The Nian Rebellion, which occurred in the north, while marginally less devastating than the Taiping, actually went on longer, from 1851 to 1868. The economic costs of these and other internal rebellions, and their toll on national confidence and cohesiveness, were colossal. It is surprising in hindsight that the Qing rulers maintained power for as long as they did.

In the final years of the Qing period, the competing pressures of an outside world keen to gain access to China's natural resources and its markets led to an increase in its internal fragmentation. Many of the country's officials and intellectual elite were aware of the need for radical change. But the central court, under a series of weak emperors and the dominant Empress Dowager Ci Xi (1835–1908) proved itself incapable of responding with anything but defensiveness. Figures such as Kang Youwei and Liang Qichao, who were among the small but increasing number that had been educated abroad, mainly in Japan or Europe, proposed a number of reforms with the support of the Emperor Guangxu in 1898. But their vision of democratic change, educational transformation and scientific development was largely suppressed, even though the Confucian exam system of key classics that had been in place for over 1,000 years, and which demanded rote learning for those who undertook it, was abolished in 1908. Riddled by a deepening internal crisis, the Qing court collapsed after a military uprising in the central city of Wuhan spread to the rest of the country in 1911–12. A regime over 250 years old, following an imperial political system that had been 2,000 years in the making, ended with a whimper rather than a bang.

Republican China, 1911 onwards

Hopes that new leaders of non-dynastic China were any better placed to answer the issues of how to modernize the country and create a sense of national identity soon proved to be misplaced. The abortive national elections of 1912 were an ominous precursor. The first and only truly democratic national elections ever held in the country to this day, they were contested by over 300 parties, and resulted in the victory of teacher and professional revolutionary activist Song Jiaoren, followed almost immediately by his assassination at the railway station in Shanghai while on his way to Beijing to become the country's president. While the looming figure of Sun Yat-sen (see Box 2.2) inspired many nationalists, by the time of the First World War China was sinking into disunity, with Tibet already declaring itself free of central Chinese control, and the country splitting into zones of influence among warlords. The one figure with enough national influence and power to broker unity in the midst of all of this, Yuan Shikai, died only a year after imperiously declaring himself president in 1915. To add insult to injury, the end of the First World War

Box 2.2 Sun Yat-sen

Sun Yat-sen (in Mandarin his name is Sun Zhongshan) remains uniquely revered by both Nationalists and the CCP in Taiwan and Mainland China, respectively, and indeed across the Chinese-speaking world. His contribution to the development of China as a nation in the twentieth century, however, is increasingly contested, with many regarding him as a figure who largely failed in his main aims, and looking at those who were around him as the real contributors. Sun, born in the southern province of Guangdong in 1866, left China to live in Honolulu with his brother at the age of 18. He was to enjoy a peripatetic lifestyle for most of his life, studying in Japan, Hong Kong and London before moving back to the USA, and returning finally to China to be the provisional president, albeit for only a year before the elections in 1912. His critical role in establishing the Revolutionary Alliance (Tongmenhui), which eventually evolved into the Nationalists, gave him prominence from 1911 onwards, even though he held no specific executive position. As China disintegrated into chaos after 1915, Sun established his power base in his native Guangdong, setting up the council for national reunification. By his death in 1925, little had been achieved, however, and the great campaigns to put China back together lay in the future.

Sun's influence at the time, and his legacy, are founded on his popularization of an ideology of Chinese national identity – and in particular through his 'Three Principles of the People' – (the 'san min' doctrine). This was articulated in the 1890s, and consists of the principles of democracy ('minquan'), nationalism ('minxu') and people's welfare ('minsheng'). The principle of nationalism, in particular, had resonance because of the issue of how to create unity in a country as vast and complex as China. Sun's writings about the five major ethnic groups in the country (Han, Tibetan, Mongolian, Hui and Uyghur), and the need to have an overarching sense of Chineseness independent from, and transcending, the dominant Han ethnicity raised issues which in some sense China still struggles with as a country. That his intellectual legacy is fought over and claimed by both the Taiwan Republic of China and the Communists in the PRC is indicative of how much symbolic impact he had.

and the armistice talks in Versailles saw large parts of Chinese territory ceded to Japan. Anger over this inspired a new generation of Chinese students and intellectuals to go onto the streets on 4 May 1919 for demonstrations across the country. Their slogan to support 'Mr Science and Mr Democracy' haunted China for the next century. Perhaps the most important outcome of the May Fourth Incident was the emergence of a Communist movement in the country (see Chapter 3). The dominant political force in China at this time was the Nationalist Party (Guomindang, or Kuomintang – GMD, or KMT), established by Song Jiaoren and Sun Yat-sen in 1912,which presented itself as the 1920s went on as a party of national unity. Sun died in 1925, long before he could realize his dream of reunifying the country. But his acolyte, Chiang Kai-shek, undertook a campaign for national reunification from 1927 onwards. To achieve this, he turned on the Communists, whose membership by then had grown to over 5,000 spread over provinces in central China, and the great city of Shanghai, undertaking a brutal purge in April 1927 and casting those that remained into the countryside.

Years of War

Through military reunification campaigns undertaken from 1927 onwards, Chiang Kai-shek was able to assert control over most of China by 1933. But from 1931 with the annexation of a large part of the north-east of China, relations with Japan grew increasingly tense, undermining this unity. International and regional issues contributed to this – the looming prospect of conflict in Europe after the rise to power by the Nazi regime in Germany, and the appearance of a more aggressive nationalism within Japan, driven by its increasingly assertive military faction. Tensions came to a head in July 1937, when Japanese and Chinese troops clashed at the Marco Polo Bridge near Beijing. Japan's harsh demands for reparations led initially to stalemate, but then to all-out war, with an invasion of the rest of the country by Japanese troops from summer 1937 onwards.

In terms of destructiveness and numbers of casualties, the Sino-Japanese war was one of the most bloody in history. At its heart, an industrialized, modernized economy threw the full force of its power against an agricultural, undeveloped one. Tragic events such as the attack on Nanjing in late 1937, which saw the Japanese army raping, murdering and brutalizing as many as 300,000 Chinese people (the exact figure has never been established, and controversy still exists about just how many suffered during that week) set the outlines of a war that was finally to radicalize the Chinese, particular in the countryside, where some of the most savage campaigns were conducted. By 1940, a third of the country was dominated by Japan, with a further third contested, and the final part under the combined control of Nationalists, with increasing large pockets run by the Communists. Mao's CCP (by 1942 it was mostly dominated by him) only survived to 1940 due a number of deft movements in the years after 1930, largely fleeing a Nationalist onslaught. Chiang had made it his mission before the war with Japan to eradicate the CCP and its nascent army, complaining that while the Japanese were 'a disease of the skin,' the Communists were 'a disease of the heart'. Eradication campaigns had encircled and then attempted to wipe out pockets of Communist influence in the countryside, forcing the CCP to undertake the celebrated Long March over 1934–5, as their main forces went north, to a more isolated, protected area in northern Shaanxi province, behind Japanese lines. At the same time, Chiang retreated west, making Chongqing (Chungking) his war capital. The Japanese established their own regime in Nanjing.

The war with Japan wholly changed the internal dynamics in China, forcing Chiang to enter into another United Front arrangement, where the Communists were accepted alongside as legitimate patriotic forces

Illustration 2.1 Tiananmen Gate, Beijing

The closest modern China comes to a sacred place, it was here that Mao Zedong proclaimed the foundation of the People's Republic after the end of the Civil War in October 1949. The place remains dominated by his image to this day.

fighting for national survival. Japanese 'slash all, kill all, burn all' methods revolted those inside China, and pushed even more towards working with the Communists. After years of deadlock, in 1944 the first great breakthrough came, with Nationalist and Communist victories in central China, and success for the guerrilla campaigns of the Maoist troops and activists. The Japanese had never planned for the way that an invasion of China would stretch their forces. They were able to control the cities, but subduing the vast countryside was a different matter. Finally accepting this, the Japanese withdrew into smaller zones of occupation as the war progressed, but it was only their final defeat by the Allies in 1945 that ended the Japanese attempt to create a 'Greater Asia Co-prosperity Zone'.

The Civil War

The victorious Nationalist and Communist forces were not able to celebrate for long. Unable to hammer out a common political programme, the country erupted into civil war between 1946 and 1949. Its infrastructure and economy, already ravaged by the anti-Japan war, were further degraded. The Civil War saw the fortunes of both contesting parties fluctuate wildly. Initially the US-supported Nationalists looked best placed. But miscalculations, poor management and greater Communist strategic awareness meant that by 1949 inflation had depleted the national economy and the Nationalist armies, at least in rural areas, were demoralized and unpopular. Even with some military support from the USA, Chiang and his forces were finally compelled to flee to the island of Formosa (Taiwan) off the southern coast of the Chinese mainland, and continue the Republic from there (see Chapter 1). The People's Republic of China, under the Communist Party, was formally declared in Beijing on 1 October 1949.

The People's Republic: Early Years

The Communists under Mao Zedong's leadership took over a country whose economy had been decimated by more than a decade of war, and whose infrastructure was almost non-existent. Their immediate challenge was to rebuild this, something that they started to do by reforming land ownership, taking all land into the hands of the state and undertaking huge, often violent, campaigns against landlords. Financial and technical support from the USSR was the one source of help in the early years. Otherwise, Mao's China was isolated from the rest of the world, and regarded with suspicion, despite the fact that many countries recognized it diplomatically. To add to the challenges, in 1950 the country was drawn into another war, when Kim Il-sung, the supreme leader of the Democratic People's Republic of Korea (DPRK) launched an attack on the Republic of Korea in the south. The war raged on, with UN forces pitted against first the North Koreans, and then vast Chinese reinforcements. Mao's own son died in the conflict. The sheer weight of numbers meant that the Chinese forces under Marshal Peng Dehuai, one of the great heroes of the Civil War, were able to push the UN back, with both sides reaching an eventual stalemate on the 38th parallel. There they stayed, until an armistice was put in place in 1953. Over six decades later, a peace treaty is still to be signed, and the Korean peninsula remains divided.

The Communist Party regarded itself as coming to power with a coalition between urban proletariat workers and, more important, farmers, who still made up more than 90 per cent of the population in 1949. The CCP constructed a national system of governance, with Party branch cells down to village level, and the establishment of new laws (the Marriage Law, granting equal rights between men and women to divorce, was amongst the first) and a national budget plan (one every five years) starting from 1953. But China's vulnerability was always in the central leaders' minds, etched there over the long years in which they had been primarily military leaders. Added to this internal vulnerability, there were border disputes with most of the 14 neighbouring countries. Tibet remained contested, with an agreement in 1951 allowing partial autonomy. Another four regions (Xinjiang, Inner Mongolia, Ningxia and Guangxi) were granted autonomous region status – though this meant little in terms of their rights to set local budgets and administer themselves. The resolution of the status of Tibet within the PRC came after an uprising of Tibetan and other minorities from 1956, with a military campaign by the People's Liberation Army PLA leading to the complete annexation of the territory in 1959, the subsequent fleeing of the Dalai Lama to neighbouring India, and the imposition of Beijing-backed leaders.

Mao worked in the early years of the PRC among a group who had gained legitimacy through winning the wars against both the Japanese and the Nationalists, and restoring China's territorial integrity. This stress on unification being their key mission was to be a feature of CCP rule through Mao and subsequent CCP leaders. National education, social welfare, security, policing and legal reforms were implemented. But in order to do this, and in fulfilment of their class-based ideology, the Party had to mount a number of mass campaigns. Some of these were directed at those identified as enemies of the central state and its policies. Landlords, capitalists, business people, and those with a bad class background (from intellectual, rich landlord, or aristocratic family background) were discriminated against. The Three Antis Campaign in 1951 and the Five Antis Campaign a year later were only preludes to a larger anti-rightist movement that followed the Hundred Flowers Campaign in 1956. In the latter campaign, the Party encouraged feedback and criticism of its seven years in power, but was taken aback by the vehemence of the criticism it received. Critics, such as the intellectual Hu Feng, an acolyte of the great Shanghai-born writer, Lu Xun were given lengthy prison sentences and sent to do hard labour or work in concentration camps in the interior of China. Universities, some of which had only just been established, and the whole work unit system set up throughout the country to provide employment, social welfare, housing and support to people, were convulsed by sessions against members of society accused of holding negative feelings towards the revolution. The Anti-Rightist Campaign was followed in 1957 by the Great Leap Forward, a movement to accelerate China's economic growth by concentrating on collectivization, increased production and industrialization.

The Great Leap Forward proved to be economically disastrous, precipitating the collapse of agricultural production, and ushering in three years of famine between 1959 and 1962. While the wars of a decade earlier saw the slaughter of over 20 million people, the three years of famine caused even greater numbers of casualties, with estimates ranging from 30 million to 55 million (Becker, 1996; Yang, 2012; Dikötter, 2010). Writers in China in the 2000s, the most assiduous of them the historian Yang Jisheng, painstakingly recreated the mortality figures for specific districts in China over this period, showing that almost every family across the countryside was affected (Yang, 2012). While the cities were provided with food, the countryside, hit by poor productivity because of the impact of the Great Leap Forward and then a series of bad harvests, became cauldrons of suffering, with people in some areas forced to eat the bark from trees, to scavenge, and in the very worst cases to resort to cannibalism. Village and township leaders falsified data about the harvests in their areas, and colluded with higher-level officials in siphoning off grain and other crops to satisfy central commands (Thaxton, 2008).

Mao was forced to listen to criticism of these policies at the internal Party meeting in June 1959 held in the Lushan area in Jiangxi. This saw the rise of a more pragmatic leadership under the country's president Liu Shaoqi and his assistant, Deng Xiaoping. From 1961, the Chinese government implemented more flexible policies, trying to win back the trust of the farmers on whom the economy of the country was so reliant. The whispered history of this era, when so many had experienced death, suffering and hunger, was to remain, however, and it ranks as one of Mao's greatest failures, and the one for which he is considered most culpable.

The Era of Radicalism: The Great Cultural Revolution

While he took a back seat, Mao maintained his crucial position as chairman of the Party, and it was from this position that he made his comeback, supporting the unleashing of one of the largest mass campaigns ever undertaken – the Great Proletariat Cultural Revolution – from 1965 onwards. One of the root causes of this epic movement was Mao's dissatisfaction with what he called the bureaucratism of the Party and the re-emergence of exactly the kinds of vested interest and local and national elites he had tried to eliminate from 1949 onwards. With remarkable deviousness, Mao slowly subverted the formal structures of power within the CCP, empowering a group of radicals around his wife, Jiang Qing, who had been an actress in Shanghai in the 1930s before they married. Initially using arguments about the interpretation of culture and the meaning of metaphor to launch campaigns against figures within the Party, the first move involved a play written by Wu Han, vice Mayor of Beijing, whose piece in the early 1960s on a Ming official four hundred years earlier removed from office because of honest advice he had given against an emperor was interpreted by Mao as a symbolic attack on himself. Rebellious student groups arose in the universities in Beijing, attacking their lecturers. Red Guards, as they came to be called, were zealous, unruly, faithful only to Mao, or their interpretation of him, and frighteningly fanatical. Remarkably, many of the veterans of this movement subsequently became senior political leaders in later decades. The Red Guard movement can be interpreted now as the beginnings of their political education.

There was also a geopolitical issue looming behind the Cultural Revolution: the falling out between the USSR and the PRC after the denunciation of Stalin by Khrushchev at the Party Congress in 1956. Mao's relationship with Stalin had been prickly. When the two met, in Mao's only journey outside the borders of the PRC, during his visit to

Moscow in 1949, the two had regarded each other with suspicion. Stalin was ambiguous about the CCP victory in China, worrying about its strong nationalism and independence streak. In return, Mao could look back on a long history of mutual antagonism and incomprehension between the USSR and Republican and Communist China. But it remained a key ally, technically and financially. However, from 1957, relations between the two powers grew increasingly tense, with the withdrawal of most of the many thousands of Russian experts based in the country by 1960. The escalating coldness between these two Communist countries meant that from 1966 one of the key modes of attack in Cultural Revolution (CR) polemics was to label someone a USSR revisionist or lackey. It was this description that was given to the leadership of Liu Shaoqi, at that time the country's president, and those around him, and it was against him in particular that the full fury of the CR campaign was eventually aimed.

The felling of President Liu in 1968, and the imprisonment of most of the leaders around him, was simultaneous with the rise of Marshal Lin Biao, another great hero of the campaigns during the Civil War that had seen the defeat of the Nationalists and brought the Communists to power. At the Ninth Party Congress in 1969 the Party membership was so decimated that almost half of the previous members were unable to attend because they had been imprisoned, dismissed, or, in the worst case, were dead. The Congress saw a number of signs that, with Liu now gone (he died of untreated cancer that same year), Lin Biao was in the ascendant, and had been chosen as Mao's successor. But his ascendancy was short-lived. Mao's suspicions and the active agitation of other competitors for the leadership meant that by 1971 Lin had lost the Chairman's favour. In mysterious circumstances, he fled China in September that year, with his wife and son, but the plane they were in crashed in the Republic of Mongolia killing everyone on board. By 1974, the country was being run by Mao's long-standing and faithful adviser, Premier Zhou Enlai, despite the fact that from the early 1970s he had been suffering from throat cancer. His illness precipitated the recall of Deng Xiaoping in 1975 over seven years after his initial felling alongside Liu, but on Zhou's death early in 1976, Deng was felled for a second time.

In the final months of Mao's life, the supreme leader of the Party for over 40 years was suffering from Parkinson's disease and unable to speak. (Li, 1996). On 9 September 1976, six months after angry demonstrations by supporters of Zhou Enlai against Jiang Qing and the circle around her, and only a few weeks after over a quarter of a million people had died in a devastating earthquake in the city of Tangshan 100 kilometres (62 miles) from Beijing, Mao died, and with him the Cultural

Box 2.3 The Gang of Four

The Cultural Revolution is blamed in official Party accounts to this day on a group referred to as 'The Gang of Four'. This group were led by Mao Zedong's wife, the former actress Jiang Qing, who had been politically inactive till the early 1960s when she emerged as a commentator on cultural matters, and managed to secure a place on the Politburo and in the Cultural Revolution Small Group which acted as a de facto Politburo during the early phases of the mass movement. Jiang Qing had a number of scores to settle from her early life in which she had been linked romantically to a number of figures in Shanghai – amongst them the father of future Politburo Standing Committee leader Yu Zhengsheng. He in particular was to suffer terribly because of persecution derived from her orders.

Alongside Jiang were three other figures, most of them linked to Shanghai, which had a reputation at the time for radical leftist politics. Zhang Chunqiao was perhaps the most significant, a former leader in Shanghai who wrote a number of important ideological manifestos against bourgeois liberalism and revisionism in the early 1970s. Yao Wenyuan, a journalist from Shanghai and the son of a well-known writer there, was the propagator for the movement, writing a number of the key polemical attacks during its inception phase and then producing searing attacks for the next decade on people figured out as enemies. Finally, a late entrant to the Four was Wang Hongwen, a factory worker in the city who was involved in the strikes of 1966 to 1967 and then became a commune leader before attracting Mao's eye and being elevated to Beijing. He was briefly talked of as a successor to Mao in 1973.

The Gang of Four held considerable powers while Mao lived. But they were only to outlast their patron by a matter of weeks, being detained in late 1976 and then put on trial in 1981 and given lengthy sentences. While they were blamed for misleading Mao in the 1981 Party Resolution (see below), this seemed harsh. At best, they were opportunistic courtiers who did what they felt was Mao's bidding. As Jiang Qing herself during her spirited defence in 1981 shouted at the judge: 'I was Mao's dog. He told me to bite and I bit.' Jiang was to commit suicide in 1991. The other members were to spend the rest of their lives in obscurity, with their demise announced through terse official announcements. Today, in China, if remembered at all, they are a byword for extremism and failed policy.

Revolution that he had inspired, supported and promoted. The radical leaders who came to be labelled as the Gang of Four were arrested less than four weeks after he was buried. And the man who he had supposedly settled on as his final chosen successor, Hua Guofeng, looked set fair to start a new post-Mao era.

Dealing with the Maoist Legacy

The PRC in 1976 was a country in which life expectancy had risen from only 32 years in 1949 to over 65; and one where literacy was high and many of the endemic health problems of the horrific pre-1949 years had been addressed. It had also gained a hydrogen bomb in 1964, reclaimed its seat at the United Nations in 1971, and been visited by an American president (Nixon in 1972). Despite the toll of the mass campaigns from 1950 onwards, and the devastating losses in the great famines of the early 1960s, the key achievement of the Communists had been to maintain a unified and largely stable country, one which had proved that it could determine its own route without outside interference. For these reasons, the outbursts of opposition and anger after the death of the popular Premier Zhou Enlai in early 1976 proved manageable.

But Mao had left a country scarred by his tireless support for internal campaigns and for creating class struggle and 'cleansing the ranks'. The Party itself had seen some of its key leaders suffer, and sometimes be murdered, from the late 1960s. Society across the country remained divided between those with good, and those with negative, class backgrounds. While many wept during Mao's epic funeral in Beijing in late September 1976, there was a sense of quiet release and relief, typified by the general celebrations when news was broadcast about the arrest of the Gang of Four a few weeks later. The leadership around the final chosen successor to Mao, Hua Guofeng, faced a country in which the critical agricultural sector was still underproductive, and in which industrialization was stunted and remained highly limited. The PRC, in 1976, was in effect bankrupt, diplomatically isolated and economically closed off from the rest of the world. It had no choice but to find another way, after the ultimate failure of Maoism.

The inexperienced Hua Guofeng, who had risen to power through provincial leadership and had few networks in the central system, had to solve the quandary of where China needed to go now that the Maoist road to Utopia had come to a dead end. There were plenty in the system who still believed fervently in engaging in class struggle. But many others knew that China had lost its way along the road to modernity and that something more dramatic needed to happen in order to get it back on track. Deng Xiaoping, who was enjoying his third return from the political graveyard, was viewed as the most credible figure in the post-Mao leadership, a survivor of the Maoist years, someone with impeccable credentials in the struggle against the Japanese and then the Nationalists pre-1949, an early member of the CCP, and a Party leader of great competence throughout the 1950s and into the 1960s. During the years when he was sent into the countryside after his first fall in 1971, Deng had spent time in rural Jiangxi. It was there, mulling over the poverty he saw around him, and recovering from the shock of hearing that his son had been permanently disabled in Beijing in an attack by Red Guards in the late 1960s, that he started thinking of the adaptations that needed to be made to China to energize the country's vast, complex economy (Vogel, 2011). The first hints of a possible alternative path were in fact spelt out by Premier Zhou himself, who summoned Deng back to Beijing in 1975, and who talked publicly once again of the need to use the Four Modernizations – in agriculture, industry, national defence, and science and technology (he had used the phrase first in the early 1960s). Deng returned to these ideas, with a group of advisers around him, from 1977 onwards.

The Start of the Great Transformation

In 1978, Deng, restored as a Politburo member and Vice-Premier, was confronted by three problems. The first was how to construct a new leadership that would be more open to reform and able to address the country's challenges as it modernized; the second was how to find ideas for structural changes in the Chinese economy that would increase productivity and accelerate industrialization; and the third was how to deal with the legacy of Maoism in ways that cleared the way for change, but did not create unnecessary problems in the country and Party by seeming to abandon Mao and his historical legacy. He was, as Deng well knew, regarded as the founder of the PRC, and as the key figure in the victory over the Japanese and the Nationalists. Deng did not wish to challenge Mao's historical role. There was too much support for Mao in the grassroots for this to be possible.

Deng saw the industrial models used in other countries, and in particular its neighbours such as Japan, Taiwan and South Korea, as offering ideas for what China could do. He paid particular attention to their rapid growth rates, and their ability to create export-oriented and globally successful industries that fuelled domestic growth. This lay behind the raft of proposals first heralded in the Party Plenum meeting in Beijing in late 1978, during which Deng outlined the need to 'reform and open up' – to allow foreign investment into China, in controlled ways, and in ways that accorded with China's national needs. From 1979, Special Economic Zones (SEZs), joint ventures with foreign companies and a raft of other reforms appeared as part of a strategy to open up China to the outside world. Deng also allowed a number of delegations, some of which he himself participated in, to visit Japan, the USA, Europe and other developed economies, to look for ideas they might bring back and apply in China. In the end, the Japanese basis was perhaps the most important, and many elements of its intense, export-oriented manufacturing model were borrowed over the coming few years.

Burying Mao

Resolving leadership issues and coming to consensus on the role of Mao were intimately connected. In 1981, the Party issued a resolution (the second major resolution since its foundation in 1921, the first being in 1945 during the war years) which assessed Mao as a great leader, a great Marxist, and the victor of the Sino-Japanese and Civil War, who had been pivotal in bringing the Party to power and leading it from 1949. The Resolution also recognized importantly that Mao had made mistakes, particularly during the Cultural Revolution – but that these had been because he had been misled. This carefully nuanced judgment meant that neither the leftists nor the reformists in the Party could become too agitated, and gave Deng the political space to push both Party and country in a different direction, allowing the creation of markets, and reducing state control over the economy, but avoiding the accusation of wholesale revisionism. Even so, Deng was to encounter some fierce resistance. As part of this re-evaluation, more by stealth than design, it became clear that, within the Party, and in the country generally, Deng had far greater credibility and support than Hua Guofeng. By 1982, Hua was moved into a largely ceremonial position and effectively quietly retired from front-line politics, dying in 2008, largely forgotten in China.

At the heart of the early reforms under the Deng leadership was the immediate dismantling of the highly inefficient commune system, and the introduction of new structures in the rural economy, which, after all, contributed over 50 per cent to China's GDP at the time (Naughton,

2006). Copying models formulated at the grassroots level in the late 1970s, by villagers in Anhui and Sichuan province in particular, the Dengist government allowed farmers to tend specific plots of land, to sell surpluses back to the state for a profit, and to use these profits to support other enterprises. The increase in productivity from 1980 was immediate, and rapid. By the mid-1980s, a country that had known starvation only a generation before was enjoying large grain surpluses. Less expected was the releasing of many from needing to work on the land and allowing them to becoming active in what came to be called Township and Village Enterprises (TVEs), locally managed collective-run entities that ranged from factories to hotels to co-operative shops. Many of these began to make goods, and lay behind the vast explosion of manufacturing, particularly in the south-eastern provinces, from the mid-1980s onwards (Naughton, 2006).

The Democracy Wall Movement of 1978–9

The 1980s were a time of heady and sometimes dizzying change in China, and were looked back on by some as the most liberal, open era in post-1949 history. Part of this might have been derived from the sense of relief after the grim social controls and uncertainty of the late Maoist period. But the Deng leadership had little interest in allowing challenges to the monopoly on power of the CCP. In fact, almost everything they did sought to strengthen the Party's role in society and to leave it less vulnerable to attack. Voices asking for more profound political reforms had begun to appear as early as 1971, perhaps as a result of the amazed public reaction to the disappearance and then disgrace of Lin Biao, Mao's once chosen successor (whose death while fleeing the country had only been announced by the Party to members in internal documents a year later in 1972, and then only gradually became more publicly known). In Guangzhou, three activists had published a paper with the title 'On Socialism and the Legal System', under the pseudonym Li Yizhe. The real challenge came, however, in the winter of 1978 and into the spring of 1979, when a wall in the Xidan area of West Beijing, close to the leadership compound of Zhongnanhai, was covered in posters debating political change. One of the most celebrated of these was by Wei Jingsheng, an electrician working at Beijing Zoo. He famously stole the Party's talk of 'Four Modernizations' and asked why this could not be increased to five, to include democracy. Others around him developed this theme (Wei, 1998). Over the years of the Cultural Revolution, people had been given a more tough-minded independence, and were less tolerant of hearing what they regarded as the Party's platitudes about implementing socialism with Chinese characteristics. They wanted the political reforms to be as bold and accelerated as the economic ones being mooted.

The leadership's response to this was swift and brutal. The Xidan free speech area was closed down in early 1979 and the posters ripped off the walls. Wei in particular was chosen as a scapegoat and given the first of two lengthy prison spells before finally being sent into exile in the USA in the late 1990s. Deng's political response was in the Resolution on Party history issued in 1981. While it was fine to talk about improvements, changes and adaptations, this all had to be done within a system in which the CCP was dominant, and in which it took the leadership in all major matters. Challenging this was not allowed. Deng was no liberal, nor a starry-eyed follower of Western liberal government models. For him, the Party was key to maintaining stability, territorial integrity and strength in China. It was not going to be challenged. Throughout the 1980s, therefore, even as the non-state sector of the economy exploded and more and more people left the state-owned work unit system, with its cradle-to-grave welfare into the world of entrepreneurialism and business, campaigns were mounted every few years, cracking down on 'spiritual pollution' and reminding the Chinese that the Westerners who were now allowed to come to, invest in, and travel and work in China were there to help the country do what the Party felt was in its interests, not to promote their own strategies of domination and control (Barmé and Minford, 1989). And to reinforce this message, Party officials could refer to the century of humiliation after the first Opium War of 1839–42, and ask who in the end had the interests of the country more at heart – the CCP, or the West?

The 1989 Uprising

Deng called the new kind of ideology guiding economic reform in China 'socialism with market characteristics' – sometimes simplified to 'market socialism'. This tapped into the Maoist language of over half a century earlier, when Mao and his key advisers had created the idea of a form of Marxism suited to China – and in particular, suited to the conditions of the Chinese countryside, where the CCP had its key powerbase. China's rapid economic changes since 1980 had come at a price, however. Party elders in 1987 had grown irritated by the increasingly freewheeling behaviour of the CCP Secretary, Hu Yaobang, and manoeuvred him out of the way, to be replaced by Zhao Ziyang. The underlying issue of need for deeper political reform to accompany the dramatic economic changes would not go away, however, and by 1989 the reforms that were ongoing in the Soviet Union had already captured the attention of many in China. Hu's death in April 1989 from a heart attack occurred as a number of cities around the country, and in particular Beijing, saw students and others demonstrate against corruption. Anger at how officials were still not held accountable and were constantly on the take alongside a sharp rise in inflation brought about for the first time since 1980 conditions which caused the economy to deteriorate.

In May, China saw the first visit by a leader from the Soviet Union since their arguments in the early 1960s – Mikhail Gorbachev. But at the same time as Gorbachev's visit, Tiananmen Square, in the centre of Beijing, was occupied daily by tens of thousands of students, some of whom had erected a papier-mâché figure modelled on the Statue of Liberty in New York, which they called the Goddess of Democracy. The Party was initially unable to find a way to respond to this outright challenge. Party Secretary Zhao was evidently sympathetic. And while the then Party Secretary in Tibet Autonomous Region, Hu Jintao, had authorized a harsh crackdown on demonstrations there in April 1989, Zhao held off in the capital. Documents later claimed to show how the CCP fought internally over ways to deal with the impasse (Nathan *et al.*, 2001). In late May, Deng summoned the key leaders to his residence in Beijing, and demanded that action be taken. Things had grown worse because of a hunger strike by some of the demonstrating students, and because there were now members of the government, the Party, and, worst of all, the military, who evidently sympathized with them. On 3 June, the Politburo with Deng authorized two crack units of the PLA from outside Beijing to enter the city and clear the central square. This they did in the early hours of 4 June. By the end of that day, the demonstrations had been dispersed. The aftermath of the event, for Deng, the country and the Party, would, however, prove profound.

For a hardened military leader such as Deng the numbers killed by tanks and live ammunition on 4 June were tiny. But for the international community and for many in the country and the Party, the government turning live ammunition on its own people was unforgivable. While a definitive number of casualties has never been established, it has been estimated that the deaths ran into the thousands (Brook, 1992). Deng, in thanking the army a few days later, stated that had he not acted, the country and the Party would have *fallen*. While he regretted the deaths, he stated that he did not regret saving the stability of the country and repelling what he called a counter-revolutionary attack (Vogel, 2011). Whether history will see things in this way remains to be seen. The twenty-fifth anniversary of the uprising in 2014 was marked by events across the world, and in particular a large gathering in Hong Kong. Despite rumours over the last few years of a reappraisal by the current Chinese leadership of the events of 1989, so far nothing has happened. It is unlikely to do so while figures like Li Peng and Jiang Zemin are still alive.

Post-Tiananmen

One of the key casualties of the Tiananmen Square uprising was Zhao Ziyang, whose apparent sympathy for the students led to his dismissal from his post and house arrest from June 1989 until his death 16 years later. His replacement, Jiang Zemin, was Party Secretary in Shanghai before being ordered to Beijing by the central senior leaders to take up the post of Party head. This appointment was a surprise. Jiang, a native of Jiangsu province, had studied engineering in the Soviet Union before becoming a manager in the state-owned enterprise sector. He had two things in his favour, however. He was regarded as having dealt with the unrest that had manifested itself in Shanghai reasonably well and without loss of life. And while no one in the Party was wildly enthusiastic about him, he did not arouse the same feelings of opposition as did some others, among them the widely reviled premier of the time Li Peng. By default, therefore, Jiang was appointed. In the end, it was to prove a success, if only because Jiang lasted in the role for 13 years and navigated the tricky diplomatic and political terrain after the massacre far more adeptly than many had expected.

The immediate impact of June 1989 was to cause China to be isolated from the international community, and for questions to be raised, both internally and externally, about where the country should now take its reforms. Those on the Maoist wing wanted more state control brought back, and demanded that the opening up of China be scaled down. Those who were more reformist argued that the problem leading up to 4 June had been too few changes made too slowly. Jiang's initial challenge was how to hammer out consensus between these, and his response during 1990, amid a widespread clampdown, with those blamed for agitating for the unrest either being put in prison or fleeing the country, was simply to make no big decisions and to preserve the status quo. Foreign companies withdrew from China, and investment levels fell. There were suspicions that China was about to enter another era of enclosure and introspection. Those of a more gloomy nature even wondered if the Party was about to fall – a belief strengthened by the collapse of the Soviet Union in late 1991.

Deng's Southern Tour

The existential shock of what had happened in Moscow in 1991 was part of the reason why Deng Xiaoping returned from 'retirement' (he had finally stepped down from leading the Central Military Commission, the extremely powerful body in the Party in charge of military affairs, in 1989) to undertake his last major contribution to Chinese political life. He did this via an impromptu visit in January 1992 to some of the successful SEZs in southern China – and, in particular, the newly built booming areas of Shenzhen just across the border from Hong Kong (then still under British sovereignty) and Zhuhai, next to Portuguese-controlled Macau. While undertaking what came to be labelled his 'southern tour', the 86-year-old Deng was taking a page from Mao's book in appealing directly to the people over the heads of officials. He spoke in the southern coastal city of Zhuhai just opposite to Macau of the need for the Party never to forget its responsibility to allow people to become more prosperous – and asserted, while looking over the dynamic buildings of Shenzhen, that the alternative to reform was simply to perish, so in that sense the Party had no choice but to continue with what it was doing.

The impact of Deng's 'imperial visit' was to embolden the reformers and encourage them to further liberalize inward investment regulations, allow more space for the internal market, and rationalize the state-owned system. From the 14th Party Congress later in 1992, the new leadership wrote Deng Xiaoping's ideas of 'market socialism' into the state constitution. They also appointed a raft of new leaders, one of whom, Hu Jintao, had been brought from Tibet and placed on the Politburo, the youngest leader to have been elevated so quickly for decades. It was only from the 15th Congress in 1997 and the National People's Congress of 1998, however, that the newly appointed premier, Zhu Rongji, set out a strategy to radically reorganize the state-owned enterprises, and to start making them productive again. Some were organizations the size of cities, with little commercial function but carrying enormous social welfare and other costs. In the north-east of the country, traditionally called the 'rust belt', the economy was stagnant. Steel production, aviation, cars and a raft of other primary sectors were often barely functional. But Zhu was aware of the costs of laying off so many from their cradle-to-grave jobs and introducing them to an employment free market so soon. Even so, it has been calculated that between 1997 and 2002 over 60 million people lost their jobs and had to find alternative work. The southern tour's greatest impact, however, was to ensure continuation of the reforms first started in 1978 of 'opening up' and creating a competitive market within China, which embraced foreign capital and was trying to upgrade its knowledge base. There would be no return to Maoist-style state autarky and central planning.

The Hu-Wen Era: The Bane of Inequality

With the death of Deng Xiaoping in 1997, a symbolic movement occurred away from the generation of revolutionary leaders who had brought the CCP to power in 1949, to those who had little connection to that time and had claim to a different kind of legitimacy. Hu Jintao became Party Secretary at the 16th Party Congress in 2002 after what was in effect the first properly smooth transition of leadership ever experienced by the CPC since 1949. His era began with the unfolding of a major landmark in the PRC's development – its entry to the World Trade Organization (WTO). This will be looked at more closely in Chapter 5. But politically, the final acceptance into the WTO fold marked the moment in which China signalled its full commitment to accepting international norms. Hu's chief accomplice in trying to fulfil the commitments undertaken in the WTO was his premier, Wen Jiabao.

The longer-term challenge of the Hu period was stated at its beginning – dealing with the increasing inequality in society. From the Maoist period, in which there were very similar levels of development (albeit with everyone being uniformly poor rather than wealthy) the market reforms introduced from 1978 onwards meant that an increasing wealth gap opened up between the winners and losers in the reform process, so that by 2004 levels of inequality had never been greater (Naughton, 2006). Some claimed they were on a par with Latin-American countries. Hu's challenge was to frame a message showing that the government was doing something about the situation. One area Hu and Wen addressed was the level of taxation on farmers. Jiang Zemin, in his final period in office, had managed to push through new regulations allowing business people and entrepreneurs to join the Party, something they had not been able to do previously. Red capitalists therefore became more politically secure, and their support was needed to employ the large numbers let go from the state sector. But many business people had seen their wealth levels rocket, giving rise to a new cash-rich echelon in society that lived, thought and acted in different ways from the Chinese of earlier periods. The wave of revolutions leading to the collapse of formerly Communist regimes and the introduction of new democratic parties in the former Soviet Union countries (called the 'colour revolutions' at the time) in the mid-2000s spooked the CCP even more, and from this period, one sees an increasing repressiveness and cautiousness on the part of the leadership (Dickson, 2003).

Evidence issued by the Chinese government's National Bureau for Statistics and other authoritative internal and external sources show that China had certainly become a more visibly contentious society as the first decade of the twenty-first century wore on. People were more conscious of their rights and were willing to pursue through provincial and central courts issues over which they felt they had been treated unjustly. Land disputes and pension claims shot up. In 2005, the final year for which official statistics were released, China saw 87,000 protests, up from only 8,000 per year a decade earlier (Huang, 2011, p. 182). Social cohesion, or its breakdown, was on the minds of the central leaders, and the mantra of aiming only for raw GDP growth became less persistent. Hu and Wen talked of 'social harmony' and of rebalancing society. They talked about changing one of the fundamental features of China, the difference in residence status between those holding household registration documents from rural areas, and those from cities. These gave different levels of access to social welfare, schooling, health support and the like. At a time when Chinese society was becoming increasingly mobile, with as many as 230 million migrant labourers having gone to the manufacturing areas in the coastal parts of China, maintaining this hangover from the Maoist period seemed odd (*People's Daily Online,* 2010). And yet, despite several discussions at the annual National People's Congresses (NPCs) from 2005 onwards, no agreement was reached. That rapid industrialization and growth had fundamentally changed Chinese society was clear – but there was no consensus between social groups, and subgroups, about what system might work better than the one the country already had under the CCP.

What was evident through the 2000s was the burgeoning role of the internet. From only two million users in the late 1990s, by 2012 there were 1 billion mobile phone users, with 677 million accessing the internet (Reuters, 2012). The explosion of communication technology in China led 2011 Nobel Prize winner and dissident, Liu Xiaobo, to declare that 'God created the internet for China' (Liu, 2012). Liu himself has used the internet to disseminate some of his ideas, particularly the Charter 08 declaration for more political freedom and an end to the CCP's monopoly on power (see Chapter 4). And while the government put enormous resources into policing its contents, and ensuring that it did not become the kind of tool for challenges to the political authorities that had happened during, for example, the Jasmine Revolutions in the Middle East in 2011, there were ways in which the internet was changing the ways that Chinese leaders governed, and the flows of information within society.

The Hu and Wen era from 2002/3 to 2012/13 was caught between being a period when China became wealthier and more prominent than it had ever been before, and when the project of modernity achieved some of its greatest successes, and a place where political reforms, while hinted at, were always delayed into the future. Hu himself in 2007 at the 17th Party Congress talked of China's dream to become 'a rich, strong country' and it was under his watch that the notion of the country achieving 'moderate prosperity' by the end of the next decade was first announced. Using concepts like 'scientific development' and 'harmonious society' he tried show that there was more to development than simply producing raw GDP. Despite this with the great financial crisis of 2008, China had no option but to do all it could to continue producing wealth, even though Premier Wen Jiabao famously announced that the Chinese economic model was 'unstable and unsustainable'. Using the mantra of 'taking people as the key thing' the Party in this decade attempted a shift towards more complex outcomes and goals, but ones which maintained their adherence to socialist ideology and morality. But it was clear after the rise of the new leadership under Xi Jinping from 2012 that the Hu and Wen decade was starting to be regarded as one where unbalanced wealth creation had grown out of control, corruption had become rampant, and a new discipline and purpose had to be instilled. This will be looked at in more detail in the next chapter.

3

The Communist Party and Politics

Understanding the Communist Party of China (CCP) is absolutely central to understanding what China as a country now is and how it functions. The CCP remains one of the least understood elements of the contemporary PRC. Part of the reason for this is that, these days at least, physically China looks, to those who visit it, as if it has a vibrant free market and a full-blown capitalist system. It seems highly contradictory therefore that there is only one party holding a monopoly of power – it is, after all, *the* Party – which still subscribes to Marxism ruling over all of this.

The significance of the CCP as a unifying institution cannot be underestimated, even in an era of increasing 'depoliticization'. Its influence can be felt in almost all areas of society, from the economy to the structure of political power. The CCP has also had an immense impact on the culture of the PRC, from the way in which language is used and decisions about the physical landscape of cities, to how literature, art and music have developed. Much of contemporary Chinese art is often interpreted as taking a position, either critical of or commenting on the powerful symbolic world that the CCP created during its rise to power, and subsequently supplemented and fortified.

What is the Party? During a discussion amongst Western scholars and members of the Communist Party Central Committee International Liaison Department in June 2014 in Europe, this question was addressed. As both sides grappled with how to understand the Party best in ways which outsiders might understand, the terms that had appeared in scholarship over the last few years were brought up: Party state, or fragmented authoritarian. Both terms, when translated into Mandarin, baffled the Chinese participants. The Party and the state were clearly delineated, they felt – one in charge of politics, the other in charge of implementation of policy. As for being fragmented, they refuted this too, arguing that the Party was flexible, strategic, supplying unity where it had to, eschewing it where it was unnecessary. They called the Party a 'learning one', one which distilled the experiences of revolution and governance of the people, represented their aspirations and hopes, and was inextricably linked to the historic mission to make China strong and powerful again. This sort of discussion highlights just how much conceptual confusion there is about what precisely the Communist Party of China actually is. How do we define it? How does it run? How do people who are members of it feel it makes their life different and in what ways do they feel like they belong to it? These are all questions that are addressed in this chapter.

How the CCP Came into Existence

In 2011, on its ninetieth birthday, CCP membership passed the 80 million mark (*China Daily*, 2011), increasing to 85 million in 2014. Were it a country, it would have been placed in the top 20 states in the world. As it was, it still only accounted for 8 per cent of Chinese people. The Party is, in fact, not like a political party in the Western sense. It does not compete with other parties for power, despite the fact that there are eight democratic 'patriotic' parties (as they are called in official discourse) which have existed since before 1949, and which are allowed a nominal existence. When it comes to deciding key military, economic and political policy, and in controlling information and personnel decisions among those with power over the distribution of key resources, the CCP maintains rigid control. And despite the demise of Communist parties elsewhere in the world, at least at the time of writing, this system looks in good health.

The legitimacy of the CCP is built on three fundamental pillars. These were spelt out in the first ever official history of the Party produced by the Central Archives and the Party History Research Bureau in Beijing (in Chinese) in January 2011. According to the second volume, covering the period 1949 to 1978, the Party had three great achievements on which its authority rested. The first was to have unified the country after the disunity of the Republican and warlord era. The second was to have won the war against the Japanese and other foreign aggressors and restored national pride to China. The final achievement was to have undertaken the great reforms from 1978 onwards.

After its foundation in 1921, largely with the Soviet Union's International Comintern support, the Party's strongest early bases were in the inland provinces of Hunan and Henan, where, according to some calculations, almost all of the first 60 members of the Party lived (Ven, 1991). The first Congress of the Communist Party was held in 1921 in

Shanghai, and then on a barge in neighbouring Zhejiang Province after being interrupted by a police raid. Thirteen attendees, two of whom were non-Chinese, represented no more than 60 Party members. One of these, Mao Zedong, was the son of moderately wealthy landlords from the central Chinese countryside, who studied at a teacher training college in Changsha, and then found a position as a librarian at Beijing University.

One of the striking features of China at this time was how small the proletariat, those whom Marx had expected to be the carriers of revolution, was in Chinese society. By 1921, the country only had two million, who worked in factories in industrial centres such as Shanghai. That these might function as a mobilizing political force for the 400 million in the mostly rural areas in the rest of the country was far-fetched enough for the Communist Party of the Soviet Union to simply tell their fellow believers in China to work as far as they could in united fronts with the more dominant Nationalists under first Sun Yat-sen and then Chiang Kai-shek and wait for more propitious times to come, decades hence. By 1927, during the first purge of the Party by the Nationalists and the ending of the earliest united front, Communist activists still numbered only around 50,000.

Mao and the Party

The influence of Mao Zedong on the development of the Party is still a matter of great controversy. Over 120 years after his birth to rich landowning parents in Hunan province, Mao remains a divisive figure, who still casts a shadow across Chinese politics (Chang and Halliday, 2005). His statues remain dotted sporadically across the country, and his image still glares down from the Gate of Heavenly Peace at Tiananmen Square. A likeness of his face appears, perhaps most disconcertingly, on all Chinese currency – something that was forbidden during his time in power and for a number of years afterwards. Called a great Marxist and a great Communist in official accounts in Beijing to this day, his contribution to the movement that brought him and his followers to power is still sufficiently sensitive that Mao's complete official works are only being issued sporadically because of the difficulty of allowing his unadulterated voice to speak even nearly four decades after his death. One of the bolder acts under Xi Jinping as President since 2013 has been to mark his influence more forcefully. On the 120th anniversary of his birth in December 2013, the full seven-strong new Politburo attended a memorial for him at his mausoleum in Tiananmen Square, Beijing. Xi has said clearly on several occasions that without Mao there would be no modern

China. For someone who had suffered personally in the Cultural Revolution, and seen his father imprisoned for over a decade, this was a striking statement. But as founding father of the country, Mao's emotional link with the Chinese public is still strong, and his inheritance remains a useful asset for a politician to lay claim to.

An objective assessment of Mao's contribution to the Communist movement and to the party he led for so long would need to include the ideological formulations he and his chief advisers made (among them Chen Boda, his main speechwriter, who was ignominiously removed in the early 1970s during the Cultural Revolution), translating Marxism–Leninism into a more Chinese-centred direction, allowing it to speak directly to the vast mass of rural-based Chinese, articulating a vision of Party structures that encompassed an active militia, and creating a raft of expressions and symbolic meanings that came to carry great weight in China as it underwent war, and then refounded itself as a country in 1949.

The great difference, therefore, between the CCP in China and the Communist Party in the Soviet Union remained the former's focus on the peasantry. It was the countryside that was to be the source of Mao's followers, when he went there for refuge in 1927 after the great purge led by the Nationalists under Chiang Kai-shek. Mao justified this as adapting the universal creed of Communism to the specific conditions that existed in China. He also used Marxism to give him the tools to produce a careful gradation of ranks and classes in Chinese society, enabling a number of internal purges and movements to be undertaken from the 1930s onwards. In the words of Jerome Ch'en, the final contribution of Mao was a highly political one – to create, in effect, a state within a state from 1927 onwards, with the CCP being almost autonomous, functioning as a military actor, a political force and an economy (Ch'en, 1967). The least palatable aspect of Mao's influence, to this day, was the tolerance he showed towards the use of violence for political ends. The only possible mitigating factor here is the extreme levels of violence in Chinese society at the time the CCP rose to power. Even so, the Party itself was to undertake a number of vicious internal purges, from 1931 onwards, directing violence towards many of its opponents.

How the CCP Gained Power

That the CCP won the long war to become the sole government of the Chinese mainland by 1949 is partly a result of the ineptitude of its opponents (the Nationalists were beset by a number of problems after 1945, but weakened themselves fatally through corruption and economic mismanagement), and partly because of its own self-discipline and how it crafted a message that won the battle of the hearts and minds of the Chinese peasantry and such urban classes as existed during the Civil War. The CCP captured critical nationalist messages, presenting itself as a defender of the Chinese nation's dignity, right to autonomy, and self-determination. These were best captured at the meeting of the Chinese People's Political Consultative Conference (CPPCC), a body made up of both Party and non-Party members to advise it, which took place in September 1949, just before the foundation of the PRC itself in October of that year. The message of strength through unity was conveyed by Mao's famous phrase, 'The Chinese people have now stood up.' The CPPCC was part of the CCP's united front work activities designed to create a broad base of support. At its founding, the Party represented both the peasantry and the proletariat that existed in urban centres.

Intellectuals, small landowners and other relatively benign classes were accorded a welcome during its early years in power – but as time went on, and mass campaigns became the Maoists' favourite means of forcing change to happen, these groups were increasingly threatened and victimized.

What Does the CCP Do?

Unlike the situation in Western liberal democracies, where neutral civil services have to take their instructions from different political parties voted into power, in China the barriers between the bureaucracy and the Party are faint. The CCP is the only political actor in China with meaningful power, which it exercises in three crucial ways: through the power of saying who is appointed to what position in the executive, the legislature and the key state-owned enterprises; through the ability to control ways of disseminating information, largely via its tight control of the media and the messages the media carries; and by expressing the dominant ideological directions of society overall – which it does through the various iterations of 'Marxism with Chinese characteristics' that have occurred over the last few decades.

Since 1949, there have been two broad periods of Party strategy. In its foundation state, before 1978, the CCP was committed to a programme of cleansing society through class struggle and the delivery of social goals through mass campaigns. Its ideals were utopian, uncompromising and often led to socially disastrous outcomes. Since 1978 it has been committed to economic growth, the construction of the primary stage of socialism, and the vision of a strong nation guided by Marxism with Chinese characteristics. These very different strategies were aimed at a single objective: the creation of a strong, rich country, with the ability to defend itself, and to preserve its sovereignty, never allowing humiliation and bullying at the hands of foreign forces again. The CCP therefore presents itself as the guardian of these national aims, as the sole agent that is able to work for their delivery. Despite the sharp difference in means before and after 1949, modern CCP leaders can argue that they are working towards the same objective. For the Party, therefore, it provides a unified ideological framework to address key issues in society. The Party, today through its key decision-making forums such as the Congresses held every five years since 1978, and their annual plenums, sets the overall political direction of society. These are then given to the government to implement. The Party also maintains an evaluative function, giving feedback on the performance of the government and of officials. All major policy documents must be approved by the Party, and through its Central Discipline and Inspection Committee it can investigate and remove officials who are considered to be failing.

In itself the Party maintains ambiguity about whether the national and Party aims are the same thing. In the last three decades, dissidents like Wei Jingsheng have questioned this. They have argued that the Party has hijacked ownership over China's future, and dictated what path it needs to take to become a great nation again. Party leaders, amongst them Hu Jintao and Xi Jinping, have stated categorically that without the unified leadership of the CCP China will not become a strong country, one able to take its place as one of the key forces, if not *the* key force, of the modern world. This focus on the CCP being the unique path towards China's national power and dominance is absolute. Current head of ideology on the Politburo Liu Yunshan has simply stated that unlike foreign political parties, the CCP is a more complete force, the expression, in his words 'of the ideals of the Chinese people for their future'.

Despite these grand words, for its many detractors inside and outside the PRC the Party remains a Leninist organization under its modernizing veneer, replacing pre-1978 language on class struggle and cleansing the people with a new more palatable discourse of serving the people and striving to deliver a more equal society, one in which there is harmony and balance. What is consistent about its behaviour under Mao and subsequent leaders is its unique focus on control and dominance of the major sources of power in Chinese society. Even in the twenty-first century, therefore, it maintains a remorseless hold on all the main levers of society in a country which, despite this, is going through fundamental change.

Party Organization: Then and Now

The Party came to power not just because it had a coherent and emotionally appealing message to China's peasants, but also because it had formidable organizational skills. Party branches existed down to the level of the smallest village in China by 1951. Members were recruited as much for their administrative abilities as their belief in Marxism. The CCP's greatest challenge in its early years in power from 1949 was to transform itself from an entity which was geared for waging revolution and forcing allegiance from people with acts of violence, to one that had to work as a party not of revolution but of governance. One of Mao's key allies, Liu Shaoqi, wrote the definitive manual of CCP member behaviour in the 1940s, *On How to Be a Good Communist*, setting out the moral and administrative standards that were expected in this new context. The aspiration here linked back to the template of a Confucian scholar-official from an earlier era. Discipline was enforced through close mutual surveillance, and through large party meetings in which central edicts were read, usually from the *People's Daily*, the Party's newspaper. The CCP control of the message and the messenger became legendary, with all newspapers, the few radio and eventually television stations that existed, and any artistic endeavours closely controlled by the propaganda apparatus. With the Xi Jinping leadership and its extensive ideological messaging and crackdown on corruption to force discipline amongst members, it could be argued that, despite all the other changes in society and politics in China, in this area things have been remarkably consistent.

The organizational structure of the CCP has changed little since the 1950s. Hierarchies of Party members remain, with jobs graded accordingly. There are still party secretaries in every state enterprise, and even in any non-state company which employs above eight people. There are training procedures for members, and specific promotion protocols, along with membership requirements. What is different now is that, with the demise of the domineering leadership embodied in a figure such as Mao, the CCP has undergone a far deeper institutionalization of its processes and internal structures, in effect becoming the sort of bureaucratic entity with professionalized cadres who spend much of their time on specific technical training and defending their privileged place in society which Mao did his best to eradicate (Pieke, 2009).

Deng Xiaoping's reforms also changed the way the CCP exercised power. He himself never took the role of Chairman (that position was abolished after Hua Guofeng, for fear of it becoming the stage for another dominant, dictatorial figure), nor Party Secretary, nor Premier, simply serving as a vice-premier until 1982, Thereafter he was simply called the 'paramount leader' outside China, and within the country the disarmingly humble 'comrade'. His real influence was via two routes – the first as chair of the Central Military Commission (CMC), which maintained control through the Party over the People's Liberation Army (which included the navy and air force as well as the army) and the second as one of a group of senior revolutionary leaders. The latter, in particular, had no formal role – but then, as with so much else in the Party, Deng and the leaders around him had had to create institutions and rules after the chaos of the Maoist period, when many of these had simply been non-existent or ignored. The only sign of the significance of these individuals (eight of them in all, nicknamed the Immortals after the Daoist pantheon of eight gods) was the existence of a senior leadership group on which they sat to advise and comment. This ceased to exist in 1987.

The key executive positions in the 1980s were occupied first by the former Party boss of Hubei, Hu Yaobang, who served as general secretary of the CCP from 1980 to 1987, and then Zhao Ziyang, who succeeded him from 1987 to 1989. They were the leaders who had to implement policies within the general direction that Deng and the senior figures around him, nominally in retirement, set out. Alongside these changes, the Party began to hold regular Congresses, introduced retirement ages for leaders, and limited terms for key positions. Work went into spelling out who had responsibility for what within the Party structure. Attempts were made to clarify the roles of Party and government entities and their respective responsibilities (see Chapter 4). From 1987, limited elections were introduced at the village level in China, partly because of the levels of state collapse that had been experienced in rural China in the two decades since 1960.

One of the core priorities for the CPC throughout its history, before and after 1949, and into the twenty-first century, has been the control and management of information and news. Xinhua News Agency was the core delivery agent of state news from 1949 onwards, although it was established in 1931. The agency shadows the Party structures, with offices throughout China down to provincial and prefectural levels, and was the main (and in the Maoist period amongst the only) source of Party and government news. Alongside the agency, the Party also established the *People's Daily* as its official newspaper, then a raft of other newspa-

Box 3.1 Party leadership since 1949

Definition of Party leadership is a more vexed issue than might be expected. Mao Zedong served as Chairman of the Politburo and the Communist Party of China from 1949 to 1976 and worked with first a President, until this office was phased out with Liu Shaoqi's fall, and then with a Vice Chairman. Deng Xiaoping only ever rose to the formal position of Vice- Premier, but was regarded as the key power holder in China from 1978 onwards. Only under Jiang Zemin did the Party Secretary position become the key one in elite politics. This can be seen partly as a process of institutionalizing the Party and its core executive positions. The standard formulation in recent years has been to talk of there being 'generations' of leaders, at the centre of which sit dominant figures. This is set out below:

First-generation leadership
Mao Zedong 1949–76
(Interim Leader: Hua Guofeng as Chairman 1976–81)

Second-generation leadership
Deng Xiaoping 1978–92
(with Party Secretaries Hu Yaobang 1980–87
Zhao Ziyang 1987–89)

Third-generation leadership
Jiang Zemin 1989–2002

Fourth-generation leadership
Hu Jintao 2002–12

Fifth-generation leadership
Xi Jinping 2012–

pers and China Central Television (CCTV). Over the last two decades, the media sector in China has marketized, with provinces having their own papers, radio stations and television companies. But the control of political news remains centralized. Xinhua has also expanded its operations internationally, with huge bureaux across the world.

Party Personnel Management

Despite these Dengist changes, in the twenty-first century the CCP remains structured with a highly hierarchical, centralized system (see

Table 3.1 Management structure of the Communist Party of China (CCP)*

Party Congresses, members of which are selected by the Central Party from party members in the various levels of Congresses throughout China and which, every five years, elect

↓

The Full (200 members) and Alternate Members (150) of the Central Committee (serviced, outside its annual Plenums, by Central Committee departments such as the International Liaison Department, Party Work Department, Propaganda Work, etc.), who elect

The Full Politburo (24). The Politburo is serviced by a Secretariat which deals with its day-to-day management, arrangement of leaders' diaries, briefing, etc.), from whom are selected

The Standing Committee of the Politburo (7 members)

* Membership numbers as of 2014.

Table 3.1). The two key entities through which it administers itself and its internal affairs are the Organization Department, based in an anonymous building in central Beijing, and run like a personnel department, making decisions on who is promoted to what position, how promotions are judged, and who is given what sort of training; and a parallel powerful organization, called the Central Discipline and Inspection Commission (CDIC), which deals with the sensitive issue of how the Party tries to police itself, by rooting out corruption. This latter entity has become particularly important since 2012 and the fall of former Politburo members Bo Xilai and then Zhou Yongkang, conducting the anti-corruption campaign that has been a signature of the Xi Jinping leadership's early phase.

That the CCP in the end is a law unto itself and enjoys a unique and privileged role in society raises immediate issues about how it can credibly achieve self-regulation and discipline. Corruption lies at the heart of this and Party leaders are well aware of the depth of the problem. According to former Premier Wen Jiabao, corruption had become one of the greatest threats to the Party's legitimacy, with more than 32,000 officials being investigated in 2005 alone, and as much as 13–16 per cent of GDP being spent on officials misusing their positions for personal gain

(Hing, 2006). The CDIC is in the forefront of attempts to combat this, with its ability to swoop on cities, provinces and other places, investigating officials right up to Politburo level, and removing those proven guilty so that they can be handed over to the legal system for judgment. In 2013, it investigated 60,000 officials for various levels of corruption, and undertook disciplinary proceedings against 8,000. This was a remarkable output for an organization made up of 1,000 people.

Corruption in the discourse of current senior leaders is less an issue of what organizations like the OECD would call classic corruption – misuse of official positions for personal gain. In many ways, this sort of networking and access to privilege and influence is endemic in the Chinese system. What has become far harder to control as China has become a wealthier country is the staggering scale of some of the venality of officials. Xi Jinping, as a Party leader in the southern coastal province of Fujian in the early 1990s, told a reporter that people should not go into politics in China to make money. But, in fact, this is precisely what they have been doing. Reporters from the *New York Times* and Bloomberg in the build-up to the leadership transition in 2012 found evidence that both Wen Jiabao's and Xi Jinping's own families were linked to huge assets abroad, in Wen's case with amounts in the billions of US dollars. For a party that had historically risen to power on a programme of addressing inequality and corruption in Chinese society, it was highly ironic that six decades later its officials would be so awash with temptation that some of them absconded abroad with millions waiting for them in foreign bank accounts. To address this issue without accepting external surveillance or a concept of rule of law that stood above the Party seemed a tall order. But this was what the Xi leadership showed they were intent on doing.

Part of the challenge of rooting out corruption is that, in addition to China being a deeply networked society riddled with mutual obligations and kinship links, it is also a place where the culture of gift giving is powerful. Deep into history, generous gestures either with money (sometimes in red envelopes), or precious goods have been accepted as a way of furthering a cause with officials or other decision-makers. This continues to this day, with patients giving doctors incentives, builders giving planners kickbacks, or offers of help made to officials' children or extended family. The lines between legitimate and venal gift giving are hard to draw, and the Xi government even went as far as to demand that the handing out of moon cakes in the Autumn festival be stopped.

There is also the issue of what the ethics of the Communist Party might be. Hu, and then Xi, with their language of taking people as the key, have tried to create a more human sounding system where public service is understood, and people look beyond themselves. Confucianism in particular has been invoked here, demanding higher standards from public officials, and internalization of these so that they are acting not from fear but because they believe their actions are right. Academics like Jiang Qing in Beijing have commented extensively on the uses of Confucian ethics with its stress on right action and appropriateness as a conceptual model that can temper some of the Party's more brutal, utilitarian tendencies. This ethical message of the Party, however, was hard to hear clearly, when its public actions swayed between expressing respect for the dignity of people collectively and the need to serve them, and its often heedless disregard for these values in, for instance, its harsh sentencing of dissidents and the punitive actions taken against their families. (Liu Xia, wife of Liu Xiaobo, springs to mind here, kept under house arrest in Beijing despite her innocence of any charges.)

Party Structure

The elite of the Party is found in the Central Committee, elected by Party Congresses which have been held every five years since the death of Mao. Congresses, as the ultimate moments of collective decision-making, were held sporadically under Mao, with a huge gap between the Eighth in 1959 and the Ninth in 1969. In this era, they were a rubber-stamp performance of no policy significance. Under the Dengist leadership, they began to have at least a more regular, evaluative function, introducing constitutional changes. The 16th Party Congress in 2002 ushered in the Hu and Wen period in power, and the 18th Congress, held in late 2012, was significant because it showed how the Party, through processes and institutions alone, could produce a new group of leaders with time-limited mandates. The Central Committee consists of approximately 200 full members and 150 alternate members (alternate members attend only some of the Central Committee meetings) (see Table 3.2). This can be described as the power elite of modern China, a balance of provincial leaders, heads of the 27 central ministries (see Chapter 4), military leaders, and heads of state-owned enterprises (Bo, 2010).

At the Congresses, the Central Committee elects a Politburo and its Standing Committee. These are the elite within the elite. The full Politburo currently has 24 members and balances the different interest areas within the Party and society. In the Standing Committee, we reach the summit of power in contemporary Chinese politics, containing all the

Table 3.2 Sections and departments of the Central Committee

The General Secretary
The Politburo
The Politburo Standing Committee
The Secretariat
The Central Military Commission

key decision-makers. Historically, the Standing Committee has ranged from five to nine members, with seven at the time of writing in September 2014. Its composition has to balance institutional and social forces in such a way that it can claim to be broadly representative. In the Xi Jinping era, the primary slot has been leadership of the Party and the Military, with the Premier Li Keqiang coming second in charge of government matters and administration. Zhang Dejiang, head of the National People's Congress, leads China's parliament. Yu Zhengsheng heads the CPPCC, a consultative body that embraces business and non-Party forces. Liu Yunshan is in charge of ideology, and Zhang Gaoli is first ranked Vice-Premier in charge of macro-economic matters. The final member is Wang Qishan, who chairs the CDIC. With the various portfolios in this group, we can map out the priorities of the Party in the second decade of the twenty-first century as it approaches the centenary of its foundation: Party domination, economic development, some controlled participation of the broader public through the NPC and the CPPCC, ideological discipline and unity and attempts to create a more ethical standard for Party behaviour.

The Party may have 84 million members as of mid-2014, but in fact the real movers and shakers number only a few thousand, and the organization is a surprisingly hierarchical one. Climbing to positions of power is not easy. To do so relies on a system of evaluation of leaders, in each job they take, whether in state-owned enterprises as managers, or in provinces or central ministries. This evaluation includes both soft and hard targets. The soft targets are social and political objectives, which are difficult to measure and are judged largely according to peer review. The hard targets are in many ways the more important ones – the ability to deliver GDP growth, and to collect taxes to be sent to the central government. Environmental protection targets have mattered less for career prospects than delivering growth, although in recent years attempts have been made to address this. Financial remuneration for officials is surprisingly low, another cause of official venality and corruption.

Table 3.3 Organizations under the CCP Central Committee

General Office
Central Organization Department
Central Propaganda Department
Central International Liaison Department
Central United Front Work Department
Central Policy Research Office
Central Taiwan Work Office
Central External Publicity Office
Central Security Office
Central Party School
People's Daily
Seeking Truth From Facts
Party History Research Centre
Party Research Centre
Central Compilation and Translation Bureau

There are a number of other important departments in the Party. The Law and Politics Department deals with the Party's guidance of the legal system and thorny issues of social balance and justice. Another is the International Liaison Department, dealing with relationships with political parties outside China. Within the summit of the elite, there are a number of leading groups, from that dealing with the economy to the leading group on foreign affairs (see Table 3.3). Under Xi Jinping these have expanded, with Xi himself chairing a leading group on reform, and one on cybersecurity. The groups are small collections of heads of ministries and Politburo members who have influence over key areas of policy and meet together to forge policy and implementation plans. It is in these groups that the Party and government interface in some way. Very little is known about their operations, and next to nothing about the specific subjects of their meetings.

While the country has a Constitution, passed in 1982 and revised several times since, the CCP also has its own Party Constitution, setting out the responsibilities and rules for a CCP member in the twenty-first century. These two documents run as parallel power texts, setting out the geography of authority in the PRC. For the PRC in the twenty-first century, one of the most extraordinary facts is that nowhere is there a clear description of the division between Party and government. Perhaps this is because everyone knows the golden rule of the modern PRC: in any organization the real power lies with the Party, not the government appointment.

Box 3.2 China's Congress: the story of the Communist Party in meetings

China's 18 Congresses up to 2012 in many ways tell the story of the Party in the last nine decades. From the first, held over nine days in Shanghai and then neighbouring Zhejiang in 1921, to the 6th, held in Moscow in 1928, the meetings were small, frequent and characteristic of a party fighting for survival. After a hiatus of over a decade and a half however, 1945 marked the start of a new era:

7th Congress, 1945, Yenan, Shanxi – Marked the final consolidation of Mao Zedong's hold on Party leadership.

8th Congress, 1956, Beijing – Held just after the Anti-Rightist campaign and before the Great Leap Forward. First Congress meeting of Party in power.

9th Congress, 1969, Beijing – Formally ended the most violent period of the Cultural Revolution, and elevated Lin Biao as Mao's successor.

10th Congress, 1973, Beijing – Marked the high point of The Gang of Four's radical leadership.

11th Congress, 1977, Beijing – Marked reinstatement of Deng Xiaoping.

12th Congress, 1982, Beijing – Marked the consolidation of Dengist reforms, abolished Party Chairmanship, marked point where Party Secretary becomes key position.

13th Congress, 1987, Beijing – Formal retirement of Deng Xiaoping, and rise of 'third-generation' leaders.

14th Congress, 1992, Beijing – Consolidation of reforms after disruption of the Tiananmen Square uprising in 1989, and of Jiang Zemin's position as Party leader.

15th Congress, 1997, Beijing – Marked high point of first phase of state-owned enterprise reform.

16th Congress, 2002, Beijing – Elevation of Hu Jintao to Party leadership role as fourth-generation leader. Admission of non-state-enterprise leaders into the Communist Party.

17th Congress, 2007, Beijing – Elevation of Hu Jintao's 'scientific development' into Party Constitution.

18th Congress, 2012, Beijing – Appointment of Xi Jinping as Party leader from the fifth generation.

Being a Member of the CCP in the Twenty-first Century

At the heart of the CCP's strength in society is its membership. For an organization of over 80 million people (see Table 3.2), maintaining ideological and organizational unity over this diverse body is a major challenge. The Party has been afflicted with divisions in the past over the pace of reform, the areas where reform needs to happen, and how the state and Party need to redefine their relationship with each other. The one great taboo area is to question the authority of the Party. Beyond that, there has been a lively debate since the 1990s about what needs to be done to modernize it in the future.

Organizationally, the Party School system, with its Central School in the suburbs of Beijing near the Summer Palace performs the dual function of think tank and internal training system for cadres at senior levels. Its importance can be demonstrated by the fact that previous presidents of the Central Party School included Hu Jintao, and Xi Jinping. The current head is Liu Yunshan, who is in charge of ideology. The Party Schools offer residential courses, some of them stretching over several months, ranging from those dealing with technical issues of administration, up to courses on ideology and Party building. Figures up to vice-ministerial level have been involved as students in training courses, showing that, under Hu Jintao, what has been called 'the learning Party' encourages all its senior figures to engage in lifelong learning. The Party School system has been effective as a means of producing an administrative elite along the lines of the great *écoles* in France or the Oxbridge system in the UK. The current generation of leaders are better trained, better educated and better equipped than ever before, to meet the demands of running a country as large and complex as the PRC.

Party Divisions

One key issue over the period from 1978 was the increasing awareness that, as more was becoming known about the Party by the outside world, it became clear that it was not simply a homogeneous entity with a unified viewpoint on all issues, but an organization with some significant divisions within its ranks. Over the 1980s and 1990s, groups resistant to the whole opening up and reform period promoted their ideas to varying degrees about how more orthodox socialism could be reintroduced into the system. One of these, the ideologue, Deng Liqun, produced a number of so-called '10,000 character' papers during the era of the restructuring of state-owned enterprises in the late 1990s, arguing that the CCP had no right to throw so many people out of secure jobs and dismantle the state welfare system. There were attacks by others on the pernicious influence of foreign ideas, with campaigns every few years from 1982 onwards against spiritual pollution and bourgeois liberalism. When in early 2012 the World Bank and the Development and Research Council (DRC) of the State Council produced a joint report on their liberal vision for China's direction by 2030, over 1600 economists and academics with leftist leanings issued an angry letter of rebuttal, showing that support for state intervention and direction of the economy was real enough among some key groups in the country. The World Bank/DRC report essentially argued that China needed to undertake more marketization, more privatization and more social and administrative reforms in order to achieve the goal of a 'high-income, creative, harmonious, innovative society' by 2030. For the leftist critics, this was capitulating to foreign influence, betraying China's socialist legacy and allowing inequality to continue unchecked. Left and right in China therefore still have resonance, even within the overarching structure of the Party (World Bank, 2012).

A model used to try to understand the linkages between elite leaders was the factional one, something promoted in the 1990s and 2000s as distinct differences in allegiance between some leaders in the Jiang and Hu period became clearer. There was a group popularly known as the 'Shanghai Gang', linked to former Party Secretary, Jiang Zemin, who had all been active as officials in Shanghai and were accused of having a particular mindset (though it was hard to discover much detail about what precisely this mindset was, apart from the individuals all knowing or having worked with each other). Another clique was associated with the China Youth League, and included people such as Hu Jintao, and to some extent Li Keqiang, both of whom had worked in this group early in their careers, and had benefited from its excellent networks among young and up-and-coming leaders. There was the Qinghua group, comprising those who had been educated at the Beijing-based university. There were the princelings, consisting of the large number who had relatives who had been high-level leaders, though once more precise definition of what constituted a former ranking leader proved elusive. There were cliques associated with particular regions and ministries. In the end, however, the most these claimed factions proved is that people had some kind of work or family link with others, and did not prove any cohesive ideological position. The most problematic aspect of the factional model to understand elite Chinese politics was that many figures belonged to a number of these networks, and some to all of the ones listed above. It is hard to say how meaningful it is to interpret Chinese modern politics in this way.

A more meaningful line at least in the 1990s and into the 2000s was that drawn between those who might be classified as reformers or liberals, and those who were conservative. This was referred to in the discussion of the 2012 World Bank/DRC *China 2030* report mentioned above. These labels operated in the same way as they did in the West, with members of each group holding distinctive views on the need for change, the role of the state and the nature of the Party's ultimate objectives. The difference in China is that the full range of left- and right-wing views exists in a single political entity, rather than forming into specific different parties.

What Does the Party Believe?

Many have declared that the PRC is a post-Communist or, in Liu Xiaobo's words, post-totalitarian country, one in which the CCP is Communist in nothing except name (Liu, 2012). Ruthless market capitalism is the norm, with Marxism reserved for a remote political elite, with no relevance for day-to-day life. The existence of 2,000 Party Schools across the country, and the amount of effort put into ideological training, however, contradicts this. Ideology, as formulated successively in the eras of Mao, Deng and Jiang Zemin, matters. It mattered enough for Hu Jintao and the leaders around him to have their own contribution to Chinese Marxist thought – scientific development – written into the state constitution in 2007. And under Xi Jinping, perhaps more effort has been put into forging ideological loyalty and unity in the Party membership than at any time since 1978.

For the vast majority of Chinese, including many Party members, the speeches of elite leaders densely filled with jargon about 'upholding the banner of socialism with Chinese characteristics' or 'building a middle-income harmonious society in an all-round way' leave them cold and uninvolved, much as for outside observers. The chief ideologue under Xi, Liu Yunshan, admitted in a speech to the Party School in 2009 that young cadres were put off by the ossified very formal language of Party speeches and documents. A phrase has even entered into Chinese discourse to describe this: *guan-hua* (officialese). Party leaders habitually use a form of spoken Chinese in public that seems stilted and formulaic, stuffed with slogans and the latest CCP buzzwords, alien in comparison to street language, with its earthy vitality and richness. The structures of power in the CCP and the language that those in the system use have dictated a great distance between those at the top and those under them. This is indicated in the ways in which people speak, with CCP elite leaders, like government ones, using a unique language that manages to be both eloquent and yet at the same time utterly devoid of any emotional impact. Hu Jintao in particular was famed for giving leaden, heavy speeches.

Ideology, however, gives CCP leaders one thing, and that is an accepted mode of conceptual communication on tough intellectual issues amongst the elite. It operates much like Latin did in the medieval Church in Europe, meaning nothing to the vast majority of people in the real world, but functioning as a non-contentious common discourse among those at the top. The political risks of jettisoning this common language, however unwieldy, are currently too great, so the Party sticks with it. In this ideology, the fundamental tenet is a form of economic-centred developmentalism where material well-being is the key objective. The thorny problems of Tibet and Xinjiang, and ethnic self-expression and identity, are all dealt with by asserting the pre-eminence of the need to have policies that deliver economic progress, stability and unity. A highly materialistic view of human nature, and of the powers of science, lies at the heart of the CCP's beliefs in the twenty-first century, and these are asserted as the ultimate solutions for China's challenges. Elite leaders are fond of batting away foreign criticism of human rights issues by saying that the CCP has filled people's stomachs, and this was the key thing on which its performance needs to be judged. These points have some traction in a country that had experience of mass starvation in living memory. As the Chinese Vice President Li Yuanchao said at a September 2014 meeting of scholars of the Party from outside China, the CCP and the PRC have been the first government of the country ever to ensure that its people were well fed and well clothed, and did not suffer from starvation. And while only partly true (malnutrition and poverty still exist in the country), it is broadly accepted that the Chinese government in the last three decades has lifted more people out of poverty than any other government in history.

The success of the Party's efforts since the end of the 1990s to impose this ideological view more consistently across society, as Chapter 8 will aim to show, is highly questionable. Xi Jinping stated in January 2012, at a meeting in the Party School in Beijing, that there needed to be more ideological guidance and training for China's teachers and students, and more 'wholesome' thought. This referred in particular to the internet, which was seen as a zone of unbridled anarchy and threat, with the need to spell out clear boundaries for what was permitted and what was out of bounds for discussion. Campaigns against Western liberalism and forms of political action were waged in China's universities in 2014, with a document issued by the Party in 2013 stating that there needed to be zero tolerance for talk of bicameral parliaments and competition between political parties as there was in Western democracies. For the CCP, while ideological struggle is its hardest task in this newly networked world, it is still something it feels is deeply important, and spends much time and effort on.

This is a long-term trend. In 2009, the editorial department of the *People's Daily*, the official paper of the CCP, issued a six-point list of the things in which it did not believe. Entitled 'The Six Whys', this became something akin to a catechism of what the CCP held to be core issues in the era that many in the outside world regarded as post-Communist. Alongside the already mentioned conviction that multi-party democracy was unsuitable for China's national conditions, and would never be implemented, there was also firm support for state-owned enterprises, and state control for core strategic industries like energy, telecoms and banking. The conclusion of this document was very simple: socialism with Chinese characteristics was the best way to carry China further towards modernization, and for this, the Party's role as unifier, director and manager was non-negotiable.

The Party General Secretary has been the final, almost papally infallible, voice of the ideology of the CCP. While in power, Hu Jintao's key contribution (or at least that of the ideologues around him who wrote his speeches) was the concept of 'scientific development', the notion that the PRC can address its issues of internal balance and unequal social and economic development with a mixture of state and non-state economic partnerships, with the CCP in charge of the political direction of the country. The stress here is on harmony and stability. The unsettling dialectics that might be found in Mao's work, where conflict and contradiction are set at the heart of social programmes and chaos is celebrated, took second place to a glorification of synthesis and unity. Despite its clunky sound, scientific development was motivated by the highly practical admission that pumping out GDP at the cost of everything, whether that be the environment or social cohesion, was simply unsustainable and a new benchmark for Party and government performance needed to be articulated. Hu's concept has been replaced, under the Xi leadership, by that of 'ecological civilization'.

What is indisputable is that differing forms of nationalism lurk beneath the surface of most of the public pronouncements of elite ideological opinion. Here we return to the mission of modernity mentioned in the previous chapter. In the late Qing era, there had been constant talk of the need to create a 'rich, strong country' that would no longer be in the shadow of modernized Western countries, and would stand on its own. In the space of only a generation, the CCP had gone from declaring that 'it was better to be red than expert' under Mao to rediscovering the need for highly trained knowledge workers. It was delivery of more power and capacity to the country and the Party that mattered most. Marxism and its concepts remained important to the power elite, but they existed in a febrile intellectual market place, its territory increasingly circumscribed and contested. Whatever ideology the CCP had was in place by 2014 because it had been shown, unlike any others, to at least supply some uniformity to the language and intellectual vocabulary of the elite and operated as a useful tool.

Democracy

The issue of corruption under Xi Jinping shows that how the CCP governs itself has become a critically important issue in contemporary China. The CCP demands a monopoly on power. Attempts by groups such as the China Democracy Party to register themselves in 1998 and 1999 were brutally suppressed. All the leading democracy activists, such as Wei Jingsheng, Xu Wenli and Wang Dang, were either exiled or incarcerated. The Constitution of the country states that it protects people's rights to freedom of expression, and China had signed the UN Conventions on Civil and Political Rights (though it had not ratified these). But for any Chinese citizen to actively attempt to set up an alternative political party is the last great taboo. Only through the CCP can a person be politically active. Hu and then Xi prosecuted brutally effective campaigns against anyone who dared to violate this code, with activists given hefty sentences for publicly challenging the Party or trying to set up their own organizations.

But the question of how the CCP efficiently governs itself is a truly unavoidable one. To have ultimate credibility, it has had to show that it has internal structures, rules and protocols that give it the right to occupy this privileged position in society, especially when so much dynamic change is happening elsewhere. For the CCP, the need to justify its existence and its way of operating has become increasingly urgent. In a meeting with Western scholars in Beijing in early September 2014, Vice President and Politburo member Li Yuanchao stated the issue baldly:

unless the Party can deliver better living standards to people and maintain their confidence it will simply fall from power. And while none of the leaders around Xi Jinping talked explicitly of any sort of social contract between the rulers and the ruled in the way that has become common in Western contexts, this was the nature of the deal for the CCP in its seventh decade in power.

From 2004 onwards, the CCP tried to solve this conundrum of internal Party governance by talking of intra-party democracy, democracy that exists within the CCP, and which justifies its mode of operating. But under Xi, this phrase became less used. Instead, grander language of a national dream which the Party was in charge of delivering has become the dominant motif. Xi has been accused of being Maoist in some of his behaviour, accruing immense amounts of power to himself, and dominating the political landscape. This is probably overblown. Mao had the power of life and death over those around him and was the most complete dictator China has had in the last century. But in respect of wanting to cleanse the Party ranks, to restore its tarnished moral credibility and to make it appeal to people's ideals and emotions, Xi had adopted Maoist strategies, though in a very different context. The simple fact was that he, and all his colleagues, owed everything to the Party as an institution, and unlike Mao they sank or swam according to its healthy continuing existence. The emperor of the new China is no single person, but the Party itself. And within this context, the Party and the Party alone can dare feel qualified to regulate and hold itself to account.

Acknowledgement of the need for openness by Party leaders is largely rhetorical. While the government has been tied since 2008 by various open governance regimes and accessibility codes, the CCP remains a highly opaque organization. Its finances, for example, are a mystery to almost everyone; and the way in which senior leaders are assessed and promoted, or demoted, is equally opaque. The 2012 leadership succession illustrated this, with no idea of what the final Politburo line-up would be till the individuals who had made it came walking out from behind a red curtain around midday on 15 November. From time to time, clues to eruptions of disagreement seep out from behind the scenes, and give some insights into how the Party has tried to organize itself.

The most revealing such moment happened in February 2012 when Wang Lijun, a former close assistant to Bo Xilai, Politburo member, Party Secretary of Chongqing, and leadership contender, sought refuge in the American Consulate in Chengdu for 24 hours. The news came like a bolt out of the blue. Only officials from the central Ministry of State Security managed to entice Wang out of the Consulate and back to

Beijing. Wang was a particularly rich source of knowledge because he had been Bo's right-hand man in the crackdown on mafia members in Chongqing in 2009 and 2010, during which many triads and members of other underground groups had been rounded up and imprisoned or executed. As the subsequent trial of Wang, Bo and Bo's wife Gu Kailai made clear, it had been the death of a British businessman, Neil Heywood, in a hotel in Chongqing on the 15 November 2011 at the hands of Gu Kailai, over what were claimed to be business dealings, that led to Wang's original flight. Claims surfaced that the Bo family had over US$1 billion held abroad. It was hard to separate the political claims made against Bo – that he was a populist who had offended many in the current Party elite – from the claims of outright illegality levelled against him.

Bo's case was revealing because it showed that behind the faces of impassive and often enigmatic leaders, there was a world as driven by passion, enmity, hatred and desire for power as in any Western context. Bo had been running a highly unusual campaign as leader of Chongqing, associating himself with populist cheap housing policies, trying to address inequality through better provision of social services, and generally canvassing for public support. This grandstanding evidently irked the leadership in Beijing, and his removal was serendipitous to many of them. Not least was the link he had with the head of security under Hu Jintao, the shadowy figure of Zhou Yongkang who, according to some reports, was the only leader to show dissent over Bo's removal from office in March 2012, and his final arraignment for corruption and abuse of office in 2013. Gu Kailai was indicted and convicted of the murder of Heywood in August 2012, and handed a suspended death sentence. For Bo, his day in court was a more delicate issue, and a three-day trial managed to run into five days. Despite censorship of his trial and heavy control, he still managed to give a spirited defence. He was expelled from the Party and also sentenced to life (Garnaut, 2013).

The upper echelons of CCP politics were always cut-throat and bloody. In Mao's time, the higher one climbed into Party positions, the more concerned one became about what fate might lie around the corner. Purges of the elite had been a mainstay of CCP actions since the 1930s. And yet, to many, cases like that of Bo proved that talk of intra-party democracy with its stress on trying to account for decisions to the wider society and having more transparent admission and operation rules was merely empty rhetoric. The CCP was saying that it wanted to have a more rules-based and accountable existence at the same time as, from 2007, it was promoting increasingly fierce campaigns against rights lawyers and civil society activists who displeased it. Whistle-blowers such as the doctor who revealed the scale of the SARS crisis in 2003 and its official cover-up, and the key activists behind the exposure of the tainted blood scandals in Henan while Politburo member Li Keqiang was Party boss there, were both feted briefly by the CCP, before being harassed, silenced and, in the case of the latter, forced to flee the country. In 2014, Xu Zhiyong, founder of Open Constitution, a campaigner for more rights protection and transparency, was sentenced to three years in jail for disorder offences. There were a raft of other cases where lawyers were threatened or silenced. In Hu and Xi's China, harmony came at a high price.

Part of this was simply because the fall of the Soviet Union in 1991, the Colour Revolutions and the Jasmine Revolutions of over a decade later, and the 2014 Sunflower protests in Taiwan against over reliance on mainland China and exposure to the threat from it had made leaders realize how easy it might be for them to be simply swept away. The Tibetan uprising in 2008 had a particularly powerful effect, seeming to come out of nowhere and convulsing the region and neighbouring provinces for a number of days. This was compounded by unrest in Xinjiang a year later, and then in Inner Mongolia in 2011. These ominous signs only reaffirmed to the Party that it had to always be vigilant, and strive to avoid falling into the traps of other one-party entities. If the price for that was massive state security and surveillance, it was regarded as worth paying. From 2008, therefore, the Hu leadership promoted a 'pro stability' suite of measures that were aimed at isolating those regarded as enemies of the regime or people trying to undermine it.

Yu Zhengsheng, Standing Committee member from 2012, encapsulated the mindset of the leaders of China well when he talked of four kinds of people that the Party had to think about: its loyal followers; those whose loyalty was bought by material inducements; those who were dissatisfied and protesting but over specific issues and not because of any problem with the Party as such; and finally the enemy – those who wished to see it fall from power. Into this last group fell all those accused of asserting the primacy of lawyers and courts over the Party, those who wanted to reign in the Party through constitutionalism, and finally the people who idolized Western models and wanted to ape these. Xi Jinping, at a speech to the National People's Congress to mark its sixtieth anniversary in September 2014, gave this final group short shrift. China had no need for Western-style liberal democracy. It would find its own way. And as long as China grew wealthier, then the vast majority of people living within it fell in the first three groups above, and the Party was able to manage things.

Fifth-Generation Leadership

The Party privileges leadership. Just as it takes up the leadership role in society, so powers are still centralized to some degree in the Party hierarchy. Mao, Deng and Jiang were each described as the 'core' of leadership for the first, second and third generation respectively. Hu was never formally accorded this title in official Chinese publications, which was read as a slight downgrading of his status. The question for the fifth-generation leadership, however, was how they would find legitimacy in a context in which there was no dominant former leader to give them any sort of benediction, and no detailed rules about who, and how, successors could be chosen.

The fifth-generation leadership succession threatened over 2011 and into 2012 to become highly destabilizing, particularly at the time of Bo Xilai's fall. Consultations of Party members and Congress participants at provincial level was extensive, but it was clear in the middle of 2012 that there were still major questions over who would finally end up in the key leadership slots, and what portfolios they would get. A summer retreat at the seaside resort of Beidaihe seemed to produce a final list, and it was this that dictated the line-up that appeared in mid-November at the 18th Party Congress.

The Hu decade had been one of explosive economic growth, a feat which was even more impressive in view of the impact of the great financial crisis from 2008 in the rest of the world. But despite this, there was a growing sense that China had lost its way, that the Party was disconnected with people and that it had become remote. All of this was acknowledged when Xi Jinping emerged as the key leader and made brief comments in the Great Hall of the People on the final day of the Congress. Questions about his ability to do anything meaningful about reform, however, were dependent on who was standing beside him. Remarkably, the former nine-strong Politburo Standing Committee had now shrunk to seven. Its membership was mostly viewed as conservative. All but one of them (Liu Yunshan) had emerged from provincial leadership positions. But in terms of any factional organizing narrative, it was hard to discern a common link between them.

Some certainly had good family backgrounds. Xi himself was the son of a former senior military leader who, in 1980, had become the First Secretary of Guangdong province and a key ally of Deng Xiaoping in piloting reforms there. Xi had uniquely served briefly in the military, then in various different levels of government in Hebei, Fujian, Zhejiang and finally Shanghai before taking up a central position in 2007. The man who stood next to him, and was to become Premier in March 2013, Li Keqiang, also had a link through his wife to a former Vice Minister of the China Youth League. A graduate in law from Beijing University, Li was rumoured to be linked through his tutor at the time to the Democracy Wall Movement of 1979. Li had gone on to work in the China Youth League in the 1980s and 1990s, complete a PhD in economics in the 1990s, and then lead Liaoning and Henan province before joining Xi on the Politburo Standing Committee in 2007.

Zhang Dejiang, the third in the hierarchy, came from a more modest background. He was the sole member of this generation of super-elite leaders who had studied abroad, though in Pyongyang in the late 1970s. From this period he had worked first in the north-east as a provincial leader, and then in Zhejiang and Guangdong before finally being made interim leader of Chongqing after Bo Xilai's fall. Zhang has been vigourously hardline in his political approach, castigating non-state companies in his speech while serving as Party Secretary of Zhejiang province, which has 70 per cent of its economy in the hands of private entrepreneurs. This sort of pragmatic accommodation sits beside a willingness to use high levels of coercion and violence when faced with unrest, as he did in the 2005 riots in rural areas of Guangdong over land appropriation by local officials. Yu Zhengsheng has a more complex background. Son of a man who had been romantically linked to Mao Zedong's wife Jiang Qing, before she married the chairman in the 1930s, Yu has perhaps the most elitist background of all the fifth-generation leaders. A close associate of the family of Deng Xiaoping, his own family were brutally persecuted in the Cultural Revolution, with his sister reportedly committing suicide, and his brother, a military intelligence officer in the PLA, absconding to the USA in the 1980s and then disappearing. He himself served in a number of provinces before becoming Party Secretary in Shanghai for five years from 2007 and guiding the city through the Shanghai Expo of 2010.

Liu Yunshan is the only leader with no provincial leadership background. A journalist from Inner Mongolia, he left the autonomous region in the early 1990s for propaganda and ideology work in the centre before being made a member of the Politburo in 2007. His promotion in 2012 was a surprise. Linked to some of the hardline conservative pushback against intellectuals and journalists, Liu has spoken a great deal about the need for the Party to strive, in the twenty-first century, to control not just the message but the messenger. Zhang Gaoli could also be categorized as a pragmatic conservative. Orphaned before he was in his teens, and from a modest background, he had worked in the state petrol sector for a number of years before becoming leader of the Party in Shenzhen, then Shandong, and finally Tianjin. Zhang's key skill has been his ability to simply produce GDP growth wherever he has gone. Shandong and Tianjin under his leadership leaped into double figures. This sort of success was mostly down to his ability to recruit enterprises from his native province of Fujian and get them to invest in the northern areas. The final member of the group is Wang Qishan, someone who is perhaps the most maverick of them all. Not even a member of the Party till he was in his early thirties, he had married the daughter of a former Vice Minister in the Ministry for Economic Affairs, and then worked in Beijing as an academic before entering politics. Party Secretary of Hainan province for two years in the early 2000s, his greatest profile had come from his role as Vice-Premier directing the Special Economic and Strategic Dialogue with the USA. But his appointment as head of the graft busters in 2012, while initially surprising, has subsequently proved easier to understand. He is regarded as someone who gets things done, and the level of anti-corruption work has certainly proved that.

Even this brief outline of the backgrounds of the fifth-generation leaders of China proves that in almost every area, from their academic and professional backgrounds, their family links, their prior records and achievements, there is no easy common threat to hold them all together. They are not uniformly technocrats, as their predecessors were, nor do they fit neatly into factions. The sole link they have is the Party. It is their loyalty to this that is at the heart of why they have risen to where they have, and their ability to serve it that will ensure that they stay there – or fall.

Power from the Barrel of a Gun: The Role of the People's Liberation Army

One of the most celebrated quotes from Mao was that power grew from the barrel of a gun. This was an admission that, in the 1920s, before the CCP became violent, it got nowhere. The formal entity to which this belief gave rise was the Red Army, founded in 1927, which subsequently became the People's Liberation Army (PLA), the fighting arm of the CCP.

One of the great misconceptions about the PRC today is that the army is a national one. In fact, the PLA reports to the CCP, and to the CCP alone. This is one of the most important sources of its power. Almost 40 years after the death of Mao, it remains faithful to his prescription to stay in charge of the gun. The CCP does this through an entity called the Central Military Commission (CMC), a group in which there are a mixture of civilian and military leaders, and which has the final say on military policy and strategy.

The PLA, with its extreme fidelity to Chairman Mao, was one of the fundamental sources of his authority and power throughout his life. In the Cultural Revolution, it was the PLA that remained the final functioning and cohesive institution in society, despite the chaos being visited by factions, Red Guard groups and contending rebellious headquarters and leaders. Many of the key members of the first- and second-generation leadership had military backgrounds and involvement. The PLA was one of the most important parts of society, and enjoyed privileged political, economic and social standing. To be a soldier was regarded as a great career, and the military was the basis for many leadership positions.

The composition of the CMC at the time of writing is testimony to the ways in which the dynamics of this relationship have changed. The principle has always been that it is the Party in charge of the PLA, rather than the other way round. This principle has remained unchanged since the 1930s, and is now underlined by the fact that the generals in the CMC have a civilian as their chairman (Xi Jinping in 2012). The chair of the Central Military Commission, it could be argued, is the key position in the country, next to general secretary of the CCP. It was as chair of the CMC that Deng maintained his influence right up to his full retirement from all positions in 1989. Hu Jintao's, and then Xi Jinping's, elections to vice-chairmanship of the body were interpreted both inside and outside China as signs that they were in a key position to lead the Party itself.

Since the 1980s, the PLA has defined its role as helping the CCP to create the right internal and external environment to grow economically and with stability, and to become a 'rich, strong country'. The PLA's command structure is through six military regions in China, and the PLA Army, the Navy and the Air Force. Two generals sit on the full Politburo, with over 20 leaders in the full CCP Central Committee. More important, all ranking members of the military must also be members of the CCP. And the approximately two million-strong membership of the PLA is the object of perhaps more intense ideological training than even the CCP membership itself.

Like the CCP, it has also gone through a period of professionalization since 1978. In 1979, it fought its last full war, against Vietnam – a searing experience where it was outmanoeuvred and shown to be operating with old machinery and obsolete strategy. The small but more experienced Vietnamese army was able to place itself in rural hideouts, thus confusing and frustrating the Chinese army. The net result of this debacle was for China to withdraw, and to think hard about ways of modernizing its armed forces.

One immediate decision was to scale down the numbers in uniform. At its height, the PLA had over four million active personnel, an enormous burden on its budget and hugely difficult to manage and train. A wave of reductions halved this over the next two decades. On top of this, a concerted campaign was undertaken to modernize and upgrade the PLA's equipment. The military flexed its muscles in 1995 during the first fully free democratic presidential elections in Taiwan, by holding unnerving military exercises off the coast of Fujian province immediately opposite the island as the elections were taking place. The net result most probably handed Li Teng-hui an even bigger margin than had been likely without this heavy-handed attempt at outside interference. Li was the main contender and one of the most vociferous voices for greater autonomy for the island. The Chinese action provoked the USA to send two of its aircraft carriers to the Taiwan Straits to guarantee some degree of peace and ensure that matters did not get out of hand. President Jiang Zemin decided, as one way of dealing with the PLA and reducing its role in politics, to remove it from the commercial business in which it had been involved – running factories and businesses, hotels and massage parlours, and force it to concentrate on becoming a more effective fighting force.

Since 1995, the CCP has mandated increasingly generous budget allocations to the PLA. There has been double-digit growth each year up to 2012, when it was claimed, particularly by the USA, that China spent as much as double its publicly stated budget of US$100 billion on military equipment (BBC website, 2012). By 2011, the PLA was able to unveil its first stealth fighter, and what looked like a refitted aircraft carrier. The PLA was also allegedly behind sophisticated cyber attacks, and had become an active force at sea again, sending ships to the Horn of Africa to protect some of its assets there against piracy.

A great question mark remained over just how effective a fighting force the PLA was, in view of its lack of combat experience since 1979. Stories are told of how the generals had watched the US attacks in the first Iraq War in 1990 and been humbled by how out of date and primitive their own equipment was in comparison. That the Party privileged the PLA with immense importance was beyond doubt. The PLA was there for national defence, to ensure that Taiwan could never declare independence unilaterally, and to project some form of power, at least regionally. In generals such as Liu Yuan, however, the PLA had spokespersons who outlined a more worrying bellicosity in Chinese thinking – the idea that now the Chinese deserved a major fighting force to take on some of its regional issues, and in particular its outstanding maritime borders and the Japanese. The memory of the Second World War, as Chapter 8 will show, grew stronger rather than weaker as time went on. But, unlike in other Communist or post-Communist political cultures, the military itself remained surprisingly politically controlled in the PRC. The CCP remained in command, despite the fact that Politburo Standing Committees from 2002 had no military figures in them. And when Hu, as Party Secretary, President and head of the CMC, wore his uniform on 1 October 2009 to mark the 60th anniversary of the founding of the PRC, the sight of him in the olive-green clothing was enough to spark surprise, and in some quarters mockery, both within and outside the country's cyberspace.

Elections

One area where the CCP did undertake reforms was in mandating at least some forms of direct elections. After 1980, as one of a number of bottom-up reforms that were initially tolerated and then sanctioned, the CCP allowed villages in selected parts of the country to have multi-candidate elections, with, in some cases, secret ballots and more candidates than positions on the village committees. Villages, as Chapter 4 will show, are below the lowest level of state governance recognized in the Chinese 1982 Constitution, and therefore were a relatively safe place to experiment without introducing constitutional change. Peng Zhen, former mayor of Beijing in the 1950s and 1960s, who was rehabilitated after the Cultural Revolution, was to be a major promoter of these reforms. The argument was simple enough. The governance of rural areas in China had been almost decimated in the period after 1966. In some parts of the country, gangs ruled or anarchy prevailed. Elections were regarded as a quick way of restoring some semblance of order as well as giving the local officials enough of a mandate and legitimacy to push forward unpopular rules such as the one-child policies introduced from 1980, the collection of taxes, and the redistribution of land.

In 1987, a draft Organic Law on Village Elections was put before the National People's Congress, and a decade later a full law which allowed elections across China's nearly 800,000 village-level areas and governments. By 2010, the PRC had seen over three million people appointed through these elections, in what was described by one commentator as the largest experiment in grass-roots democracy the world had ever seen.

By 2003, only a year into the Hu Jintao period, there was talk among some think tanks that advised the Party in China of rolling these elections out to townships, the next level of governance above villages. In the more administratively innovative provinces such as Sichuan and Jiangsu, some attempts were made to do this, though this measure failed to gain the support of the Party at the centre and was abandoned. From 2004, therefore, township elections have been put on hold despite the fact that in more developed areas such as Shenzhen there was talk of allowing direct elections for mayors of specific districts, and even for certain Party positions. The bottom line is, therefore, that in the contemporary PRC, no official with any meaningful control over resources or finance is directly elected (Brown, 2011).

The CCP's Future

Since the unrest in 1989, many have declared that the CCP, like the Communist Party of the Soviet Union before it, would fall, and that its days in power were numbered. For many, it has been trying to do the impossible, by maintaining a market system with a socialist political party in control. This strikes many as an attempt to square the circle. The CCP itself admits the need for reform, and has allowed discussion, at the Central Party School and elsewhere, about what options might be workable. It has looked at systems in Europe, elsewhere in Asia, and in North America. Singapore, Japan and Taiwan have all been offered as potential models for what the CCP itself might do, in allowing organized political opposition, but not risking instability in moving towards this objective, nor, more important for the CCP, losing its power.

The sort of instability and uncertainty that democracy seems to bring with it, however, remains unappealing to the current Chinese Party elite. For them, the collapse of the USSR was followed by a decade of poverty and chaos. They are wary of regarding democracy as some sort of panacea and more comfortable with regarding it as linked to American hegemony and control. While the Basic Law for Hong Kong had promised consultations on universal suffrage by its Chief Executive in 2017, the central government from Beijing scotched this in 2014 with a proposal that would mean future prospective leaders would need to be picked for a highly limited franchise. This in particular shows just how tepid the Chinese leadership is about even the most limited political reforms. PRC leaders have talked of the reform path taking many decades. The CCP claims that, in fact, democracy of a type suitable to conditions in China already exists. Hu Jintao and other elite leaders use the word democracy heavily, and argue that the West, especially after the economic problems of 2008, hardly offers the all-encompassing, perfect answer that some thought it might a decade before. For Wang Hui and other intellectuals, such as Pan Wei at Beijing University, the West's arrogant assertion of the excellence of its own system over all others is increasingly hard to maintain in view of the problems that Western-style democracy has faced in terms of public participation in voting, economic performance and credibility.

Even so, there is wide awareness that reform needs to be ongoing, and that in critical areas such as the rule of law, dealing with contention in society, and trying to allow civil society to develop to build social cohesion, it seems very necessary. In this, the CCP is facing an enormous challenge, and one that its leaders are often quite open about. The complexities of governing the PRC will be addressed in Chapter 4. As regards the future of the CCP, however, there is a strong awareness in the elite that merely appealing to its historical legitimacy will only get it so far. For Xi Jinping, as for his predecessors, one of the striking issues they shared is that they see the Party as the force that sits at the forefront of China's engagement with modernity, and with modernization. They probably also fear (despite the claims of their critics that this is merely self-justifying expediency) that they are the sole unifying force in a society of great complexity, which is divided socially, ethnically, culturally and, despite the various forms of Mandarin spoken across the country, linguistically. Xi has tried to address this by mobilizing people with talk of a China Dream. In the abstract, this seems to work. But in detail, it often looks in danger of collapsing into shrill nationalism.

What does the CCP stand for in the twenty-first century? Many see it simply as an organization focused on power, and power alone. For them, the CCP's sole objective is to maintain itself in power, and to crush all opposition. But that seems overly simplistic. Power is always a means to an end. Having it as the sole objective would pretty soon prove limiting. The Party historically has articulated visions. In the late Maoist period, the vision was a utopian one, working towards the Marxist vision of a withering away of the state and a world without class conflict, where all were considered equal. The vast communes in which people were forced to work were the ultimate expression of this. The disbanding of these in the 1980s marked the end of that experiment, and an acknowledgement that such utopian goals were best left far into the future, so they did not touch on current policy. For the CCP after this, the core aim became wealth creation, and the production of GDP. On these terms, since 1978, the CCP has been successful.

As long as there is good economic growth, the CCP will probably be able to maintain the social contract in which people are on the whole indifferent to, or at worst alienated from, politics to such an extent that they simply get on with their businesses, making money, or getting by, and looking forward to a tomorrow that is better than today. Since 1978, again, this has been the case. Growth has been strong. China has been becoming more prosperous. As long as this continues to be the case, the majority of people will probably live with the status quo rather than seek disruptive change that might threaten their lifestyles.

What happens either when growth falls, or when there are sufficient numbers of people in the middle-income bracket – the usual point at which democratic movements really kick in – is another matter. In that sense, the CCP is in a strange sort of pact with the devil. It sees around it a world in which many other one-party states have delivered what it is now delivering (albeit on a smaller scale), only to be turned out of power, or forced to compromise and allow organized political competition. Despite this, the CCP has no choice but to continue on the path of economic reform and wealth creation. Deng stated in 1992 that the opposite of this reform was 'perdition'. In 2007, Hu echoed this, saying that reform alone was the surest path for the CCP and the country. Haunting the elite leaders, however, are the kinds of questions that surfaced in the memoirs of Zhao Ziyang, the Party leader until he was felled by the Tiananmen Square uprising in 1989. The memoirs were smuggled out of the country while Zhao was living under house arrest, and published in Hong Kong in 2008, three years after his death. For him, the question was not whether the CCP needed to make the final reform and embrace democracy, but *when*. Zhao had concluded in the long years under house arrest from 1989, that to pretend the CCP's current modus operandi might represent the sole political direction of the country was wrong (Zhao, 2010). There were alternatives, and their attractiveness would only grow with time. The idea that a rising Chinese middle class might, uniquely in the world, have no interest in being involved directly in decisions over who led them and how they performed, was not feasible. In all sorts of areas, from the use of courts, to blogs, to petitions and protests, these people were showing that they had an interest in their self-determination and wanted a say in how they were governed. For the CCP in the twenty-first century, despite its historical roots as a party of revolution, the key issue was to consider how to finally engage with this new society born from the economic reforms it had allowed, what to do about its own reformation, and how long it had in which to do this. Much of this was hinted at in comments made during 2011 by former Premier Wen Jiabao, when he talked of the CCP needing to undertake deeper and faster political change to improve the current system. But at this time, his was a lone voice. Perhaps the succeeding generation of Chinese leaders will be more supportive. As of 2014, it is impossible to predict when this will be.

4

How China is Governed

Governance of today's PRC is a complex, demanding process. In any week across the country there are protests and clashes between different groups, with people vying with each other to promote their businesses, family or political interests. In that sense, contemporary Chinese society is in ferment. Since 2001, this has only increased. In 2011, there were as many as 180,000 protests (Orlik, 2011), two of which (concerning a high-speed rail crash in Zhejiang, and the treatment of land repossessions in a town in Guangdong) attracted international attention. Whatever else it might be, the PRC of the second decade of the twenty-first century was not a calm or relaxing place.

The task of managing this complex, vast and rapidly developing society falls to the government under the guidance of the CCP. In some senses, the CCP takes a remote position above society, performing what one critic called an evaluative role and outsourcing the actual implementation of policy to the organs of government (Wang, 2011). This chapter will look at how the PRC is governed, and who does the governing.

The State Council and the Premier

On some levels, there is a quick answer to this question. The 1982 Constitution nowhere sets out any clear divisions between the Party's area of influence and control, and that of the government. What it does do, however, is to clarify five levels of administration, from national down to provincial, prefectural, county and township. China's 800,000 villages are considered to be 'autonomous' and are not included in the formal structures of national governance – hence the holding of village elections in these areas (see Table 4.1). Perhaps the easier way to see the Chinese government in its various guises is as a vast executive agency on behalf of the CCP. The CCP decides the general policy ideas, and the overall direction for the country, then the government has to implement all of this and shape it into a workable policy. The key tools it uses, from market mechanisms to allowing non-state actors and creating social

Table 4.1 Levels of administration in China

1 centre
32 provinces (including Taiwan)
333 prefectures
2,861 counties
43,500 townships
Informal levels
800,000 villages

Source: Data compiled from Lai (2004).

Table 4.2 The Secretariat of the State Council, September 2014

Premier: Li Keqiang
First Vice-Premier: Zhang Gaoli
Second Vice-Premier: Liu Yandong
Third Vice-Premier: Wang Yang
Fourth Vice Premier: Ma Kai
Secretary General: Yang Jing

welfare structures, can only go ahead as long as they do not violate CCP orthodoxy. Of course, as the period since the early 1980s has shown, there is immense interchange and dynamic cross-fertilization between Party and government, so a clean division between the two is not a straightforward thing to define.

At the national and provincial levels, however, at least in terms of structure, things are simple enough. It is the State Council, under the premier, that runs the country through the Secretariat of the Council (Table 4.2). The State Council functions like a cabinet. It consists of the heads of the 27 different ministries, with the premier standing as something like a chief executive. It also consists of a range of other functional job holders, in particular the governors of the various provinces and autonomous regions. It is these who have to meet each year to answer to the NPC.

For a continent-sized country, that the PRC is run by such a slender bureaucracy is surprising. In the past, there were as many as 46, later reduced to 38, central ministries. Each one could, in theory, be a power foothold. Attempts to streamline these ministries to create greater efficiency were championed by former Premier Zhu Rongji in the 1990s. Under Hu and Wen, the bureaucracy has been slimmed down even further (see Table 4.3).

Table 4.3 China's ministries

1. Ministry of Foreign Affairs
2. Ministry of National Defence
3 National Development and Reform Commission
4. Ministry of Education
5. Ministry of Science and Technology
6. State Ethnic Affairs Commission
7. Ministry of Public Security
8. Ministry of State Security
9. Ministry of Supervision
10. Ministry of Civil Affairs
11. Ministry of Justice
12. Ministry of Finance
13. Ministry of Human Resources and Social Security
14. Ministry of Land and Resources
15. Ministry of Environmental Protection
16. Ministry of Housing and Urban–Rural Construction
18. Ministry of Transport
19. Ministry of Industry and Information Technology
20. Ministry of Water Resources
21. Ministry of Agriculture
22. Ministry of Commerce
23. Ministry of Culture
24. Ministry of Health
25. National Population and Family Planning Commission
26. People's Bank of China
27. National Audit Office

Looking at the State Council and the range of ministries, however, one is struck by two things. The first is that there are still surprising gaps. Attempts to create a Ministry of Energy were begun in the 1980s. In view of China's burgeoning energy needs, this would seem to be a natural area of policy concentration, with the need for an executive decision-making body and bureaucracy. In fact, a range of vested interests, among them the powerful state-owned energy companies, such as PetroChina, prevented this happening. The most China now has is a National Bureau for Energy, which functions on a quasi-ministerial basis, but is not defined as a ministry.

The second is that there are a group of ministries with responsibility for macroeconomics, begging the question of who is responsible for what, and how they relate to each other. Is there, in the end, a formal hierarchy? There is the Ministry of Finance, the Ministry of Foreign

Commerce, and finally the National Development and Reform Commission. Who has the ultimate say over economic matters in a way similar to the Chancellor of the Exchequer in the UK or the Secretary of State for the Treasury in the USA?

In fact, there is a division of responsibilities. The National Development and Reform Commission (NDRC) exists as the remnant of a state economic planning structure, and was called, until 2007, the State Planning and Development Commission, with powers to enforce budgets from ministries, and to allocate funding to different provinces from central resources. In the marketized Chinese economy, the primary function of the NDRC is to be the guardian of the Five Year Programmes. In that sense, the NDRC has immense influence, though little executive responsibility.

Under the formal ministries, there is a raft of other bodies answering to sponsoring ministries, but with defined areas of responsibility, such as the State Administration for Taxation, the National Bureau of Statistics, and the General Administration for Customs. There are bodies such as the China Regulatory Commission, the Chinese Academy of Sciences, and the National Council for the Social Security Fund. Below these are bureaux dealing with areas such as science and technology, cultural issues and even sections such as the post, or regulation of the state tobacco monopoly. The full body of the State Council meets every six months. Its executive, chaired by the premier, with his executive vice-premier, three vice-premiers and five state councillors, meets every week. This is the body that, at least in terms of administration, can be said to run China.

The central bureaucracy in all these ministries is, by some estimates, surprisingly small. People both inside and outside China have often complained about the highly bureaucratic nature of decision-making in China – but looking at the numbers in some of the central state entities, it is hard to see vast waves of central functionaries running the whole country. In Beijing, perhaps 50,000 work as civil servants in the central ministries and the agencies and bodies under them. Some, such as the Ministry of Foreign Affairs, consists of only a few thousand people. The Ministry of the Environment reportedly had only 400 officials when it existed as a State Environmental Protection Agency before being elevated to ministerial status in 2007 (Economy, 2005). In 2002, the whole state bureaucracy across the country included no more than ten million people – two-thirds of them employed by sub-provincial entities (Brødsgaard and Zheng, 2006, p. 106). The state employs many people, through state-owned enterprises, town and village enterprises, and the military and security services – but these are not working in the offices of the central or local arms of government. In that sense, governance in the PRC is remarkably light in terms of personnel.

The final issue for ministers and members of the State Council is that they do not need to be CCP members. In 2007, two ministers (science and technology, and education) were not Party members. At the provincial level too, deputy governors were often not Party members. In terms of gender composition, however, there are overwhelmingly more men than women in the State Council, in the CCP and in almost all areas of the country's public life apart from business. In 2007, at the 18th Party Congress, 80 per cent of CCP members were men, as were members of the NPC in 2012 (Guo and Zheng, 2008, p. 7). The archetypal government and Party official of contemporary China, therefore, is male and Han.

Trying to Reform the Central Ministries

As part of the reform process since 1978, the central Chinese government has attempted to slim down and streamline the bureaucratic structure. There have been a number of rationalizations, with a reduction from almost 50 ministries in 1990 to around 40 during the Zhu Rongji and Jiang Zemin period from 1997 to 2003, and then a further round of cuts in the Hu and Wen period, bringing the number down to its current level of 26. The lack of a national-level ministry specifically dealing with transport policy, previously divided between the Ministry of Railways and the Ministry of Transport, was rectified by a surprising move in 2013 at the National People's Congress to unify these into one super-ministry. This was regarded as one of the earliest signs of the purposefulness of the Xi administration.

This national structure is reflected in the provinces and the prefectures, with departments for finance, transport and other administrative areas carrying out national policies at the local level, but sometimes sponsoring their own variants in order to reflect local conditions. In that sense, Chinese governance might look like an inflexible bureaucracy, but it has considerable scope within it for change, adaptation and innovation. Where the greatest constraints on local government's actions exist is in terms of who funds specific ideas, and how resources are distributed.

How Is All This Funded?

One of the most striking features of contemporary China is the funding of government services, and the ways in which the government is held to account for the money it spends. Government expenditure as a proportion of GDP in the PRC is 22 per cent, much lower than the UK, at 40 per cent, and Japan, at 33 per cent (CIA, *World Factbook*, 2014. The annual budget of the government centrally came to over 8 trillion RMB in 2011. From this, over 70 per cent is sent back to the provinces to be spent on health care, education, social welfare, fixed investments, pensions and other costs. The fiscal imbalance between the centre as a tax-raising entity, and the provinces as places where money is spent, is a convenient reminder that China has in some ways a highly centralized administrative system, but security and policing budgets are often decided at the local level.

Taxation is a contentious issue in China. Reforms in 1993 meant that there was greater clarity over what state-owned enterprises, corporations, individuals and foreign enterprises had to pay in tax. A consumption tax was also made more consistent. Even so, for such a major economy, the structure of personal taxation and corporate tax remains unusual. Less than 10 per cent of tax comes from individuals, with a tax rate on their salaries of over 40 per cent for high earners, similar to levels in other developing countries (Lin, 2009, p. 24). Enterprises involving foreign investments contribute a fifth of central government receipts. The bulk comes from state-owned enterprises, which hand over substantial amounts of tax, but which also have, since their restructuring in the late 1990s, become significantly more profitable.

The Chinese government spends marginally more than it earns from taxation. But at the provincial level, many officials are able to raise money on the lands they can sell, or other smaller taxes – but many of these attract passionate public opposition. There has also been much research in recent years into how local governments in China are able to demand that banks, almost all of which are state owned, have to fund their projects and sometimes act like branches of the local treasury. This lack of clarity over the division between banks and government is a major structural issue, and one that may have led to the accrual (though because of the lack of transparency, no one really knows the extent of this) of hundreds of billions of RMB on bad loans (loans still accruing interest, but where there is almost no possibility of the debtor being able to pay them off).

The National People's Congress

The question within the governance structure is therefore how any of its functions and expenditures is given any proper scrutiny and by whom. The standard view is that in China the government decides everything and the people simply follow. This is, of course, a gross simplification. Hu Jintao, in 2007, during his speech at the 17th Party Congress, talked of 'public participation in decision-making' largely to deal with the explosions of anger at official incompetence and inefficiency. Every year, in the spring, Beijing is host to the 3,000-plus delegates to the annual National People's Congress (NPC), the prime means to try to incorporate this element of participation. It is this Congress that formally approves the policies of the State Council, the budgets and its personnel proposals when they are made. Delegates from the NPC come from all of the PRC's provinces, autonomous regions and directly subordinate metropolitan areas, and from the special administrative regions of Hong Kong and Macau. Even Taiwan has a symbolic presence.

The NPC is presented as the highest organ of state power in the Chinese 1982 Constitution. In many official statements it is called China's parliament, though it is not bicameral, and, even if it had the appropriate constitutional powers, it meets too infrequently to be truly effective. When a Chinese journalist declared in the late 1990s in a PRC publication that the NPC was purely a rubber-stamp body, she was jailed for several years. In fact she had written what everyone knew, but no one dared to say. The NPC might have the powers to analyse Chinese laws, and to approve budgets, but these are highly controlled. And while it is true that the NPC, since the controversy in the early 1990s over the granting of permission to build the Three Gorges Dam in south-western China, has become more vociferous in its opposition on certain issues, on the whole it has proved a compliant body. This is largely because the membership of every single delegate is approved, selected and vetted by the central government and the CCP.

Those who observe or attend NPC annual gatherings are struck by the high element of theatre that the meetings present. National minority delegates come dressed in their supposedly ethnic clothes. In recent years there have been celebrity delegates, with singers, actresses and other public non-political figures being co-opted. The meetings themselves are heavily stage-managed to ensure there are no nasty surprises. A government work report is read by the premier, as the highlight, and a press conference is given. Once the Congress has been disbanded, the rest of the year's business is overseen by an executive committee of about 150 members.

The Congress is held at the same time as the Chinese People's Political Consultative Conference (CPPCC), a council made up of Chinese individuals from diverse backgrounds, representing the various different forces in society, stemming from its foundation in 1946 to link up with the KMT and other parties that existed at that time (see Table 4.4). The CPPCC is presented as offering non-binding advice to the CCP. It has no significant powers, and a national membership of around 3,000. The CPPCC has nine committees, and its membership is drawn largely from these worlds: economic affairs; resources, population and environment; education, science, culture, health and sports; legal and social affairs; ethnic and religious affairs; cultural and historical issues; foreign affairs; Hong Kong, Taiwan and Macau affairs; and a general office for handling proposals.

Many argue that the whole Congress system is ripe for reform, as part of a process of democratization within the CCP mentioned in Chapter 3. Scholars at the Central Party School in 2007 proposed that, in many ways, the Congresses and the CPPCC could become far more representative, but in order to do so they needed to be reduced to a more manageable size, and have some direct link with constituencies for which they could be said to stand directly. Membership of the NPC and the CPPCC at the time of writing has a largely ceremonial flavour. The Central Party School was proposed by Wang Changjiang; Zhou Tianyong and Wang Angling (Wang, Zhou and Wang, 2007) simply to reduce the number of Congress members dramatically so that each represented about three

Table 4.4 China's eight democratic parties

Name	*Membership*	*Date of Foundation*
Revolutionary Committee of the Kuomintang (KMT)	65,000	1948
China Democratic League	135,000	1939
China Democratic National Construction Association	85,000	1945
China Association for Promoting Democracy	81,000	1945
China Zhi Gong Party (mainly for returned overseas Chinese)	20,000	1925
Jiusan Society	85,000	1946
Taiwan Democratic Self Government League	1,800	1947
Chinese Peasants' and Workers' Democratic Party	80,000	1930

million Chinese, meaning that the whole NPC membership would fall to about 400 people. This would mean that Chinese Congress members would represent about the same numbers as senators in the USA. In addition,the book suggested that the NPC should hold more regular meetings, and have a more meaningful oversight of national budgets. They pointed out that the passing of the immense annual budgets, running from January to December, usually happened three months into the period in which they were due to run, and involved delegates being given huge printouts with rafts of figures but hardly any time to examine the material meaningfully.

That the NPC and CPPCC are natural objects for reform is clear from the ways in which the government and Party talk about the need to have more political participation in decision-making. Innovations have been introduced to obtain feedback on government services and, to quote Hu Jintao, to make people 'the key thing'. In his speech at the Party Congress in 2007, Hu stressed the need to open up more ways for people to be involved in decision-making. Having more competition for membership of congresses might be an easy route. Even so, the head of the NPC from 2003 to 2013, Wu Bangguo, typified the differences of opinion between the government and CCP by consistently taking a hard-line approach. His declaration in 2011 that Western-style liberal, multi-party democracy would never work in China, and that the state-owned enterprises were the keystone of the economy, something that would never change, became a rallying call for other hard-liners. The subsequent leadership of the NPC under Zhang Dejiang has so far offered no startling innovations.

Local Congresses

The central government structure is mirrored at provincial level. In each province, there are governors and a range of vice-governors, and in each city a mayor and up to nine deputy mayors. These act as a kind of local cabinet in charge of decision-making, executing commands from the centre and translating them to local conditions. This structure was duplicated down to prefectural and county level. Cities as entities of sub-regional governance exist at both prefectural and county level. For these levels of governance, there were congresses, but the lower down the tree of power, the more latitude there has been to experiment. Town congresses, in particular, are places where citizen activists have been able to stand for election without CCP support.

From 2010, the government's promise to make these local congresses more representative and allow non-Party figures to take part in them was exposed by the huge hurdles that activists were confronted by when they wished to put themselves forward for election. In one case, in 2011, Liu Ping, who was standing on a non-Party platform in Jiangxi province, found her candidature cancelled on a technicality. Her persistence was rewarded with further harassment by local officials, and she was detained in Beijing by security agents in March 2012 during the annual meeting of the NPC. At the level of rhetoric, to continue building the United Front and to create the sort of 'big society' about which the Party talks a great deal, these outside voices have, in theory, been welcomed. One successful township election candidate in the late 1990s and early 2000s in Hebei, Yao Lifa, managed to call in almost half of the laws and regulations passed by congresses for greater scrutiny. But in the much more anxious and cautious latter part of the decade, such discordant voices became increasingly unwelcome.

Local Officials

Local officials occupy a specific place in the feelings of the nation. According to a survey in 2009 carried in the magazine *Xiaokang* ('Moderately Well Off Society'), Chinese people trusted farmers the most, lawyers second, doctors third, and sex workers fourth. In terms of Party and government officials, things became more complicated. National government leaders were on the whole still trusted, in the sense that when all else failed then at least a direct appeal to them might lead to some delivery of justice. Attitudes to local leaders were, however, quite different.

Leaders in the centre, such as Wen Jiabao, played to this, with an avuncular, patriarchal style, appearing during the terrible snowstorms in early 2008 at the Chinese New Year to reassure stranded migrant labourers trying to get home for their single most important annual holiday that he understood their pain and was trying to do something about it. But of the nine million petitions made to the central government in 2009 when avenues of protest had been used up locally, according to Yu Jianrong at the Chinese Academy of Social Sciences, only 0.2 per cent were ever dealt with satisfactorily (Yu, 2010). So, while central leaders were still trusted, the level of that trust, according to internal surveys, has fallen since the early 2000s.

What was clear from the survey, however, was that local officials were the most loathed and detested of all those working in modern China. They were regarded as brutal, corrupt, untrustworthy and morally debased. In a report produced in 2000 by Chen Guidi and Wu Di, two Anhui-based journalists, it was the local officials who came out as the most vilified, and the most villainous, of the characters in the rich firmament of the New China (Chen and Wu, 2006).

The disdain for local officials could be imputed to one fact. It was they who did the state's dirty work at the most visible level – collecting taxes, imposing unpopular policies such as the diverse forms of the one-child policy that had been brought in to varying degrees across China from the 1970s and early 1980s, and dealing with land distribution issues. Local officials were on the front line in relationships between one of the most difficult groups in contemporary China, the farmers, and the state. That many local officials were corrupt, rent-seeking, greedy and violent was borne out both by the stories that Wu and Chen told, but also by a range of other material contained in newspaper and magazine reports and elsewhere. This was motivated to some extent by the restraints on the officials' ability to raise taxes and find funds (covered earlier in this chapter). The anti-corruption campaign from 2013 was targeted at some of this larceny, ordering officials to stop huge expensive banquets, be more careful with public money, travel abroad less, and conduct themselves more appropriately in public. The campaign seemed to have some effect, reportedly putting a raft of expensive restaurants and hotels out of business because of the falling off of government patronage.

Local officials, after all, might argue that they were ostensibly on very basic salaries, and they had heavy responsibilities placed on them, so needed more inducements. The most talented were soon promoted upwards. Few wanted to linger in the rural districts, or in backward towns. For those who had to stay, seeking some reward beyond what they were paid was not hard to understand. A blog kept by one official, who wrote under a pseudonym in the late 2000s, expressed the frustration of someone trying to administer spotlessly in an environment where almost everyone was corrupt. To be honest in this sort of world attracted bewildered attention, not least because often the whole name of the game locally was how to implicate everyone else in the world of mutual back-scratching and favour-giving practised across the rest of the country. Trying to opt out of this, as the blogger showed, attracted suspicion above all else.

Measuring the corruption of local officials is difficult. One local official was accused of having amassed huge debts through having more than 146 mistresses. Another famous case covered in the Chinese media described how a leader in a small township in Shaanxi had acquired 17 mistresses, the husbands of a number of whom ganged up angrily and denounced him for cuckolding them. Local officials were accused of misspending government money by going on trips abroad (something tightened up with new rules from 2009 limiting international travel), hosting lavish entertainments for each other, and being drawn into major business deals contrary to Party and government regulations. Where they were often most vulnerable was in the ways in which their children and relatives were also drawn into this world.

The negative impact of local-level corruption on public confidence can never be underestimated. In the late 1990s, Lai Changxing, a Fujianese businessman, is claimed to have built up an immense smuggling business largely through looking after officials in the customs bureau and at other levels of local government through paybacks, favours and running his famous 'red mansion', a brothel-cum-exclusive nightclub in which high-level local leaders were entertained. The exposure of this case in the year 2000 led to Lai fleeing to Canada, the felling of a number of important local leaders, and numerous rumours reaching right up to the Standing Committee of the Politburo itself. His extradition was requested by the Chinese government, and he was returned to China to face trial in 2011 after assurances from the authorities that he would not be executed. He was sentenced to life imprisonment in 2012.

The Rule of Law

Since 1978, the official view often found in government and Party documents is that China has moved from 'rule by man' under Mao Zedong to 'rule of law'. Chinese reformulations of this state describe the internal aspiration as becoming a system where there will be 'rule by law'. Law and legal procedure in the PRC is under the guidance of the Party, through the judges, courts and lawyers that have been trained since the early 1980s.

The creation of a functioning legal system has been a critical part of the reform process. Since 1978, over 460 laws have been passed, and a raft of new regulations introduced. In the final years of Mao Zedong, judges were mainly long-retired military figures, working in courts where cases that were dealt with had no right of appeal, and heard with a swiftness that meant most trials, even for the most serious cases, were decided and the culprits executed or imprisoned all within a day. The recognition by the leadership in 1978 that in order to develop economically and to attract foreign investment, the country would need better legal structures inspired the wholesale adoption of many pieces of legislation from Japan, Germany and other jurisdictions. Many countries, from the USA to the UK, Germany and Australia, partnered China in helping it in this process, seeing this as also being in their own interests. The NPC and the State Constitution were all part of this immense legalization process, each with a defined role in scrutinizing or laying down the parameters of rights.

Courts exist throughout China, from the township level upwards, with a Supreme Court in Beijing, the office of Procurator-General and the Ministry of Justice. China passed important laws to cover contracts, bankruptcy and investment protection from 1990 onwards. But the vastness of the country meant that there were highly uneven standards in terms of the quality of judgments and the application of law. Beyond this, the even deeper issue of the real validity of the rule of law persisted, especially when faced with the almost super-legal existence of the Communist Party, which was clearly never going to allow courts or lawyers to start challenging its right to act unilaterally and beyond the constraints of law when it chose.

This unevenness manifested itself in two ways. Courts often gave judgments that were sound and well reasoned, but having these implemented proved far harder. Foreign business people have filled books with tales of woe about working in the provinces, or in the urban centres of China, and having their contracts overturned, or their intellectual property stolen, and, despite getting help from the Chinese courts, finding this useless when confronted with trying to implement the court's decision on the ground (Clissold, 2005; Midler, 2011). In the most contentious legal cases – those regarding counter-revolutionaries (as they were defined until the year 2000) and subversives (their label after 2000), the rights granted to citizens in the state Constitution were of next to no value. For this reason, international lawyers talked of the Constitution being the weakest legal document in the country. Legal scholars often called the Constitution a 'sleeping beauty', full of excellent words and great notions, but of no great force as yet. Chinese political activists, Liu Xiaobo, was detained in 2009 for over a year against the stipulations of the Criminal Justice Law, where limits to detention for those not charged with crimes were clearly set out. The case of rights lawyer, Gao Zhisheng, was even more striking, with his complete disappearance, without any legal explanation, for several years from 2010. News of his release from jail finally in 2014 revealed that he was still under a form of house detention in Xinjiang. In sensitive areas, the rule of law has remained highly negotiable, with clear limits to its strength.

Human Rights

For many citizens in China, there has been increasing awareness of their legal rights, and their ability to pursue these formally through the courts, since 1978. The number of lawyers has increased dramatically, and local courts at least have become clogged with civil cases involving the same kinds of things as anywhere else in the world – land disputes, property rights, and claims for compensation from government or corporations over perceived wrongs. The desire for justice is as strong in contemporary China as in any other society among citizens, with many keen to exercise their rights and spending large sums of money pursuing cases through the courts. In the Hu and Wen era there have been surprising moves to liberalize some parts of the law, despite evidence that elsewhere this was a controlling and repressive period. In particular, an Open Governance Law was passed in 2008, allowing people access to official information along the same lines as freedom of information legislation in other countries. The province of Guangdong posted its whole budget online in 2010, creating a massive file that took up two gigabytes on the computers of those who downloaded it. It is hard to judge to what extent these moves are the most harmless concessions by a government that knew it had to compromise but was reluctant to do anything too dramatic. Cynics may look at what the central and provincial government has acted on so far and say these are strategic choices by rulers who are still highly controlling and wish to make little progress to a more open society. In the end, the budgets of both the CCP and organizations under it are shrouded in mystery, as are most of the financial arrangements between local banks and the Chinese state which runs them.

One course open to disgruntled citizens is to petition the local and central governments directly when they have exhausted formal legal options. This draws on ancient precedents of subjects sending letters of protest to the imperial court. In cities such as Xian, vast areas in the middle of the city have been set out for 'reception of petitions and letters of complaint'. Showing his support for this peaceful means of lobbying the government, premier Wen Jiabao visited a petition reception centre in Beijing during the spring festival in 2011, the first central leader to do so since 1949. He made statements about the need to deal with people's complaints in a timely and efficient fashion. There were even internet-based ways of expressing complaints against officials.

Those who took this route may have been inspired by the case of one complainant in 2007 who had managed to penetrate Wen's security and hand a petition directly to him. This was, of course, dealt with quickly, for public perception reasons, if for no other. But the anxiety of leaders at both local and national levels about the rising numbers of petitions (nine million in the year 2009 alone, on one estimate) was put down to the fact that the levels of these petitions were one of the criteria by which officials were marked for promotion or demotion. It was in their interests, therefore, to ensure that complaints were kept to a minimum, by fair means or foul. One study showed that many who made complaints suffered some kind of recrimination as a result (Human Rights Watch, 2009). Others simply got dragged into a Dickensian world where they wandered from one part of the bureaucracy to another, without getting any satisfaction. An American citizen petitioning on behalf of her Chinese boyfriend reported how even her attempt to physically hand the letter to the correct office in Beijing proved challenging, with many doors being slammed in her face, and office workers declaring that, despite the clear instructions on the door, the matter was nothing to do with their department. In Beijing, as the 2000s went on, separate provinces set up central reception centres for petitioners. It was to these that unhappy plaintiffs came. But as numbers rose towards the end of the decade, many local governments decided to use unorthodox means to cut numbers down, simply getting private security companies to take the most stubborn into a system of illegal detention called 'black jail', and having them taken back to their home provinces to be dealt with by the local authorities there.

As in any other place in the world, justice in the PRC boils down to how the system is funded. Courts are funded by the government at the level at which they are functioning. Town courts have their money from town governments, right up to provincial level. Funding cases without a legal aid scheme is a problem. And there are real issues about how local courts are ever, in commercial cases, likely to attack vested interests locally that might have powerful political patronage. China's legal system is therefore a thing in flux, but also an area of increasing importance in the modernization of the country and the attempts to create a more predictable environment.

Law Enforcement: The Role of Security

In the Maoist period, the country was divided into neighbourhood committees, which acted like the most local form of state direction and law enforcement. The whole system often resembled one of mass surveillance, with committees able to report on citizens in their areas if they suspected crimes were being committed, but also to ensure the political reliability of people. These local committees still remain, these days in a somewhat different form, as semi-elected bodies representing citizens' and residents' concerns in urban and some rural areas.

China after 1949 was a society moving from a period of high militarization to a more civilian, peacetime mode. So the creation of a public security bureau (PSB) to undertake the work of civilian security and peacekeeping seemed natural. The PSB exists to this day as the equivalent of the national police force in other countries – but is helped in its vast challenge of maintaining law and order and dealing with crime in China by another organization, the People's Armed Police (PAP), which was given enhanced powers after the uprising in 1989, and exists as a domestic riot police. All these organizations are funded and directed at both the central and the provincial level.

Unique to China is a vast (and burgeoning) internal security apparatus, the Ministry of State Security (MSS), which covers both keeping control over a number of domestic threats, but also working as the Chinese equivalent of the US Central Intelligence Agency (CIA) or the British Secret Intelligence Service (SIS) in promoting what are stated to be China's key interests abroad. In recent years, state security has focused on terrorist threats, and on the issues of Tibet, Xinjiang and other sensitive border regions. They have also mounted large campaigns against religious groups such as Falun Gong, whose belief systems and practices are seen as inimical to the CCP.

Unlike the situation in the Soviet Union, the security services have never been a power base in their own right – the Godfather of the Chinese MSS, Kang Sheng, one of Mao Zedong's key allies, never presented himself as a potential competitor to Mao, but ensured that the agencies he directed were reporting directly to Party imperatives. In that sense, they mirror the position of the PLA. Even so, the sheer numbers of state security workers at the time of writing, and the budgets they are granted, show that they are the most shadowy, but perhaps one of the most powerful, elements of contemporary Chinese society.

Conclusion: The Challenges of Governing a Society in Ferment

The year 2011 offered two cases that illustrated the complexities of trying to govern a society that was undergoing deep and rapid material and economic changes. The first, the tragic high-speed rail crash of May 2011, highlights the role of over-ambitious central ministry plans, and the response of local government to crises. The second, from the town of

Wukan in Guangdong province, brings to the fore the issue of how the government deals with groups in society that have deep grievances.

The collision between two trains on the high-speed track near Wenzhou, Zhejiang province, was blamed on the poor quality of the concrete in which the track was set. The PRC, under the Minister of Railways, had undertaken, from 2002, the most ambitious construction of a high-speed railway the world had ever seen. A network of bullet trains was established across the country in the space of a few years, dramatically shortening travel times. The journey time between Beijing and Shanghai was reduced from 12 hours to five, for example. Trains like these were seen as the solution to many of China's problems – the creation of a good internal logistics infrastructure, which was relatively non-polluting, and which accommodated larger numbers than planes were able to, and at a cheaper price. It was also useful in trying to wean some Chinese off their new addiction to cars. But the rapidity with which the new rail network was developed struck many experts as over-ambitious and fraught with potential problems. One story tells of a contractor for concrete simply showing procurement officials the best batch of material he had, but handing them a wad of money on the understanding that the real material he would supply would be of an inferior, cheaper quality.

What was most striking about the accident was the initial response of local officials, who simply imposed a news blackout, and then buried one of the damaged carriages, without a proper investigation. This showed they were behind the times. Netizens (individuals involved in online communities) exposed the case, with the government locally letting the management of the story run away from them. Within a few days it was clear that the issue had escalated to such an extent that the central government needed to become involved. Wen Jiabao reportedly rose from his sick bed to deal with the crisis. Minister Liu was removed, an investigation was begun, and the issue of how to compensate the victims and deal with their anger was addressed.

The unrest of Wukan in wealthy Guangdong province illustrates different but related issues. For the local officials, what had started as a clumsy land acquisition against the will of the local people, something all too frequent in a PRC where the value of land has been growing in recent years, led to a huge uprising by almost every member of the 20,000-strong town, with local security officials being ejected, and provincial police blocked from entering the area. For several days in November and December 2011, a stand-off prevailed. But the canny way in which locals had invited international and local media to witness what was happening meant that the image-conscious local government was unable to act as it once would have done, using hard-line tactics and simply bringing in members of the People's Armed Police to deal with the situation. By mid-December, the local provincial Party secretary, Wang Yang, mandated new negotiations, the outcome of which was the innovative idea that a series of local elections be held in which the leaders of the rebels would be able to stand. These allowed the restoration of at least some stability.

China in the twenty-first century presents immense challenges of governance. This is clear on an almost daily basis. On any given day, officials at every level within the PRC wrestle with the contending demands of members in a society that is growing more complex, and more aware of its rights. Chapter 6 will look at the structure of Chinese society in a period that has been called 'an era of contention'.

5

The Chinese Economy

The Chinese economy is one of the wonders of the modern world. From constituting a tiny part of global GDP in 1978 at the start of the great transformation, China stood, in 2011, as the world's second-largest economy (it had overtaken Japan in this position a year earlier), making up over 15 per cent of the world's economy. It was the world's largest holder of foreign reserves, its largest exporter, second-largest importer and the largest user of all energy sources, apart from oil, where it stood a very close second to the USA. In terms of productivity, Chinese leaders were keen to say that, since the early 1980s, China's economy had grown by 10 per cent per year. Even after the onset of the global financial crisis in 2008, China managed to add 40 per cent to its economy at a time when the rest of the developed world was stagnant. In the decade after its entry to the World Trade Organization (WTO) in 2001, China quadrupled the size of its economy. In terms of the rate and gross size of growth, China was either at the top of data tables, or very close to it. Predictions of when it would overtake the USA to be the world's largest economy varied between 2015 and 2035 – it was a question, in any case, not of *if*, but *when* – and the end date for this to happen was frequently revised downwards (BBC News, 14 February 2011).

The Chinese Economy in 2014: Basic Data

One of the first things most people notice about the PRC is that it is a country of big numbers. At the top of these sits the Chinese GDP rate. Since 1978, it has increased on average by 10 per cent each year, lifting China from 17th place in global rankings in 1979 to second in 2011 (World Bank, 2010) (see Figure 5.1). In 2013, of its (in purchasing power parity, or PPP, terms, a measure which takes into account the relative spending power of different currencies in their own economies rather than by determining a global absolute value) US$13.39 trillion-strong economy, agriculture made up 10 per cent, with the remaining 90 per cent being split almost evenly between services and industry. It was the largest

Figure 5.1 Chinese gross domestic product, 1978–2012

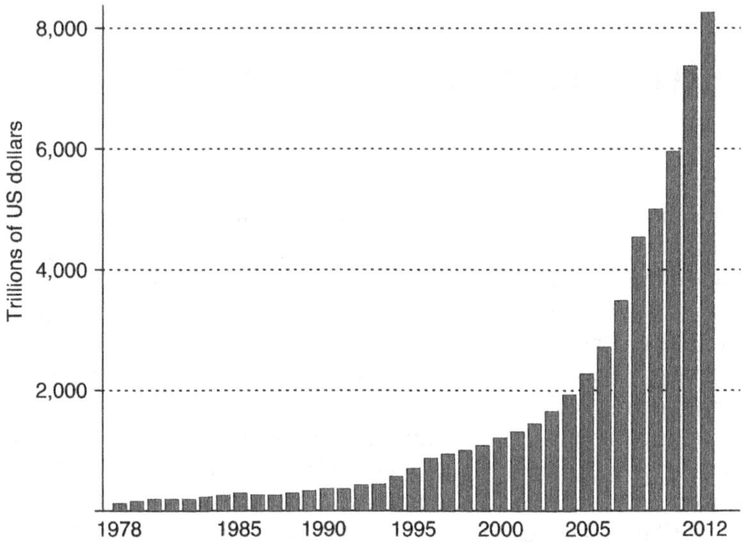

Notes: GDP in current US$; not adjusted for inflation.

Sources: World Bank, *World Development Indicators* (2015).

exporter in the world, sending US$2.21 trillion of goods abroad, consisting mainly of electrical and other machinery, including data-processing equipment, apparel, textiles, iron and steel, and optical and medical equipment. It was also the world's second-largest importer, absorbing US$1.95 trillion in value, consisting of electrical and other machinery, oil and mineral fuels, optical and medical equipment, metal ores, plastics and organic chemicals (CIA, 2014). By the end of 2012 there was a stock of almost US$1.344 trillion of foreign direct investment within China, and US$541 billion was invested by China in the rest of the world. One of the most remarkable characteristics of the Chinese economy since the 1980s has been the large proportion of annual GDP that is invested in fixed assets and infrastructure – 46 per cent in 2013, making it the world's second highest. Only 36 per cent of GDP was from domestic consumption (CIA, 2014).

One of the most remarkable measures of China's development since the 1980s is its accrual of foreign reserves (see Figure 5.2). As a country that has imported less than it has exported, China has been able to build what is known as its capital account (the balance between money paid for goods and services leaving and entering China – something like a current

Figure 5.2 China's foreign currency reserves, 2000–2013

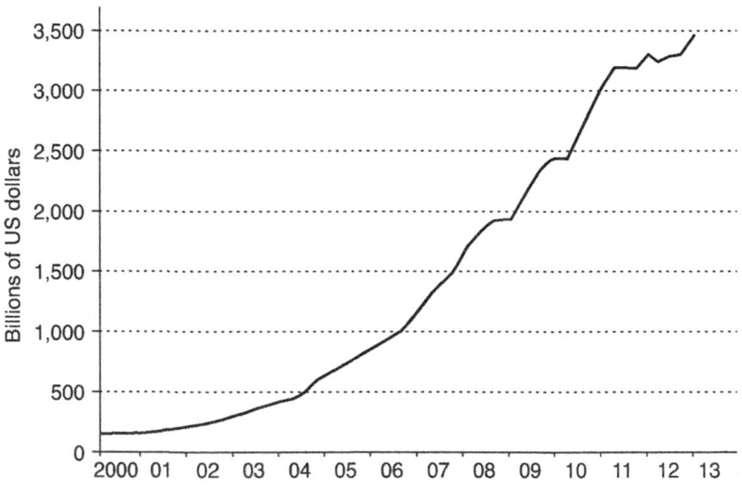

Sources: Data compiled from the State Administration of Foreign Exchange, People's Republic of China; the People's Bank of China; and the author's own figures.

account for an individual in a bank). In 1978, China exported and imported next to nothing. In 2006, it overtook Japan as holder of the world's largest stock of these reserves. By 2014, it had over US$4.5 trillion.

The Sources of Chinese Growth: Reform of the Agricultural Sector and the Special Economic Zones

Down the centuries before 1978, agriculture was the prime sector for the Chinese economy. It employed the vast majority of the people, and accounted for most of the country's GDP. Even after three decades of Maoist central planning from 1949, China remained a predominantly agrarian economy, with very limited industrial infrastructure. One of the key objectives of the 1978 reforms was to move China away from this agrarian model, and to modernize the economy through deeper and more rapid industrialization. This was after all one of the key targets of the Four Modernizations set out first by former Premier Zhou Enlai, and then by Deng in the 1970s. But, in order to do this, China had, first, to feed itself sufficiently, and then be able to increase productivity in the countryside to such an extent that labour employed there could be freed for use elsewhere.

The remarkable success of the Household Responsibility System, as it came to be labelled, allowing farmers to sell surpluses back to the state for a small profit, achieved these aims. From 1980, because of this incentive, productivity in terms of grain production increased markedly (Naughton, 2006). But this had the unintended consequence of releasing many from working on the land to work on industrial enterprises (that this was unintentional was something Deng Xiaoping was to recognize publicly a few years later, when he said explicitly on his 1992 Southern Tour that it was never the government's initial intention to see this happen). Whole new areas of economic activity came into existence. By 2014, those working on China's farms had decreased to only a third of the population, with only half the country living in areas categorized as being rural (Chinese National Bureau of Statistics).

A fundamental tool of the early strategy of opening up was to attract foreign investment. This was not only to enjoy the use of foreign capital, but also to gain access to intellectual property and management know-how. Deng and his colleagues, in their tours around the world in the late 1970s and early 1980s looking at other economies to pick up ideas about what to do, were aware of how backward China had become in terms of technology, education and expertise. The only quick option was simply to start buying this expertise through partnerships with foreign entities. The first joint venture law was passed in 1979. One of the earliest multinational companies to work in China was Coca-Cola, which set up a bottling plant in Tianjin. From 1980, in particular, large numbers of Japanese companies went to work in China. But the real impact was made less by changing the national laws than by establishing, from 1980, a number of Special Economic Zones (SEZs) in locations where they were able to leverage proximity to non-Chinese industrial centres, and allow for a safe (from the CCP's point of view) interface between China and the outside world (Brown, 2008).

Shenzhen, next to Hong Kong, was to prove the most dramatic of these. A fishing town with fewer than 300,000 inhabitants in 1980, it was designated as a zone that would be attractive to the many business people in Hong Kong who wanted to expand their manufacturing facilities and gain access to cheaper labour and land because of the dearth of these in the highly urbanized, land-poor city. Shenzhen was given a special status, and a raft of rules were passed allowing tax breaks for those who came to invest. The key activity was to manufacture and re-export. Only in 1996 was Shenzhen finally permitted to make goods for the domestic Chinese market.

The other SEZs were in Zhuhai, a little further to the west along the coast from Shenzhen, next to Macau; and Xiamen, facing the island of

Taiwan. Deng was eventually to sanction the establishment of 14 SEZs, culminating with Shanghai being declared an SEZ in 1990. By 2002, the kinds of benefits that were granted to investors in the SEZs were effectively extended to the whole country. By this time, however, Shenzhen itself had boomed to become a city of 10 million inhabitants, which in some years in the 1980s had seen year-on-year growth rates of over 40 per cent. Its skyline of skyscrapers became the definitive image of the new CCP-controlled capitalist country (Koolhaas and Leong, 2001).

Shenzhen's great benefit was plentiful and inexpensive land, but also the access it gave foreign multinational companies to vast pools of cheap, well-educated labour. Accounts of the explosion of manufacturing, first in the city, and then in the whole province of Guangdong which it was located in, show how many millions were to migrate from inland China into vast new cities in the Pearl River delta area, serving in factories that sometimes had workers numbering in the tens of thousands. The social and economic impact of this was, and remains, immense, with as many as 200 million migrant labourers moving around the coastal areas, in particular, going from factory to factory. By the 2000s, China had become, as the former premier, Zhu Rongji, said, 'the factory of the world'. It had plants producing 90 per cent of the world's microwaves, and one city that was responsible for the vast majority of the world's socks (Kynge, 2005). And while, initially, manufacturing produced relatively simple consumer goods and electrical appliances, quite soon more advanced technological products were coming off Chinese factory assembly lines. PRC-located factories were supplying most of the world's laptops, mobile phones and personal computers, no matter what brand names the goods might be carrying. Companies such as Apple, Siemens and Volkswagen began to locate major parts of their supply chain there. By the late 1990s, China became amongst the world's top destinations for foreign investment, liberalizing its laws further to allow companies to set up wholly-owned enterprises, and attracting more than US$0.5 trillion in investment, and 600,000 separate joint ventures and foreign investment enterprises across the country by the middle of the decade (Kynge, 2006).

Entry to the WTO: Global China

The logic of the early moves to allow foreign investment into the country was to open up the Chinese economy so that it could upgrade its technology and processes, and undertake accelerated modernization. It was certainly not China's aspiration to become simply a vast workshop for the rest of the world, producing goods that were then shipped away to be enjoyed by middle-class consumers elsewhere. The manufacturing focus was only a means to an end. The final objective was for China itself to grow wealthy through this, and then in turn enjoy some of the fruits of its hard work.

The great challenge for Chinese policy-makers, even as investment flowed into the country, was that rather than rely on imported technology, know-how and brand, China wanted its own enterprises to start innovating and moving into higher-value products. It soon found that there were impediments to achieving this. The US, Japan, Hong Kong, Taiwan and other major investors on the whole used a model whereby they shipped partly finished goods into the country, had them finished and then shipped out. The real intellectually valuable part of the process was still done elsewhere. Chinese companies had very few proprietary intellectual property rights (IPR). While patents registered by the Chinese rose exponentially from 1990, there was little sense that Chinese corporations were trend-setters in the global marketplace. While a company such as Apple could become the world's most valuable corporation over the space of a few years, succeeding even in breaking into the tricky Chinese market itself, Chinese companies were far less visible.

Exposing the Chinese economy to international competition in a managed way was, therefore, the key challenge for central policy-makers. Chen Yun, the most eminent economic thinker of the 1980s, had famously described the Chinese economic model as a 'bird in a cage' – there was some allowance for innovation and freedom, but within limits. The bottom line was that the state through state-owned enterprises and other means maintained control over key parts of the economy, but avoided the excesses of uncompetitive, bureaucratic behaviour that had typified so many state companies in the past. An Organisation for Economic Co-operation and Development (OECD) report in 2005 had stated that more than 50 per cent of Chinese GDP growth came from the non-state sector. Even so, the state still had to control as much as possible, for political and economic reasons (OECD, 2005). Over-reliance on foreign investment was not, in the long term, good, however; China had to stand on its own feet.

Entry to the WTO might have seemed an odd way to achieve this. The WTO, after all, is the key organization promoting Western norms and an international, neo-liberal order on global trade. But the WTO, on some interpretations, would at least allow central policy-makers to introduce much-needed competition into Chinese state companies and break some of the entrenched vested interest and conservatism that prevailed there

(Foot and Walter, 2010). Internal reform was not likely to work so quickly. Chinese leaders therefore cleverly let external demands do the trick. In the same years as they talked of promoting Chinese global champions, they also finalized the epic negotiations for WTO entry; these were signed in November 2001.

The road to the WTO for China had been a long and arduous one, taking more than 14 years. The final stretch had been particularly exhausting, involving detailed arguments with the USA and the EU in particular over problematic sectors like finance, telecoms and services. What was ultimately agreed involved, at least on the surface, wide-ranging liberalization by the Chinese over key sectors such as financial services and agriculture. Both of these had posed thorny problems because of their strategically vital role in the Chinese economy overall.

For financial services, the agreements which the Chinese government signed allowed entry to the domestic banking retail market by foreign banks and financial service providers after five years from 2001. This was a tough proposition. In the 1990s, the banking sector had been beset by poorly performing loans across the PRC, creating major headaches for the government. As explained in Chapter 4, state control of banks meant that they often acted as the servants of local government, who had placed increasing amounts of debt on them in order to fund local projects. This had imploded in 1998, causing the central government to set up more stringent rules, but the problem of over-close relationships between banks and officials never went away. While foreign banks and insurance companies looked hungrily at one of the world's great untapped markets, the central Chinese government was aware of just how unprepared the banking sector was locally. Some foreign banks were allowed to take up to a fifth of the shares of Chinese banks. Others gradually began to work abroad. The China Development Bank even took a 3.5 per cent stake in Barclays Bank in the UK in 2007. And the Industrial and Agricultural Bank was partially listed in Hong Kong, New York and then London, becoming one of the world's most valuable companies for a while, at least on paper. For agriculture, it was more a case of Chinese farmers worrying that they were simply unable to take additional competition from foreign suppliers. They lacked the production techniques and the economies of scale to be able to compete with farmers in the USA, Australia or elsewhere in Asia. Protection of a sector that still employed as many as 400 million people in the PRC remained one of the most contentious issues during negotiations. It is one which the Xi and Li leadership have finally tried to address by simply shifting more of the population to the cities, so that there is less labour dependency on living off the land.

By 2007, only a year after most of the implementation period for the agreement had passed, it was already clear that despite the initial worries the Chinese government had managed its entry into the global economy with huge success. Forces of productivity had been unleashed, which saw a steep rise in exports, and steady positive GDP growth. The fundamental strategy of the government was simply to allow external competition to sharpen up domestic companies, and to a great extent this was achieved. Banks largely recovered from their difficulties of the 1990s, and the agricultural sector was stable, its problems mainly caused by farmers' irritation over rights to the title of their land and the taxes placed on them (taxes that were lifted in 2007), rather than foreign competitors.

The internationalization of the Chinese economy, however, was mainly through China's role in global supply chains rather than the part its companies played in international business. One of the most remarkable aspects of WTO entry was the way in which even more multinational corporations crowded into China, placing large proportions of their manufacturing or supply chains there. Wal-Mart alone was sourcing US$18 billion of goods in the country by 2008. That this shift happened so quickly meant that Chinese manufacturing companies were able to become far more assertive towards foreign customers (Midler, 2011). Problems with the quality of goods surfaced in 2007, when Mattel, who had more than 10,000 companies supplying their toys across China, discovered the use of disallowed lead paint on some of their products and had to recall them. However, so great was their dependence on the work done for them in China that they subsequently had to apologize to the Chinese government for complaining so publicly in the first place. Tales of how hard the Chinese market was to make money in had to be set alongside the reality that, for volume, few other countries had the logistics, or the labour force, or the capacity to supply, so many goods. Rising labour costs from 2012, however caused some manufacturers to consider going elsewhere, or looking for cheaper, better deals more deeply within China. The collapse of some of the Western export markets from 2008 too made the Chinese policy-makers start to pay attention to raising consumption at home to stimulate demand. Despite these efforts, however, in 2013 consumption as a proportion of GDP was still stubbornly set at the same figure it had been for over two decades – a third of GDP. Chinese people, on the whole, continued to prefer to save rather than go out to spend.

The economic impact of the years of China's export-led growth, when over a third of GDP growth came from making or finishing off goods to sell abroad, was huge deficits between China and most developed markets. This problem was particularly acute for the EU and USA, whose consumers had developed a quick dependency on cheap goods manufactured in China and then shipped to their markets. China's current account balance (the difference between exports and imports) in 2013 came to US$182 billion, the second highest in the world. The brunt of this was born by the EU and USA, which created major political problems, with Western politicians complaining that Chinese companies had caused the loss of millions of jobs through their protectionist, cost-cutting ways, despite the counter-argument that people had generally benefited from being able to buy cheaper goods. There was a more fundamental issue behind this – the claim that Chinese goods were so competitive because of the use by the government of subsidies. The EU, in particular took exception to this, refusing to grant China market-economy status because so many of the factors of production that were marketized in developed economies – electricity, water and land, for example – were subsidized by the central and local states in the PRC. The chief complaint from foreign companies after 2008 and the economic crisis was that, as their Western markets dried up, there was still a lack of take-up by Chinese consumers, who, apart from some luxury goods, were largely unwilling to buy the same kinds of things and accrue the same kinds of personal debt that Westerners lived with. In the end, Chinese consumers were hard

Illustration 5.1 Fast trains at Shanghai Airport

The breakneck speed at which the Chinese economy has developed is symbolized by the explosion of infrastructure in China, from high-speed train lines and airports to top-grade motorways – the largest infrastructure programme ever undertaken in such a short space of time.

to sell to – careful with their hard-earned money, very demanding of the products they bought, and at least up to 2014 unlikely to want to buy much by internet from foreign suppliers.

From 1980, in term of investment into fixed assets, China had committed an unprecedented 45 per cent each year of all government expenditure. This was triple the proportion of most developed economies. In addition to the high-speed train links, Beijing and Shanghai were able to construct in five years the world's second- and third-largest subway systems by 2010 respectively. The vast new airport in Beijing was built for the 2008 Olympics in only three years. But it was mirrored, albeit on a slightly smaller scale, by provincial airports across the country as Chinese people took to the air rather than sit for days on trains. China currently has 160 airports, with plans to build another 70 by the end of 2015. It runs the world's third-largest train network with 86,000 kilometres, over 11,000 of which are high-speed lines, the longest in the world. Even remote outposts like Lhasa and Kashgar are supplied with train links, the Tibetan plateau one involving burrowing through pure ice. Since the late 1980s, China has constructed over 100,000 kilometres of roads, 8,000 of them added in 2013 alone, in what is termed the National Trunk Highway System. Energy infrastructure has also been improved, with the two national grids upgraded and smart systems introduced to improve efficiency. Vast hydropower (over 700 in all) and nuclear stations were built, often in very controversial circumstances. The infrastructure demands fuelled resource booms in places as far away as Australia or Brazil where raw materials like iron ore were sourced. As a symbol of this often breakneck growth, in the late 2000s skyscrapers were being constructed with a storey added each day.

The Complexity of the Chinese Economy

As the PRC economy liberalized and reformed, it became clear that the country was highly segmented. Some political economists talked of China being 'economies' in the plural, rather than a single entity (Huang, 2008). There were three broad swathes. The coastal area had exploited excellent logistics and immediate proximity to global supply chains to kick-start its development after 1978. By 2010, therefore, the provinces alongside the central and southern coasts of Zhejiang, and Jiangsu, had a per capita GDP of around US$10,000, compared to the country's average of US$4,500 (Chinese National Bureau of Statistics database, 2011). They were places of widespread entrepreneurialism, with places such as

Zhejiang in particular being bastions of non-state companies. The area of Wenzhou within this province became a byword for this, with a uniquely non-state model; the use of informal loans between family members; a widespread national and then regional and international business diaspora; and huge success in building up companies to which manufacturing was outsourced. Coastal China saw excellent living standards, and the start of the appearance of the new, wealthy Chinese. In the north-east and in central China, however, things were more complicated. There were pockets of business dynamism, with the creation of science parks, and then open zones modelled loosely on the SEZs. These areas subsequently became more competitive as costs for manufacturing, labour and land in the coastal regions grew more expensive. Central China had more limited infrastructure development than coastal China, though some provinces compensated for their logistics handicaps by exploiting resources that coastal areas did not have. It was in this way that the landlocked Inner Mongolia was able to become one of the wealthier provinces because of its abundant coal deposits and its proximity to Beijing and other major cities. The least developed area of China was the great western region, consisting of half of China's landmass, but sparsely populated in large areas and the home of most of China's ethnic minorities, some of whom had been problematic and dissenting towards the central government. Tibet, Xinjiang and Inner Mongolia alone had huge borders shared with other countries, and, in the case of the first two, infrastructure which was less developed than in the rest of the country. In the western region, state-owned enterprises continued to dominate because of the restricted business environment, although there were plenty of examples of lively entrepreneurialism in service and technology areas. Xinjiang, making up 18 per cent of the whole of the PRC's land area, had gas and coal reserves, and served as the nuclear testing area for the nation, much to the anger of some of its local residents – yet the allocation of profits made by the key corporation in the autonomous region, the Xinjiang Bingtuan or 'Army Corporation' were largely channelled back to the central government, creating major resentment in the area, particularly by Uyghur Muslims who felt that this illustrated just how exploited their region was by a central government that did not devolve meaningful powers locally. The discontent from this was one of the contributory factors to the riots in July 2009, when more than 200 died. Another was high levels of youth unemployment amongst Uyghur youth and heavy-handed centrally mandated social and educational policies.

Beyond these three broad zones with their different levels of development and dynamics, there were major variations between the 31 provinces and autonomous regions, and even within them. Many provinces had different arrangements for tax, for the payment of road fees, and for establishing businesses. The fragmentation of the Chinese economy meant that one of the great challenges when the WTO agreement was signed in 2001 was harmonizing a vast raft of local laws so that they accorded with national ones. Truck drivers taking goods across the country had to pay for a range of permits in different provinces, often meaning that it was simpler to manufacture on the coast for export than to try to do inter-provincial business. These internal imbalances were initially partially addressed through a scheme whereby wealthier provinces were meant to support poorer ones. Zhejiang, for example, had investments in Tibet. In 1999, the central government took things a step further by launching an 'Opening Up the West' campaign, in which it declared that, after seeing so much development in the coastal provinces, China now needed to see its western areas advance. Effort was put into attracting foreign investment to go into building airports, roads, ports and other key parts of the infrastructure. Officials were given inducements to work for a period of their career in the area, to start turning back the regional brain drain that had been happening for a number of years. Even so, per capita GDP figures continued to show that inhabitants of the western provinces earned far less, and lived shorter lives, than those on the coast.

Despite no longer being a command economy, China still maintains Five Year Plans (called the more user-friendly 'Programmes' since 2006). These set broad macro-economic targets and policy goals. The 11th Programme running from 2011 was heralded as the 'Green Plan' because of the ambitious targets it set for energy efficiency, cutting emissions and marketization of the energy sector. While the impact of the 2008 global crisis at first sight seemed shallow in China, creating the impression that it was last into the turmoil, and first out, it did force the government to implement a massive fiscal stimulus programme. This saw over US$600 billion pumped into the Chinese economy. While the Chinese government issues no figures on government debt, many suspect that taking local and national public debt together these might be well over 200 per cent of GDP. The priority of recent leaders, however, has been to produce raw growth no matter what, and going from that benchmark, the double-digit growth that China produced from 2010 was a decent enough return.

Despite these various inducements to spend more, Chinese consumers have remained resistant. Household savings come to 50 per cent of GDP. Chinese are inveterate savers. In many ways the Chinese economy remains one in which through low wages Chinese are indirectly taxed, with the government the major player in most parts of the economy. The classic reliance on government investment as an economy starts to modernize was something seen in Japan, Taiwan, South Korea and other developing economies as they industrialized and travelled up the value chain. The transition from an investment-intense model to one with more consumption will have profound social implications for China, as well as economic ones. It will see a different role for both government and citizens. They will increasingly become tax payers, and are likely to want to participate in decision making over the direction of their economy. Interest rates and the exchange rate are also currently set by politicians rather than by market forces. This too creates structural anomalies, and has been a source of tension between China and, in particular, the USA which believes it gives Chinese exporters a huge unfair advantage, being able to sell goods more cheaply with a weaker dollar onto the global market place rather than according to a proper rate. The combination of low wages and lack of investment opportunities for citizens has been an issue for some years. Bloggers in 2009 complained bitterly that their government, through its entry to the WTO, had managed to sell Chinese cheap labour and help to create comfortable Western lifestyles on the sweat and blood of local workers. They referred to the widespread exploitation in factories throughout China, with people working 18-hour days, sometimes in Dickensian conditions. One factory saw over a dozen people die because they had been locked into an assembly-line room and were unable to escape when a fire broke out. In another, the vast Foxconn plant in Shenzhen, employing over 400,000 workers putting together products for, among others, Apple, there was a series of suicides in 2011. The company's response was to put up wages, but also to add a clause in workers' contracts saying they were not responsible for people taking their own lives and could not therefore be sued by angry relatives. Chinese people, as anywhere else, did not want a life of permanent sacrifice. They aspired to enjoy the fruits of their work at some point; they were looking at the kinds of Western lifestyles they were now able to see on television or the internet. There was also a structural problem, as one study showed when it calculated that for every Barbie doll sold in the USA for US$40, the Chinese producer was paid only a few cents (Pascoe, 2011).

Part of the underlying challenge was that Chinese embarked on their research and development (R&D) activities, on which higher-value production was dependent, late in the day. Their education system had to be rebuilt from scratch after the closures of schools and universities

Box 5.1 The USA, China and the EU: the world's economic engine

The European Union, China and the USA account for half of the world's GDP. Put together, they are the engine of its growth. But their economic relations are complex, highly competitive and often contentious.

Since 1978, the USA and EU have become huge export markets for China. From 2001, this escalated, with the deficit between the two becoming more politically problematic. The USA focused in particular on what they called China's manipulation of its exchange rate, setting it according to political rather than market considerations and keeping the RMB low in order to give it more favourable trading conditions. The US Treasury Department threatened a number of times to name China as a currency manipulator and the issue figured in the US–China Strategic Economic and Policy Dialogue. For the EU, the main issue was as an intellectual property partner. Through projects like the Galileo space programme and the mapping of the DNA project, Chinese and European partners worked well, with a number of technology transfer agreements. Despite this, a series of contentious trade disputes from 2007 complicated the relationship. The largest was over solar panels which were accused of flooding the European market from 2011 and being produced through unfair subsidies in China. The EU started a formal process of naming Chinese manufacturers in this area as targets for tariffs into the EU. A nasty trade war was avoided through a compromise agreement in 2013.

during the early Cultural Revolution years. So, while the country had sent over a million and a half people to study abroad and pick up advanced skills since 1978, just how many of these have come back to China to work, and how well used their skills are, is a hotly debated subject. Building capacity within Chinese universities too has been a priority. The Ministry of Education attempted to create 50 elite, world-class universities from the 2000s, and a number of these actively recruited scientists and scholars from abroad. However, building up this sort of capacity cannot be done overnight.

Chinese Companies Going Global

One of the guiding imperatives of the original 'Going Out' Policy declared at the 16th Party Congress in the final days of Jiang Zemin's and Zhu Rongji's stewardship of the Party was the need to create international champions among Chinese state and non-state companies. There were two contributory issues here. The first was the increased competition likely to be introduced to Chinese enterprises within China by the country's entry to the World Trade Organization (WTO) in November 2001; and the second was the need to continue the reform of the state-owned enterprises (SOEs), which had been ongoing under the premiership of Zhu Rongji since 1997, and which had seen the key state industries reduced in size, with a large number of workers being laid off as part of a concerted attempt to make them more productive and efficient as businesses. By 2007, in terms of potential market capitalization, China had some of the largest corporations in the world (*Forbes* magazine, 18 April 2012). And yet, companies such as SinoChen, PetroChina, CNNOC, Huawei, ZTE, Lenovo and others were barely known beyond China's boundaries.

The attempt by Chinese companies to purchase foreign brands was one solution to this low profile and lack of awareness. But it was also motivated by the desire to obtain technology which would otherwise have been more difficult to access. Just as the wave of foreign investment into China from the 1980s often brought with it benefits in terms of technology transfer and management know-how, all in deficit in China, so outward investment was an additional means of accessing these. The most celebrated example is the purchase by the Beijing-based technology company Lenovo (previously called Legend) of the US IBM Think Pad brand in 2003. Failed acquisitions, however, were more common. Thomsons, the French television manufacturer, after its sale to the Chinese TCL group in 2005, underwent a number of challenges. From problems with the old technology that had been bought, to issues of how to understand the union laws in France, to problems over which markets the acquisition might best access.

In August 2010, Chinese manufacturer Geely completed the 100 per cent purchase of the European carmaker, Volvo, from Ford, its owners since 1999. It was, according to the chairman of the Chinese company, Li Shufu, 'an historic day', costing them US$1.3 billion. The sale included commitments to maintain the car plants in Sweden and Belgium, along with the sales networks throughout Europe.

The purchase of Volvo was the largest single Chinese acquisition in Europe up to that point. In 2009, Chinese overseas direct investment (ODI) stock in Europe was only US$8.6 billion, making up a mere 3.5 per cent of its global amount. The Volvo–Geely deal increased this by over 15 per cent. That it was in the automotive sector was appropriate, as, since 2000, China had seen some of its strongest domestic demand grow in this sector. Germany was the only country among the EU-28 states that was able to run a trade surplus with China because of the strength of China's demand for cars. Volkswagen and BMW in particular were able to export to China, and set up successful plants within the country. Since 2008, China has become the world's number one purchaser of cars, overtaking the USA. However, with only 30 cars per thousand people in 2009, compared to 800 per thousand in the USA and 500 per thousand in the UK, there was still plenty of room for growth, making this one of the priority areas for both non-Chinese manufacturers and exporters, and for the Chinese government looking to deal with the very low rate of domestic consumption as a proportion of GDP.

Chinese involvement in overseas car manufacturing, however, has not been particularly happy. In 2005, Nanjing Automobile Corporation had finalized an agreement to purchase the UK's MG Rover brand and its plant at Longbridge, Birmingham, UK. This happened after a prolonged discussion with the Shanghai Automotive Factory from the late 1990s and into the 2000s, discussions that were finally stalled by the huge pension liabilities of the company. It also only happened after lobbying at the highest level (letters were sent from the then UK prime minister, Tony Blair, to the Chinese premier, Wen Jiabao). And 6,000 jobs were lost in the UK. In 2009, Nanjing Automotive reasserted its desire to produce 15,000 cars a year, and create 1,200 jobs, but at the time of writing this has come to nothing. This in spite of bold talk by one person involved in the deal in 2005 that 'the fact that Nanjing has bought the entirety of MG is an indication of their bigger intention to become a global automotive company'.

The case of the energy company Unocal in the USA in 2005 shows the involvement of Chinese investment in strategic sectors to be a sensitive area. Brad Setzer, of the US Council for Foreign Relations, interviewed in November 2007, stated: 'The rise of sovereign wealth funds represents a shift in power from the US to a group of countries that aren't transparent, aren't democracies and aren't necessarily allies.' The Chinese Investment Corporation (CIC) was one of the key targets for concern. Californian congressman Richard Rombo, referring to the specific case of CNOOC and Unocal, said that, if the bid had been successful, it would have had 'disastrous consequences for our economy and national security'. It was not just the Chinese who were regarded with suspicion – the purchase by Abu Dhabi of the P&O port and ferry business was among the most heavily watched news stories in the USA, creating huge anxiety and opposition over the potential sale of what was viewed as a key strategic asset to a foreign company. 'Europe may be seen as a geopolitical irrelevance,' *The Economist* report of 30 June 2011 stated, 'but the

Chinese feel more welcome there than in America.' In addition, with the onset of the euro crisis from 2009, the need for Chinese money increased (Brown, 2008). From 2012, the China Investment Corporation did start to take up strategic stakes in some major European infrastructure projects, particularly in the UK which under the Coalition government from 2010 made attracting Chinese money a priority. The fund took a strategic stake in London's Heathrow Airport, and also in Anglia Water. A Chinese investor also took over Weetabix, an iconic British cereal brand. Chinese investment increased dramatically in Australia, particularly in the mining and agribusiness sector. Chinese companies were also highly active in parts of Africa and Latin America. Despite this the strategy remained cautious. Of global stocks of ODI in 2013, China accounted for less than 2 per cent, and remained far outranked by the UK, the USA or Japan.

One of the great success stories of the outward strategy was the flotation for over US$20 billion of Jack Ma's Alibaba company. Ma, who had originally been an English teacher in Zhejiang, had set his original internet company up in the early 2000s as a Chinese competitor to companies like Yahoo and Amazon. Despite an early strategic alliance with Yahoo, Ma took the company back wholly into his direction, and made it one of the most dynamic and diverse in the world. His initial public offering on the New York Stock Exchange in September 2014 was hugely successful, and made Alibaba one of the most visible indigenous Chinese companies.

The Chinese Stock Exchange and the Financial Services Sector

The entry of China to the WTO opened up one area of great interest to foreign companies – China's financial services sector. The increase in wealth levels meant that the PRC started to see something approaching a middle class with expendable levels of wealth approaching those of the middle-income countries. Cities such as Shanghai were at the forefront, with per capita income levels of around US$10,000. For these people, banking, investing on the stock exchange, and arranging for their retirement and insurance for their properties, their health and their future became as important as it is for people in the West.

While the Chinese population on the whole showed little interest in taking on personal debt, and credit card take-up in the country (at least up to 2012), has been very low, there has been increasing interest in financial products. For banks, insurance companies and other financial service providers, China has become one of their most important markets. But it has proved to be a tightly controlled and complex one.

One of the few areas where the aspiring middle class was able to invest money was on the stock exchanges created from the early 1990s across China, but centring on those that set up permanent bases in Shenzhen and Shanghai. If anything represented the dynamism of the modern PRC it was these exchanges with their volatility and the intense interest that people showed in the movements of shares. The Shanghai stock exchange was the largest, with volumes of trade increasing exponentially during the first decade of the twenty-first century. Shanghai stood as a potential competitor to the international stock market centre in Hong Kong, with excited journalists sporadically declaring that the city was the new Hong Kong of Asia. Hong Kong's greatest assets, however, the rule of law and a predictable legal environment, were something that Shanghai was still only able to aspire to. From 2000 to 2004, the Shanghai stock exchange lost over 40 per cent of its value. Similar collapses happened in the period after 2008 during the global economic crisis. The H-type (available to foreign investors through dual listings in Hong Kong) and A-type shares (only for domestic investors) on the Shanghai exchange allowed some foreign enterprises and joint ventures to list, and allowed some foreign investors to participate. Even so, more than most other exchanges, Shanghai often seemed like a gambling casino.

Shanghai municipal government regarded itself as the potential place for an indigenous financial services hub, building up a viable centre that was suitable for the rapidly expanding internal market. The Pudong area of the city, south of the river, dominated by farmland and warehouses up to 1990, was redeveloped dramatically after Shanghai was declared that year to be an SEZ. But historically, the city still lived under a shadow of mistrust by the centre in Beijing, which regarded it as an untrustworthy entrepreneurial free-for-all, which never quite bought into the grand socialist experiment promoted from Beijing (Huang, 2008).

Historically, this was an odd view. Shanghai had been the centre of radical politics in the 1920s and 1930s, and the home of the extreme left-ist Gang of Four during the Cultural Revolution. It was from here that they promoted their onslaught against 'bourgeois capitulation' in the period just before the death of Mao Zedong in 1976. That the city had a rich past as a place where foreign enterprises had been established right from the first engagements between Western capitalism and China in the nineteenth century was not in doubt. Companies such as Shell, Standard Chartered, Jardine Matheson and others had all settled in the city from the nineteenth century onwards, meaning that Shanghai accepted the overwhelming bulk of foreign investment before 1949. But by the 1950s, the city had been purged of all its capitalist entrapments and a particularly vicious battle took place throughout the Cultural Revolution. For those visiting from the West in the 1970s, just as China was starting to open up again, Shanghai's colonial architecture seemed a poignant reminder of another era, its great Bund water frontage a run-down shadow of its heyday more than half a century before.

The city's geographical location at the end of the great Yangtze River, with a huge water frontage, was a great economic asset. And the city had always been adaptable, changing from being a fishing centre in the Qing dynasty to one of the great entry points of Chinese style capitalism in the 1930s, dominated by triads, gangsters, radical groups and foreign adventurers. The ornate dance halls and florid hotels from this period stand as testimony to an era that is still celebrated and recreated in films and documentaries. But Shanghai was also a place where writers such as the great Lu Xun were able to live and work, and where the early Chinese film industry developed, a place of creativity, visited by figures like Albert Einstein, Bertrand Russell and Charlie Chaplin.

Shanghai now declares itself to be one of the key banking centres of modern China. But its complexity is easy enough to uncover. In American-based economist Yasheng Huang's view, there is plenty wrong with the city. For those looking out over the great modernist cityscape that greets them when they arrive in Shanghai and take the hyperfast Maglev train from the huge Pudong Airport into the city centre, it prefigures the future, and is what the rest of China aspires to in the decades ahead. But to those with a more enquiring mind it reveals itself to be a city whose economy is dominated by state-owned enterprises, whose middle class have grown no richer even as enterprises have, and whose stock exchange and financial services sectors are mere shadows of those that exist in other countries (Huang, 2008).

In September 2013, the central government announced the foundation of a Shanghai Free Trade Zone. While light on policy initially, as the year went on and the Communist Party Plenum made its announcement in October, it was clear that the Zone was intended to play a pivotal role in the development of a Chinese finance sector. Transactions in RMB by foreign banks based in the area were allowed, with talk of it playing a major role as the Chinese government liberalized its capital account in the coming years. As of 2014, however, there remains scepticism that the city can quickly become a major international finance centre because of the lack of a free press and the rule of law.

Box 5.2 China's science and technology zones

Deng Xiaoping was not a scientist, but according to Ezra Vogel's epic biography of him, he had a deep respect for them, and he made the development of China's abilities in science a priority in the reform process.

Science's link with modernization was clear enough, and in the eyes of many of the country's political elite, it was science that was going to solve China's energy, environment, and, indirectly, social and development problems. Vast resources were poured into educating people about science at schools and universities. Many Chinese students were sent abroad from 1984 to study at Western universities. The Five Year Plans and Programmes became key to setting targets for scientific innovation, with R&D spending being increasing from about 1 per cent of GDP to 2.5 per cent over the period 1990 to 2014. The Chinese Patent Office claimed it was receiving more applications than any other country in the world by 2009. Citations of Chinese scientists' work in international journals increased rapidly. One of the ways in which the government encouraged scientific innovation from the early 1990s was by establishing a national network of science and technology zones, spread across the country, in provinces and major cities. These areas, sometimes covering many hundreds of hectares, served as miniature SEZs that allowed foreign enterprises to go to China and establish ventures with local partners, enjoying tax breaks, good logistic support and a range of preferential policies. For the Chinese, beyond the commercial gains this was a way of encouraging foreign enterprises to do more technology sharing.

Some of the science parks were spoken of as the Silicon Valley of China. The huge Zhongguancuan area in Beijing, linked in particular to Qinghua University, was one of the first to be established and hosted companies such as Microsoft (despite the fact that in 2007 Microsoft complained that 98 per cent of its software in China was being copied). In the central city of Xian, there were two huge development zones, dominating the outskirts of the city. In Suzhou, a city famed for its tourism and history, the Singaporean government established a technology zone with the support of its legendary prime minister, Lee Kuan Yew, only to find a competitor supported by the local government had set up next door. By 2014, China had, according to the Ministry of Science, which was nominally in charge of these zones, 54 science parks, but these ranged in size and capacity. There were another 30 which were not under the central ministry and run by local governments.

The Non-state Sector

The non-state sector effectively ceased to exist in some senses in the PRC after 1949. Those labelled as capitalists either fled to Hong Kong, Taiwan or elsewhere. The ones that stayed watched as their property and assets were requisitioned by the state. A small number made accommodations with the CCP and managed to continue – Rong Yiren was the most famous of these – a wealthy Shanghai businessman who was able to operate as a political figure for the CCP after 1949, and who survived into the 1990s, allowing his son Larry Yung to continue his business after him. They were the exceptions, though.

In the 1980s, a period of liberalism, enough space opened up in the Chinese economy for people to set up small businesses – shops, restaurants and manufacturing – and even to obtain loans from local banks. But the mantra 'getting rich is glorious' was anathema to many hard-line leftists of that era, and throughout the 1980s into the 1990s figures such as Deng Liqun launched spirited attacks on the non-state sector, calling its growth an outright attack on traditional socialist values. This was balanced against the simple fact that as the 1990s progressed, the proportion of national GDP created by non-state companies increased. The private business sector was responsible for employing more and more people who had been laid off during the restructuring of the state-owned enterprises, so creating an increase in the proportion of national GDP created by non-state companies (Dickson, 2003).

The pivotal moment for the enfranchisement of the non-state sector was 2002 when, after changes to the Party Constitution, business people were allowed to become CCP members. This had been justified ideologically by Jiang Zemin who, from 1999, had talked to the 'three representatives' – those who represented the advanced forces in society and were therefore part of a new united front to deliver modernization, one of the CCP's key tasks. One businessman, Zhang Ruimin, the chairman of the partly private company Haier based in the coastal city of Qingdao, was even allowed to sit on the Party's Central Committee as an alternate member from 2002.

Despite its importance as an ally for growth, the non-state sector operated in a different way from its equivalents in developed economies. Non-state companies were excluded from many sectors, lacked access to credit, with most companies operating on loans from family or networks, and had very little formal banking support. This gave rise to the shadow banking, unregulated sector which became so prominent from 2012. For these businesses, the international market was often far more benign than the one in their own backyard. They had to develop strategies to deal with rent-seeking and interfering local officials, and to ensure that they did not come under political surveillance.

Since 2008, with the onset of the global economic crisis, the state-owned enterprise sector has become more empowered. There is still a political pecking order in the Chinese economy, with the non-state actors being seen as the most vulnerable (Huang, 2005). It is likely that state-owned enterprises will dominate key strategic sectors like energy, telecoms and finance. But in most other areas, the non-state sector is more profitable and more dynamic. In 2013, it produced 7 per cent profits, compared to 5 per cent by the state sector. In a China with a falling growth rate from late 2013, and searching for what the Premier has called 'the empty spaces for growth within the Chinese economy', the non-state sector is likely to play an increasingly important role. This was only given greater recognition in the 2013 Plenum Decision, issued in Beijing by the top Party leadership, which recognized the role of non-state companies and their increasing need for support as the country's demand for their diversity and dynamism grows. Companies like Alibaba, the drinks manufacturer Wahaha, the real estate company Sohu, and the internet giants Tencent and Weixin were all highly representative of the new generation of non-state companies.

Energy and Environment

China's development since the 1980s has made it an energy- and resource-hungry nation. This hunger has pushed it into investing in Africa and Latin America, and sourcing its materials from across the world. Despite the PRC's vastness, it is a country surprisingly barren of easily accessible energy and resources. The only major oil field, Daqing in north-east China, has already reached peak production. Elsewhere, at the time of writing, exhaustive searches for new sources of oil have so far yielded little that is economic to exploit. With regard to aluminium, copper and other metals, China's hunger has pushed it to being the world's largest user.

As the factory of the world, China's need for energy and raw materials in its manufacturing process was clear enough. But the impact of how it gained, and used, these in its environment, was becoming a global issue by the late 1990s with greater awareness of climate change. China's energy needs rocketed through the 1990s and into the 2000s. Its dependence on fossil fuels such as coal, from which it drew 70–77 per cent of its energy, was a major cause of carbon emissions. From the extraction of coal from one of the many thousands of mines dotted across the country, to its transport, to its uses in energy production, there were problems. The coke-producing towns and cities of Shanxi Province were under a permanent pall of thick pollution most of the year, and the World Bank declared Lanzhou to be the world's most polluted city in 2005.

Attempts to shift China's energy usage profile from coal to other forms of fuel were problematic. Petrol and oil supplied 20 per cent of the country's needs, but half of this had to be imported, frequently from unstable areas where Western competitors were unlikely to become angry if China muscled in; Saudi Arabia, Iran and Sudan were all suppliers. Attempts to use more nuclear power led to a plan to build 30 power stations in the decade after 2010, though this plan was slowed down after the Fukushima disaster in Japan in 2011. Even with the construction of these power stations, though, only 3 per cent of China's energy needs would have come from nuclear power. The country has also become the world's largest user of solar and wind power, as at 2011, with vast wind farms scattered across the flat landscape of Inner Mongolia and Gansu (Ernst and Young, 2011). Zhejiang-based Sun-Tech became one of the world's most highly regarded solar panel and technology companies before overproduction and a trade spat with the EU in 2013 caused the bottom to fall out of the market and the company to collapse in debt. Despite this, though, the combined contribution of all these to China's energy needs has been only 1 per cent. The addiction to coal seems as if it will continue well into the future (see Figure 5.3).

One solution has been to improve energy efficiency. On one calculation, China was, per unit of energy produced, six times less efficient than Japan and four times less than the EU. The government set itself tough efficiency improvement targets over the periods of the 11th and 12th Five Year Programmes (2006–16), but it was hard to see how these were to be met when the imperative for officials at both local and national levels was to pump out economic growth no matter what. The complaint made by many in China was that it had been forced into highly polluting manufacturing industries by its export-led growth model, meaning that many developed countries had simply outsourced their pollution to China. In 2011, a trade argument between China and the rest of the world about the mining and production of rare metals, critical for use in mobile phones and other appliances, showed that the PRC was the source of 99 per cent of these, even though the metals existed in places such as the USA and Australia. Their highly laborious and polluting mining made clear that

Figure 5.3 China's energy consumption by source, 1982–2012

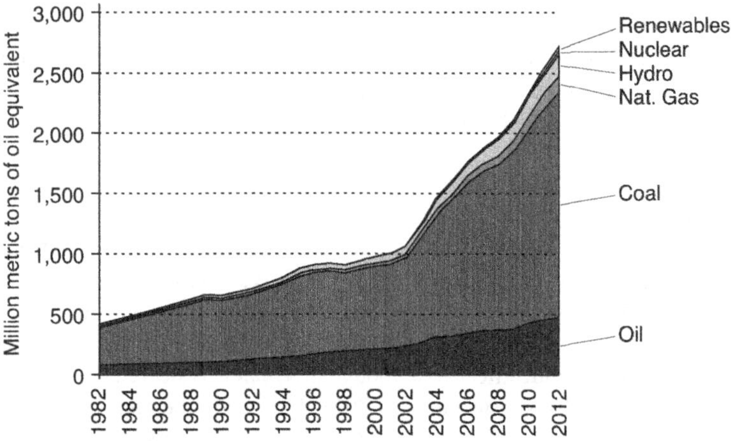

Source: Gail Tverberg, 'The Close Tie between Energy Consumption, Employment and Recession', ourfiniteworld.com (2012).

one of the reasons why other countries were not active in this area was simply so that China might bear the brunt of the environmental outfall.

Pan Yue, head of what was then called the State Environmental Protection Agency, but was changed to the Ministry for the Environment in 2007, famously stated in the mid-2000s that, for all the wealth that China had accrued over the period of the reform era, it would have to spend a sizeable chunk of this on cleaning up the mess from intense industrialization. Visitors to China from the early 1980s saw the visible impact of this industrialization on the landscape, in terms of the air quality, the state of water and the rivers, and the degradation of the natural landscape. Even the most remote parts of the country did not seem to be immune to the reach of China's pollution.

China had become the world's second-largest economy on two great pillars: the enormous effort of many millions of migrant workers who had come to the companies originally in the coastal region to make them the factory of the world; and exploitation of its environment, which had paid a shattering cost for parts of China to industrialize and enter the global supply chain. These aspects of the Chinese miracle, as some called it, were no joke. Millions were affected by the poor air quality. According to surveys conducted by the Chinese government itself, the air in the cities was one of the Chinese citizens' biggest grievances. During the 2008 Olympics, many wondered how marathon runners would be able to run in the pollution-laden air of a hot Beijing summer. They also had to worry about the sandstorms that were becoming increasingly fierce and prolonged in the capital because of the deforestation and desertification of Inner Mongolia, along the northern border of the country. Things worsened in early 2013 when massive smogs blighted the capital's air for many days. A similar problem occurred in Shanghai the following year. These were irrefutable signs that the country's air quality and its environment were at breaking point, and that the environmental protection measures needed to be accelerated.

As worrying as all of these issues, though, was the fact that the PRC was a country without clean water – a country in which, from some estimates, 70 per cent of the water it had was polluted and undrinkable, and in which the great rivers that were the veins and arteries for the land were sometimes so badly clogged with substances that they turned into brown, poisonous sludge (Economy, 2005). In one infamous case, Taihu Lake in Jiangsu, local activists who protested against the toxic nature of the water were persecuted into silence. The Songhua River running through the north-eastern city of Harbin became highly toxic during the winter of 2010 because of the spillage of pollutants upstream. Fish stocks plummeted, and such fish as could be harvested were often uneatable.

The government, led by people who were more scientifically literate than in most of the rest of the world, knew about the water problem, and had plentiful data about it. They accepted discussion on environmental issues as early as the first UN-supported environment conference in the 1970s. China was supportive of the protocols passed at the Kyoto Earth Summit and the Rio de Janeiro summit in the 1990s and 2000s. But its position was complicated because it needed to maintain high growth, and without that the government feared instability and unrest. The Copenhagen Summit on Climate Change in December 2009 was the moment at which China pitted itself not just against the developed world, but also against the developing one. There was a simple reason for doing this. While, per capita, carbon emission levels in China were as much as a quarter less than in the USA, in terms of overall size the PRC had become the world's largest polluter by 2008. If China didn't act, then the fear was that whatever was done by other countries would be largely irrelevant (Watts, 2011). In another unwelcome record, China produced more emissions in 2013 and into 2014 than the EU and USA combined.

China's environmental problems are perhaps its most serious current issue. The simple fact is that the economic resource-intense and energy-inefficient model that the country has used over the last three decades is now at the end of the line. The 12th Five Year Programme from 2011 called itself a 'Green Plan' and did start to set out targets for emissions. But from 2013, the language changed to 'ecological balance' with a recognition that enterprises, state and non-state, now had to enforce far higher compliance levels to ensure that they controlled their emissions. The government could sometimes implement powerful measures to address environmental worries. A tree planting scheme in the early 2000s had partially stopped the very bad sandstorms from blighting spring days in Beijing. Renewable sources of energy were also rising, with 60 per cent of new energy from 2013 coming from there. The attempt to move to a more service sector-orientated model was also crucial. But it is hard to see how China in such a short space of time is going to turn around its degraded natural environment, with melting ice caps in the Tibetan plateau, profoundly polluted water sources and the increasing occurrence of natural disasters figuring as short- to medium-term challenges, without a period of accelerated innovation.

Death by a Thousand Cars

Cars were an excellent illustration of this. In 2007, for every thousand people in China there were nine cars. Cars were a luxury in a society in which many people still used bicycles, even in cities such as Shanghai and Beijing. On the whole, they belonged to state-owned enterprises, companies or the government. Personal car usage was a rare luxury (Ng *et al.*, 2010, pp. 5–6). By 2010, things had changed dramatically, however. China had become the world's largest user of cars, and the largest car importer. Volkswagen, Toyota and Ford all had major plants in the country making cars, and the myriad of Chinese car manufacturers were trying to increase the volume of production. BMW, Bentley, Rolls-Royce and Mercedes were just a few of the luxury brands that could seen on the streets of even middle-sized cities in the western regions.

There were two immediate results. The first was that congestion in the cities worsened. Beijing and Shanghai experimented with schemes to prevent too many cars clogging the streets. They built respectively the world's second- and third-largest subway systems to take people off the roads. Even so, as many visitors and locals alike soon found out, getting stuck in traffic jams could eat up significant amounts of one's time, and the aspirational middle class in cities simply wanted to use their cars. A famous jam on the freeway into Beijing from the north, running by the Great Wall at Badaling, continued for a week in 2010. Pundits quipped that while the Great Wall couldn't be seen from the moon, the Great Traffic Jam probably could. The second result was the impact on air quality, where cars added to all the other sources of pollution competing to ruin people's lungs in the main cities. Chinese people's love of the car also pushed up the demand for petrol so that the country became an even bigger importer, sourcing half of its need in the problematic and unstable Middle East.

Cars also give an illustration of the possible solutions to the PRC's current energy and pollution quandary. BWD, a Chinese automotive company, began producing electric cars from 2009, promising to make them a real alternative to conventional petrol-driven vehicles. This local innovation was advertised widely as an example of how, under the right conditions, PRC enterprises could be trend-setters. The case illustrated that, without rapid technical change, the problems as they were laid out in 2012 were fearsome. In the giddy space of five decades, the PRC had travelled from starvation for many millions of citizens to becoming a country so heavily populated by factories that it was in danger, instead, of causing the deaths of most of its inhabitants through poisoning. This shows the tragically double-edged nature of China's economic success.

An Unsustainable Model

For all its great dynamism, the consensus inside and outside China coming into the Xi Jinping and Li Keqiang period in power was that the Chinese economic model which had been used so successfully until then was unsustainable. It was too capital intensive and resource intensive, and had massively impacted on China's environment. The Plenum meeting in late 2013 addressed these issues by stating that there needed to be a new phase of growth which was 'ecological' and balanced.

At the heart of this was a strategy to have more Chinese live in cities, rather than in rural areas. This was because the aspiration, as China doubled GDP from 2012 levels to 2020, was for it to become a much more service sector-orientated economy, rather than just a manufacturing and exporting one. Let down by the collapse of export markets from 2008 after the crisis in the rest of the world that year, the Chinese leadership looked to make China's economy more reliant on its own latent growth. That meant building a more reliable legal framework, liberalizing financial services so that people could invest more in China, and having a middle class based in cities who would be able to supply the services sector with labour, rather than working in factories that were producing less value added to the Chinese economy.

Sustainability was as much a philosophical as an economic issue. This was the link with the ideology of the Party, discussed in the previous chapter. For the first thirty years of reform, the objective had been simply to improve the material wellbeing of people. But now that more and more were enjoying moderate to very good levels of wealth, more complex questions of what sort of lifestyles they wanted to live arose, and how to articulate other benchmarks of development. Chinese leaders used words like 'creative' and 'innovation' frequently, and this indicated the direction they wished to travel in. For them, the 'China Dream' that President Xi alluded to for much of 2013 and into 2014 was about a good quality of life and a sustainable one, where people lived in a better environment, felt they were in control of their destinies, and that they could trust the air they breathed, or the water they drank, or the food they ate. In all of these areas, however, China in 2014 was a work in progress. Food was often subject to contamination scares, the air was too often unbreathable, and the water undrinkable.

The government therefore had to outline a more complex national aim than simply becoming wealthier. It had to have policies that addressed people's aspirations to a lifestyle that was about more than just earning lots of money. For this reason, the communiqué issued in late 2013 when the Party Central Committee Plenum finished its deliberations reads in many places like a manifesto on how to make all areas of the Chinese economy and its development strategy sustainable. Sustainability as a word became one of the most heavily used amongst Chinese leaders. But the simple fact remained that in 2014 China was maintaining a model that was unlikely to last for another decade without major new technology and ideas to solve its underlying problems. An innovative China was emerging daily, but whether it would really come into its own before being overwhelmed by environmental, resource and associated problems remained one of the great known unknowns of the twenty-first century.

Conclusion: The Next Step in Internationalization – The Renminbi

One of the great anomalies of the modern international economic system is that the second-largest economy has, at the time of writing, a currency that is non-convertible. While most other major currencies, from the euro to the US dollar, to British sterling or the Australian dollar or Japanese yen, can be used to settle invoices overseas, or traded against each other in global currency markets, the Chinese RMB (renminbi, or 'People's Money') is non-convertible. At a basic level, this means that one cannot buy it at foreign currency bureaux overseas, but only in the country itself. It also means that, in theory at least, it cannot be taken into or out of the country. Those who visit China have to fill out forms each time they change currency, and undertake to change whatever local money they still have back into foreign currency before they leave.

At a higher level, for Chinese exporters, this means that when the Chinese sell their goods abroad, they then take whatever currency they have been paid in to the central bank in Beijing, and this is converted into RMB. The foreign currency itself is kept in the central system. In practice, exporters often use a variety of methods to handle currency, sometimes working through banks in Hong Kong or offshore. But this system is part of the explanation as to how the government in Beijing has managed to accrue the vast foreign currency reserves mentioned at the start of this chapter.

The Hu and Wen leadership have argued that having a non-convertible currency means they are largely free of the sorts of speculative attacks that led to the Asian financial crisis in the late 1990s, when Hong Kong, Indonesia and other countries in the region saw their currencies collapse dramatically. For the Chinese leaders, the current arrangement gives them a firewall. The central government has set a narrow band within which the RMB can vary against the American dollar, which accounts for the small variations that sometimes take place. But this is a rate set by the government, not the market.

Since 2008, this system has come under increasing attack, particularly by the USA, which has argued that China is maintaining an artificially low rate for the RMB against the US dollar. They argue that, in this way, China is able to enjoy a competitive advantage over other manufacturers when it exports because its goods are automatically cheaper. The Obama administration threatened the Chinese government several times in 2009 and 2010 with labelling it a 'currency manipulator', largely with the aim of forcing Beijing to revalue the RMB upwards, and making it a much more expensive currency.

There have been increasing moves since 2010, however, to allow for the settlement of international invoices in RMB. China's central bank, the Bank of China, which is in charge of RMB rates and China's foreign exchanges, has said that some time in the next decade the RMB will become a fully convertible currency, and that it will then be used just like the US dollar and other currencies. At that point, China will indeed be part of the international global economy. One of the main outcomes of this move, if it happens, will be to see Chinese individual investors appearing much more actively abroad. This, therefore, is likely to be the next step in China's internationalization strategy.

6

Chinese Society

The traditional image of Chinese society is of a rural one, based on the sort of 'elastic links' that the great sociologist Fei Xiaotong talked of in his classic and controversial study of Chinese society from 1947, translated as *From the Soil* (Fei, 1992). For Fei, Chinese social structure derived from a world in which everyone knew everyone else, a world in which contracts and legal niceties were unnecessary because people only did business with those they knew. Everyone in this world lived in an environment rich in trust. It was a world in which there were multiple layers of relationships in the centre of which each individual sat, practising a kind of sovereignty over his/her own realm, a society that was highly networked, but also very localized, and in which, according to Fei, people operated fundamentally selfishly. Gender relations were highly stratified, so that men hung out with men, and women with women, each working in their preserved domain, with the only contact between them being producing children. In many ways, Fei was describing a society with a highly defined structure, in which there was a rigid hierarchy: a patriarchal, and, to its critics, misogynistic society, where there was almost 'caste-like' rigidity over the class into which an individual was born and its impact on his/her later life choices.

For this society, the power distances between the leaders and those being led were immense. The sole means of upward mobility was by passing the Confucian administrative exams to obtain a place in the civil service, but the abolition of these exams at the end of the Qing Dynasty in 1908 meant that the routes to transforming one's social position were narrowed even further. In contemporary China, this world is often portrayed through cultural productions, television, film and literature with a great deal of nostalgia. But in much of the early propaganda of the Communists, this world was accused of sterility, injustice and inequality.

The Xinhai Revolution of 1911–12, which saw the fall of the Qing, the chaos of the early Republic period and the tragedy of the Sino-Japanese War from 1937 – these are just some of the external events that led to profound changes in Chinese society. But none of them compare with the reform period and its impact from 1978. The net impact of this has been profound, for two reasons: for the first time in its long history under various guises, China is now a society in which just as many people live in urban areas as in the countryside. And it is also a society in which people have never been more mobile, in which as many as 20 per cent of Chinese people belong to the 'blind masses', the migrant workers who have been one of the great forces of modern Chinese life, working in the vast manufacturing areas, in the factories in which much of the country's new wealth is earned. China today is an environment infected by constant change.

China under Communism: The Class Wars

Mao may never have understood the further reaches of theoretical Marxism that clearly. But he understood how to apply class theory to Chinese society. Many of his works throughout his long political career, either emanating directly from himself or written in his name, come back to the issue of class in China and its specific configuration. Class trumped issues of ethnicity (see Chapter 1) and regionalism. It was the fundamental identifier for an individual. The effort put into assigning their correct class label continued almost from the moment the Civil War ended with Communist victory in 1949, to Mao's death in 1976. In his major speeches in the 1950s, and particularly the 1957 'On the Correct Handling of Contradictions Amongst the People', he spoke of the Chinese population being divided between the proletariat, the rural workers, the comprador bourgeoisie, the landowning classes, intellectuals and capitalists, and how best to manage the relationships between them. In the mid-1950s, every citizen of the PRC was given an officially designated class status that determined to a large extent what they could and could not do, how they were treated and their access to specific jobs. Class struggle was the key function of Party rule during the Mao era. Despite the fact that it led to immense social unrest in the Cultural Revolution, and to major internal battles before and after, it was something that Mao regarded as important enough to adhere to, through thick and thin, until the day he died.

The Role of Intellectuals

The treatment of intellectuals offers a good case study. Recognized as being important for the construction of the new China from 1949, they were the targets of increasingly intense attacks from the first – the Three Antis in 1951 – to the Anti-Rightist Campaign in 1957, and the culmination of all these, the onslaught of the Cultural Revolution. This obsession with intellectuals is even more striking when considering how small the actual number of those classified as intellectuals was. This was true even if a very broad definition is used, encompassing teachers, writers, artists, journalists and scientists, all of whom were lumped into this category. Simply doing work that involved using a pen rather than manual labour was enough to be placed in the intellectual category. The literal translation of the Chinese term 'zhishi fenzi' is 'knowledge element' and that captures as well as any other their core identifying attribute. Their role in Maoist society was highly contradictory – partly vitally needed, but also partly regarded as contaminated, untrustworthy and forever needing regimes of severe correction.

Post-1978, China's issues with intellectuals have never wholly disappeared (witness the demand in 2013 by the Xi leadership that academics do not talk about liberalism, democracy or other unwelcome ideas in their lecture theatres or classrooms), but the need to make knowledge a key part of economic rebuilding meant that they were restored to a more privileged role. As the reform period went on, the issue was more about how to develop a benign, less uneven way of classifying groups in society, and forging unity, rather than developing antagonism and conflict which had been the Maoist tactic.

The Household Registratation System (Hukou)

The most elemental source of social division was also the one that was to undergo the most change: between rural and urban. The household registration system ('hukou') introduced along the lines of the internal passport used in Stalin's USSR, was a key means of social control in the early PRC, and in its earliest form classified people as 'agricultural' (rural) or 'non-agricultural' (urban). Originally it had a dual purpose, supporting the maintenance of social order but also ensuring enough people worked in supplying cities with foodstuffs as they led the modernization campaigns of the early Maoist years. Only over time did it start to mark a larger social division, with those with urban residence status getting better access to social welfare, better education and higher wages. In the period of the great famines they were also those who were given priority in relation to food. As one economist stated, in this period the countryside literally starved to feed the cities (Naughton, 2006). The inevitable impact of rapid industrialization in the 1980s was to see urban areas increase, and a steep rise in people's mobility. Even so, the household registration regulations have never been fully removed, no matter how mobile and urbanized Chinese society has become, and the 'agricultural' and 'non-agricultural' division remains. This has created a number of contradictions. Many now living in cities have to practise a variety of strategies and deceits in order to get the same rights as those with urban documents, but reclassification is time-consuming and difficult. To be a citizen in modern China is, therefore, to live in a two-tier system, with significant differences in rights depending on whether the person falls into the rural or urban category.

In July 2014, the State Council stated that the whole *hukou* system would be reformed, with transfer limits to small cities removed, restrictions on medium cities relaxed and new qualifications set for the largest cities. Despite this promised liberalization, some commentators were sceptical. Distinctions between rural and urban divisions might go, but the fundamental one between local and non-local would remain, and this in the end affected the access to social welfare from education, housing and healthcare. An even larger problem was that agricultural residence status at least gave access to land rights, and rural holders are reluctant to give up on these in view of the rising prices for land now. A number of incentives have been introduced, with varying success. *Hukou* reform therefore has proved immensely complicated, and varies from region to region across China, acting as a classic example of just how varied implementation of central state policy is in the country.

One of the issues that sit beside *hukou* reform is that of urbanization. From only 15 per cent of people living in cities in 1978, China by 2010 had, for the first time ever, as many in the urban as rural areas. Including migrant labourers, this was perhaps nearer 60 per cent of Chinese. Cities have become important in China as the forefront of the new economy, service sector orientated, higher consuming, and generally places where the middle-income, more innovative China that its leaders foresee for it is already coming clearly into view. A city like Shanghai typifies this fast-track urbanization, a place with a population in 2014 of 23 million which increases by half a million a year in the space of a mere 630 square kilometers. Shanghai's ability to absorb so many people has been a challenge for its environment, its infrastructure and its social cohesion, with perhaps only a third of people being originally born in the city. Despite this challenge, Shanghai is a place of dynamism with high per capita GDP and a relatively peaceful environment. Other cities lack the happy geographical location of Shanghai and its excellent logistics links – but it has been estimated that over the decade from 2000 China saw over 250

Illustration 6.1 Modern building in Beijing

Since the early 1960s, Chinese society has urbanized, Westernized and grown more complex. Modernist architecture is the supreme symbol of the new China, dominating the great cities in which more than half of the Chinese population now live.

cites emerge with more than a million people living in them. Whatever else is clear about China's future, its urban nature is indisputable. It is likely that as early as 2030 two-thirds of Chinese people will live in cities.

Class in Contemporary Chinese Society

How can one make sense of the society in a country that encompasses a fifth of all humanity, and covers a continent-sized area, and which, as the first chapter showed, contains huge cultural and ethnic diversity? This has been a challenge to sociologists, analysts and historians searching for the right framework within which to look at the society and how it has evolved in today's PRC. One issue is the significant regional differences. Society and the social structure in north-eastern China are different from those in the south-west. The ethnic composition is different, the economies are different, and the kinds of elites that work in these areas are different. Even within provinces there are major differences, right down to specific communities. One of the issues that the process of village elections revealed was that, in many places, specific tribes worked for their own interests against each other. Village elections gave, on one level at least, an insight into the power structures that existed in post-Maoist China – in some areas, mafia and the 'black society' of crime and corruption dominated communities, recruiting officials to support their interests, and controlling the economy. In other areas, ethnic groups vied with each other to gain the upper hand, trying to win representation on village committees through the elections. In many regions, it was simply a case of those with the same family names collecting around a sense of their joint interest, and pushing against others who were seen as opponents or outsiders. Sun Yat-sen famously complained that Chinese society was like sand because of its granular quality and the lack of formal definition across different groups. Mao took this a step further, calling the Chinese a blank sheet across which could be written identities that would then be used to shape people's actions. But for many who look at society in China, one of the most striking qualities is its diversity and complexity, even at a very local level. Those assuming homogeneity do so at their peril. Despite these regional differences, and those between rural and urban dwellers, there are some broad categories of class that can be used to try to understand people living in China now. The ones with the perhaps highest profile because of their new-found and growing wealth are the entrepreneurs. Business people outside the state sector lived subterfuge lives for much of the last six decades. Under Mao, they were targets of elimination campaigns in the Deng China where 'to get rich is glorious' was one of the key phrases; those in the non-state sector were blamed for involvement in events like the 1989 uprising, and subject to nervous scrutiny by authorities. Only in 2002 were they fully enfranchised – one of the most pragmatic moves of the final period of Jiang Zemin's rule when acceptance of the the importance of their past contribution to the Party state's delivery of the all-important GDP growth targets (see Chapter 5) highlighted their value. Such entrepreneurs constitute perhaps less than 0.1 per cent of Chinese society, but their prominence derives from the role that similar classes have played in bringing radical change in other environments, and their existence as slightly outlawed, unorthodox members of a society still dominated by the state's privileged role. For all their dynamism, Chinese entrepreneurs as a class have proved to be politically unadventurous, with most keeping well away from political issues. Pragmatically aware that some on the CCP still regard them warily, about a third have become Party members, the highest proportion of any social group (Wright, 2010). From time to time entrepreneurs have figured in the Central Committee, though their main ostensive political representation is on the CPPCC. Unlike Russia, China has so far avoided a class of oligarchs, though some of this has been because individuals with deep networks in political elites are working as business people, able to leverage off their high, powerful links.

While entrepreneurs can be neatly grouped because of their relatively small number, the professional middle class are less easy to categorize. In the decade since 2000, figures of 100 million upwards have been used to quantify the numbers that make up the new Chinese middle class (Wagner, 2010). It is this group above all that Western companies have in their sights when they try to sell their luxury goods or educational services. But the middle classes, from such evidence as exists, are under the same amount of pressure that their equivalents in other countries suffer, having to finance their mortgages, fund their city lifestyles, and make sure they have enough savings for health care and the education of their children, where the provision and cost vary widely across the country. It is this group that has saved most of the staggering US$2.5 trillion that had accrued in Chinese bank current and savings accounts by the end of 2013. For as much as one can generalize about the various kinds of middle class that exist across China, and within specific provinces, they are unlikely to be a source of major threat to the CCP. Many have profound vested interests in ensuring that the country is stable, with property, good careers, and the same pressures to be socially conservative as the middle classes elsewhere. As long as the Party maintains stability they are unlikely to be restive. Perhaps the most important issue about them is that they are becoming more demanding of government services, more willing to speak up when they are dissatisfied and much more assertive towards officials.

A third social group is the migrant labourers who live between the countryside and the cities. These have contributed most to the economic development of the PRC since the end of the 1970s, moving from the rural areas to the great manufacturing centres in the Pearl River delta and along the coastal regions of China, where logistic links have made the areas attractive for companies to be established that are geared to export industries. Before 1949, such mass migration as occurred in China was largely a result of war and internal unrest, with people fleeing from one area to another to gain sanctuary. The Sino-Japanese war led to the displacement of over 50 million people. From 1949, with stability returning, mobility was largely restricted to the 'sent down movements', where urban residents were relocated as part of mass campaigns to work in less

Box 6.1 The entrepreneurs of modern China

To be a capitalist in China was once a label that would either have meant spending years in prison, or, at worst, a death sentence. The capitalists were the exploitative classes, against whom the 1949 Revolution had been a major blow, at least according to official narratives and ideologies. But since the Reform Era began in 1978, they have become more important and, as long as they keep away from politics, valued. The stories of some of China's most well-known 'red capitalists', as they have come to be called, are all very different – but each shows a streak of strong determinism and patience.

Yin Mingshan, founder of the Chongqing-based motorcycle and car manufacturer Lifan, was born during the Sino-Japanese war in 1938, and spent the period from 1960 to 1979 in jail as a rightist. After his release, he sold books by the roadside in the city, but noticed that there were an increasing number of motorcycles being used as the reforms progressed and the economy opened up in the 1980s. By the end of the 2000s, his company had over US$1 billion turnover.

Pan Shiyi and **Zhang Xin** are the husband-and-wife team that runs one of China's most successful real estate developers. While Zhang Xin spent a number of years in Hong Kong, and then the UK, where she studied at Sussex and Cambridge Universities, Pan remained in China and built up a small property empire based in Shenzhen. He joined forces with his wife to work in Vantone, a company he founded in 1992 and eventually listed on the stock exchanges within China.

While men may dominate the world of politics in contemporary China, among business people the gender balance is a little more even, and there are a healthy number of women who have succeeded in becoming billionaires. **Yan Cheung** typifies this, a woman who was reportedly worth over US$2 billion in 2007 according to Forbes Rich List, and who has made her fortune on the back of waste-paper recycling through the Nine Dragons brand. Yan started her business while based in Hong Kong with US$4,000 savings she had accrued there. Her unique idea was to use the empty containers coming back from the USA to China to take recyclable waste from Hong Kong, which was processed in China.

developed rural areas, particularly in the western regions of China. There were a high number of such people during the Cultural Revolution who were resettled, usually temporarily, from cities such as Shanghai to provinces such as Xinjiang. Some eventually returned to their home cities, while others settled where they had been sent.

By 1980, the first waves of the so-called 'blind mass' appeared, trying to improve their situation by moving to the newly established SEZs. For this generation, migration was a purely economic issue. Many had been freed from work on the land because of the dramatic improvement in agricultural productivity resulting from household responsibility system reforms. By the 1990s, there were over 100 million migrant labourers settling en masse from specific regions of China into cities such as Beijing, where they famously created small-town-sized communities of people from the same province or city. A 'Zhejiang City' in the capital was particularly prominent.

At the NPC in 2010, migrant labourers were said to number over 150 million. Because of the household registration system and prejudice against them in some of the communities where they went to work, there were a range of issues about how to deal with such a large number of people permanently on the move, going from one factory to another looking for a better life. The SARS crisis in 2003 alerted the authorities to the challenges of trying to keep control of a society on the move when there was the threat of a pandemic. Many migrant labourers were ordered back to their home villages at that time. Every Chinese New Year is a reminder of the sheer size of this group, when the national transport system becomes clogged with people trying to get to their original homes.

Leslie Chang, in a study of women who had gone to work in the huge factories in Guangdong province, describes how aspirational this class is, despite the huge sacrifices they have had to make since the early 1980s. Many have had to leave families and children behind as they go to find work, sending back remittances to the countryside. For many of them, days of up to 16 hours of work are possible, with only one or two days off each month. Since the start of the 2000s, reporters and analysts have found communities of migrants living in squalor and working for tiny wages, often producing goods to sell in the export markets. Companies such as Nike and others have been accused of using suppliers that employ under-age labour, or do not honour China's own factory laws. The migrants that have succeeded have created companies of their own with the money they have made, and many others have been able to rise into better-paying managerial or professional work. Since 2010, migrant workers have been able to be far choosier about where they work, as factories have started to open in the hinterland of China, capitalizing on the developing infrastructure there, cheaper land costs and the growing internal market. Migrants have organized demonstrations and been the source of many protests against poor payment and dangerous factory conditions. But their mobility means that, as a social group, they lack cohesion and this diminishes them as a political threat should they begin to unite around a specific grievance (Chang, 2010).

China's Farmers

The final major class of modern China is the farmers. Farmers occupy a privileged place in the modern social universe. They were the political base for Mao's version of Marxism with Chinese characteristics which he devised after fleeing to the countryside in Jiangxi in 1927. Farmers were the key group fighting in the wars the Communists waged in order to come to power. And as the CCP itself proclaims in its official history, published in 2011, farmers, along with the small urban proletariat that existed then, were the foundation of the United Front and the most important contributor to the CCP's rise.

Despite this, famers have often had a hard time under Communism. The worst period was in the great famine of the early 1960s, during which the countryside, which comprised more than 90 per cent of the population at that time, literally starved so that food could be sent to the cities. Yasheng Huang writes of the largely anti-rural policies of the central and local governments since 1978, during which they tried to take as much land as they could away from rural use and exploit it for construction (Huang, 2008). Many parts of the so-called Chinese countryside in the twenty-first century appear densely urban, with almost continuous building development.

Until 2006, farmers also laboured under a disproportionate tax burden, needing to pay separate taxes on their net income, their property, their output and their consumption. While many of these taxes were lifted by the central government in 2007, farmers are often at the mercy of local officials who take land at will for commercial use, or simply extort money in other ways. The greatest single grievance of China's farmers in the twenty-first century, however, is that they are unable to use the title of their land for security against loans. This issue has been discussed at numerous NPCs, with excited reports that modifications to the country's property law would allow people in the countryside to have more security over the land they tend. To date, however, the principle that the land belongs to the state has not changed, and is not likely to do so in the foreseeable future.

China's farmers are at the forefront of two great modern battles in the PRC. The first is that they are wrestling with the country's profound environmental problems. Lack of water blights harvests in the north and central areas, with pollution of water, as noted earlier, affecting up to 80 per cent of China's rivers. Those who fish or rely on water from streams for their livestock often experience devastating blights from toxic contamination. A drought in Inner Mongolia in the early 2000s coincided with viciously cold winters, and as a result countless herds of sheep were killed. In the north-east of the country, a similar extended drought later in the decade meant that some places did not see rain for over a year. At the other extreme, flooding has become more common, with particularly bad examples in 1998 along the Yellow River. There have been sporadic floods almost every year since then.

The second is that Chinese farmers are the most difficult group for the modernized CCP to try to interest. They are a vast source of discontent, even though their support is crucial for the legitimacy of the Party, and yet they are marginalized increasingly in a society that is urbanizing rapidly. Of the nine million petitions from citizens to the central government in 2009, well over half came from rural households (Yu, 2010). Aware of the long history of dynasties being brought down by agrarian uprisings, the CCP does its best to keep a lid on the discontent in the rural areas. Under Hu Jintao the mantra was of 'a socialist countryside'. For Xi and Li, it seems the strategy is simply to move people from the countryside to the cities as quickly as possible. But the challenges this poses for social cohesion are multiple. Families, the mainstay of so much of Chinese rural social history, are under stress as never before, often scattered between different localities, with a rise in divorce, elderly people being left behind in rural ghettos, and a country which increasingly looks as though it has a two-track economy – rural and urban. Placating the rural dwellers of China will undoubtedly be one of the great challenges of the current and future leaderships as this process of rapid urbanization proceeds.

A Society in Ferment

Nobel Prize laureate Liu Xiaobo, in his critique of the modern CCP culture, talks of a society in which public values have been degraded to such an extent that the country's nightclubs – where officials and businessmen love to do deals in a world dominated by vested interest and personal connections, sometimes directly against social good – have become the ultimate symbol. Levels of distrust have increased as the country has grown richer (Liu, 2012). One shocking case in 2011 illustrates the kinds of deep emotional dislocation to which Liu referred. A truck driver in Guangdong ran over a two-year-old girl as she wandered into the street, away from her distracted parents. Instead of immediately seeking emergency help, the driver reversed over the girl, running his truck's wheels across her numerous times. The whole harrowing episode was caught on camera and released on the Chinese version of YouTube (youKu.com). What shocked people the most, beyond the mindless callousness of the driver, was the way in which more than a dozen passers-by and bystanders did nothing to help. One finally summoned the emergency services who took the little girl to hospital, where she died of her injuries later the same day.

Interviewed after his arrest, the driver explained that, had the injured girl survived, he would have been liable to give much higher compensation to the parents, but once she was dead, the most he would be punished with was a one-off fine. The anger on the Chinese internet over the event caused widespread public soul-searching. Some explained it as a lack of 'good Samaritan ethos', referring to the case a few years earlier of a man who had become involved in an accident as a bystander, trying to help someone, and then been sued successfully by the person he had tried to help. Others simply complained about a collapse of values in a society that had grown wealthy too quickly.

A similar debate occurred during a spate of shocking knife murders in schools carried out by aggrieved individuals in 2008. This was echoed by more attacks in schools in Northern China in early 2014. One case saw a disabled man in a wheelchair so aggrieved at his treatment that he appeared in Beijing airport with a home-made bomb strapped to him, threatening to detonate before being led away by police. In a society of over 1.3 billion people, however, it was not surprising that the PRC had its share of the bad, the dangerous and the downright evil. Serial killers have begun to be recognized since 2000, with one particular case reportedly responsible for as many as 50 deaths. Those convicted of murder are usually given death sentences, which are carried out quickly. The country shifted in the mid-2000s from execution by firing squad for most provinces to death by lethal injection, and the public executions that had been one of the features of the country after 1949 became rare. Even so, in 2013 the country was responsible for executing around 1,000 people, according to estimates by those outside China. However, other informed sources claim that the real figure was possibly in excess of 3,000, which was more than the rest of the world combined. (Economist, 2013). In 2007, the NPC requested that all death sentences passed by provincial courts be sent for final approval to the central Supreme Court, giving at least a further degree of scrutiny. The execution of a British national of Pakistani origin in December 2009 for drug smuggling was a reminder, however, of how incomplete the Chinese justice system was, even when it involved deciding if someone was to live or die. According to the lawyers representing the accused, Mr Akmal Sheik, no psychological reports were requested (he was reportedly suffering from bipolar disorder), and no mitigating factors were considered when he was finally sentenced for bringing over four kilos of heroin into Xinjiang. His execution was the first case of an EU national in the PRC since 1952, and was carried out despite approaches at the highest level from the EU and the British government to the Chinese leadership.

China is similar to many countries in the fact that the public, according to the surveys that have been undertaken, are mainly supporters of the death sentence. Even so, in 2011 the government reduced the number of crimes that carried the death sentence as the ultimate punishment, removing it from many largely financial, non-violent areas. The case of Wu Ying, a businesswoman convicted of corrupting officials, raised the issue of how just the death sentence was when her appeal for clemency was refused in 2012. Many bloggers in the PRC felt she had been dealt with harshly, and that imposing the death sentence on a woman who had once been an admired entrepreneur was unjust. Her appeal to the Supreme Court was finally successful in May 2012 and she was resentenced to death but with a two-year suspension – in effect, life imprisonment. Public anger over sentences had worked before. A nightclub waitress who was accused of stabbing to death an official who demanded sexual services from her had her sentence remitted to life imprisonment on the lesser charge of manslaughter after national outrage at her treatment in 2009. Once again, public outrage had an effect. The final highly symbolic case was that of Li Yan, who had suffered horrific domestic abuse at the hands of her husband before finally stabbing him to death. Her original death sentence on being convicted of the crime was commuted to a suspended one in 2014 after a national and international outcry.

The China that foreigners fondly remember from the 1970s and early 1980s, where leaving even a small item of clothing in a hotel room could result in it being sent on to the visitor, and where crime was seemingly unheard of (at least for foreigners), seemed to disappear as the country grew richer. According to official statistics, murder, rape and violence against the individual were all increasing, and while these were on the whole much lower than in the USA and many other developed countries, there was a nagging suspicion that such figures as existed were huge understatements. Domestic violence was horrifically common in many areas of the country, with high levels of alcoholism, and prejudices against the disabled. Mental health problems were largely ignored, except in the major cities, where psychiatric units began slowly to appear in hospitals in the first decade of the twenty-first century. Homosexuality was finally removed from being regarded as an illness in the late 2000s, though persecution of those who were openly gay persisted, despite highly visible figures such as the singer, Li Yuchun, winner of the national Supergirl talent contest in 2005, who was reportedly a lesbian. Perhaps as a sobering comment on the general view of mental health in the PRC, particularly problematic dissidents have, according to a number of reports from Human Rights Watch and others, been placed in psychiatric wards, which, from the accounts of those who finally succeeded in escaping, are little different from prisons.

With divorce rates increasing dramatically from 2001, China has become a society afflicted with many of the problems of developed economies. One of the most striking is the explosion of the sex industry. Prostitution and pornography are illegal in the PRC. One of the most symbolic acts of the CCP when it came to power in 1949 was to outlaw prostitution and to support programmes to find new careers for former sex workers, especially in Shanghai, which had been famously chaotic in the early part of the twentieth century. By closing down brothels, the government had aspired to a lifestyle that, at least on the surface, was puritanical. The division between the sexes remained; acceptance of sex outside marriage, and (despite its legal permissibility) tolerance of divorce were low. With the onset of the reforms, there were areas in which greater freedom was allowed, but frequent 'strike hard' campaigns from the early 1980s saw many 'bad elements' simply taken off to jail in mass justice rallies. This has done little to hold back the tide of moral turbulence, and in the PRC currently there may be as many as seven million sex workers, with some areas of the large cities looking like the red light districts of the West.

The sex industry in China, according to a report by the Economist Intelligence Unit in 2001, was already vastly profitable despite its underground nature. Lai Changxing, the corrupter of officials in Fujian who was forced to flee to Canada after the multi-million dollar smuggling scam he had operated was exposed in 2000, ran a brothel in Xiamen, which was exposed in the press in painstaking detail after his case had come to light. The plush karaoke rooms, private dining areas and sauna facilities were, however, nothing different from what could be found throughout the length and breadth of the country. Hostesses who worked in these places, many from the countryside, boasted of earning more in a day or two than most of their fellow villagers who had gone to work in factories made in a month. For many, the aim was to find a marriage partner quickly after they had reached what was regarded as the age limit for this work, usually their late twenties. Many, however, became bar managers and even graduated to owning their own places. As part of the Xi Jinping anti-corruption clampdown, a place reputed to be the centre of the Chinese sex industry, Dongguan in Guangdong, was the subject of a huge police-led operation in early 2014, with hundreds of sex workers rounded up, along with their clients. This sent a chill through the rest of the industry in China. Officials caught in brothels or massage parlours known to offer sexual services were humiliated on TV. In a country where change was happening so quickly, however, and with family structures under daily attack, the Dongguang clean-up had apparently only short-term impact. By the summer of 2014, many of the businesses closed down seemed to be back in operation.

Another unwelcome tradition from the pre-1949 era was the return of the keeping of mistresses. Both Bo Xilai and Zhou Yongkang during their falls were accused of keeping multiple mistresses. This lent the anti-corruption drive a puritanical flavour. But a deeper associated question was the position of women in society generally. For much of its dynastic and modern history, China has been a patriarchal place, where women were granted a highly limited political and social role. The repulsive custom of foot binding under the Manchus in the Qing right up to the twentieth century symbolized this, with young girls effectively crippling themselves because of the high premium placed by elite males on the erotic and aesthetic qualities of small feet. Mao had led a revolution which proclaimed that 'women hold up half the sky.' And while women had been granted more rights, on paper at least, in the 1951 Marriage Law, their role in society expanded only gradually. Even in 2014, for leadership positions, there was a clear glass ceiling. No woman had ever been a member of the Standing Committee of the Politburo. There had only been two female governors of provinces since 1949, and just a handful of Party Secretaries. In 2014, only 20 per cent of Party members were women. In the upper echelons of business, however, there was a better proportion of women succeeding.

Despite this, a number of social changes were strengthening the role of women. The most important of these was the impact of the one-child policies introduced in the 1970s to bring China's booming population under control. This had seen imbalances between the number of girls and boys born, with a national ration of 118 men to 100 women by 2010 (Branigan, 2011). Projected into the future, this meant that by 2030 China was looking at 50 million more men than women. Many of these men would spend their lives unmarried. The issue of farmers finding it hard to find partners became more pressing from 1992, when there were a series of abductions of women from towns or cities who were simply taken to remote areas to be forcibly married to rural residents. Women were therefore paradoxically becoming more necessary at the same time as society remained male-dominated and patriarchal. And while the rural desire to have male children is fading, partly as a result of huge public education campaigns, it is still powerful enough to mean that scanning to check the sex of a child before birth remains illegal, and reports persist of murders or abandonments of unwanted infant girls.

Daily Life in Modern China

No society has undergone such large-scale changes in such a short space of time as those that have happened in contemporary China. In the 1970s, it was a place in which, on the whole, people lived and died in relatively small communities, in which everyone knew everyone else, in which there was limited technology, and where many of the key life decisions even in a person's personal life were made by agents of the state, usually at work unit or neighbour committee level. All this has now largely disappeared. Since the 1990s, young Chinese have had to make their own way in the world, finding work, either through public advertisements or, more often than not, through networks. They can choose who to marry, what to study at university, and where to live. The state cannot, and does not want to be involved in these personal decisions, and the private sphere now exists as much in China as it does in Western countries with their high levels of individualism.

Despite this, China remains a deeply networked society. Everyone, from the day they are born to the day they die, relies on networks, to secure work, to promote their businesses, to sort out legal or other problems, to find marriage or sex partners, or simply to socialize and survive. This is characterized as '*guanxi*' in much of the literature, a broad and highly contested concept, more talked about than properly understood. A better word might be 'network'. For many Chinese today, there is a strong awareness of needing to have a good, broad network of those known or available to them, so that the many unexpected challenges of life can at least be faced knowing there might be sources of help.

For most young Chinese, urban life is much like it is in the West – enduring traffic jams to and from work, dealing with the pressures of office work, having to pay bills, keeping up with the living expectations of their peers and families and so on. Many are living away from their home areas, and have to create new networks through their work, through friends, and through socializing. Perhaps one cultural constant has been the importance of food and eating in all of this – most modern Chinese cities are crammed with restaurants, all usually crowded at lunch and in the evening. Eating is a major activity for most Chinese people, important as a time to do business deals, to form deeper links with people around them, or to celebrate important occasions. As though to recognize this, there is a hierarchy of food, with expensive seafood at the apex and then meat and other exotic dishes. The ways in which the Chinese greet people, even in the twenty-first century, recognizes the importance of food in a country which, until recently, knew famine, with the common greeting 'Have you eaten yet?' echoing the memory of this anxiety.

What strikes most observers of this urban lifestyle is how globalized it is. Many of the songs, films and trends popular in the West are also followed keenly in China. Football, and to a lesser extent basketball, are very popular, with Yao Ming, the basketball player who joined the NBC league in the USA being one of the country's greatest contemporary heroes. Just as in the West, young Chinese people watch endless hours of TV (there are over 200 television stations). At cinemas, the young people watch many of the same films as are popular in the rest of the world, with more local patriotic fare, such as the film released in 2011 celebrating the 90th anniversary of the foundation of the Communist Party, largely a resounding flop (it was only saved by free ticket issues to groups, who were then obliged to go and watch the film). Impartial critical opinion was damning. Karaoke, drinking and shopping remain major national pastimes. Much of this lifestyle has penetrated deep into the so-called rural areas of the country.

Family Structure in the Era of Mobility: The Little Emperors

In the early days of Mao's China, high rates of fertility were encouraged, with large families being the norm. Mao reportedly liked the idea of a huge population, and shocked Russian visitors once when discussing the calamity of a dropped nuclear bomb by saying that China could lose half its population and still have more than other countries in terms of the number of its people. Even in the late Maoist period, however, the size of the population began to worry leaders, with Zhou Enlai, according to his English translator, once looking at a packed school yard and asking out loud what on earth the country was going to do with all these mouths to feed. From 400 million in 1930, China's population rose to 800 million by 1970, and to over a billion by 1980. The first attempts to control the growth of the numbers of people were made, in fact, before Mao's death, but a national attempt was not in place until 1978, when the so-called 'one-child policy' was introduced, limiting the number of children a family could have unless they were members of an ethnic minority. This policy, according to some estimates, has prevented China having a population of over two billion by 2015, but its implementation, with reports of forced abortions and infanticide, has been controversial. In the late Hu and early Xi era there were moves to liberalize, with two people living in cities who were both single children able to have two offspring. Policy-makers were aware that a shrinking population meant an ageing one, and that the social and pension costs for this would be vast.

The general impact of the policy on family life has been profound. In the space of only a single generation, families have gone from six or seven children to just one. Those violating the laws have had hefty fines and other punishments imposed. The whole structure of Chinese family life has changed, with the appearance of the phenomenon of 'little emperors and empresses', children with 'six-pocket households', in which mothers and fathers, and two sets of grandparents, dote on them, supporting them and looking after them, frequently pooling their resources so that children can attend good schools, and often even study abroad.

Perhaps most striking of all has been the appearance in recent years of obesity among the population. In a society which has had famine in living memory, there could perhaps be no more powerful symbol of how China has transformed than the fact that now people are dying from being overweight, rather than from malnutrition. As more meat-based, fatty diets have become the norm, McDonald's and Kentucky Fried Chicken, served with Pepsi or Coca-Cola, reach into almost every province. Rice has been replaced by French fries. And heart disease is starting to rise to the same rates as in the West, through clogged arteries and high cholesterol levels. These problems are not helped by the very high levels of smoking in the country. This rapid diet change added to smoking is starting to be the main drain on hospitals and the resources of the national health service (French and Crabbe, 2010).

What the outlook of the young people born in the era of the one-child policy might be is hard to state with any certainty at this point. The generation that remembers the Cultural Revolution had plenty of experience of poverty and hardship. Those who were coming to maturity at the beginning of the 1980s when the reforms were having an effect have a different outlook, one in which China has been growing stronger and richer year by year, and in which the same feelings of entitlement and ambition that exist in the West have come to the fore. Young people related to high officials famously career around the country as though it were a private playground, with one of these, in Hebei province, whose response, when he ran over two students in his expensive car in October 2011, was 'Go on, sue me, my father is Li Gang' becoming an internet sensation. Li Gang was a senior local public security official, and the imperious attitude of the son captured the sense of immunity that those with good links to officialdom and the CCP frequently have. After one of the injured students died in hospital, however, public anger grew, with Li Gang himself confessing tearfully on television that he had brought his child up irresponsibly. The son was eventually sentenced to six years in prison. The story captured the lives of the privileged young in new China. There were plenty more examples of the well-connected trying to, and often succeeding in, literally getting away with murder.

One of the saddest statistics of the contemporary PRC has been the steep rise in suicides, particular among young women. China's development has created many winners, but for too many the new world is disorientating and meaningless. A spate of suicides at the Foxconn factory in Shenzhen, makers of many appliances found in the West, such as the Apple iPad and iPod, drew attention to this in late 2010, when its Taiwanese owner, Terry Gao, was forced to appear before the press and defend the safety and welfare record of his vast 450,000-strong factory. Commercialization has created huge pressures on people to be successful, to keep up with their peers, and to push themselves as hard as they could. That these suicides had occurred in a factory keen to showcase its decent sports and recreation facilities puzzled many, but a life in which there were six-day weeks with long working hours and very little time to escape the work environment was of limited attraction, however alluring the amenities appeared.

Great Social Challenges for China's Future

Another impact of the one-child policy was the quick transformation of China's demography. It was becoming not just one where men outnumbered women, but also one where the old were starting to outnumber the young. In twentieth-century China, retirement was a luxury created when life expectancy shot up after 1949. In Republican China, the average age at death was in the early thirties. But by 2000, it stood in the mid-seventies for both men and women (CIA, *World Factbook*, 2014). The greying of the Chinese population is set to have profound consequences for the labour market, the social welfare system and the shape of society overall.

China currently has no national pension system which only compounds matters. Pension provision was arranged up to a point by state-owned enterprises in the cities, but with the slimming down or privatization of many of these in the 1990s there was a problem over who would service the liabilities. Many simply stopped providing subsidized housing, access to healthcare for the elderly or monthly pension payments, causing some of the fiercest protests. Pensions were in fact the largest single financial outlay of the Chinese state, with provinces such as Sichuan spending, in 2009, as much as 90 per cent of its funds on servicing them (Frazier, 2010). China's looming ageing problem means that the issue of pensions is not likely to go away, and as in the West, the issue of how workers can save today in order to look after themselves tomorrow has become a pressing one. Attempts to create a national pension fund were unsuccessful under Premier Zhu Rongji. Some local authorities, such as that in Shanghai, attempted to set up their own pension funds in an attempt to deal with the impending financial demands. It was the claimed mismanagement of these which led to the fall of the Party Secretary of the city up to 2007, Chen Liangyu. Under Li Keqiang, the construction of a workable pension scheme is one of the government's core challenges. Study of superannuation funds or other systems used outside China has only made it clear that the country is trying to do something on a scale never before attempted. As yet, there is no clear blueprint. A secondary issue was the problem of the breakdown of the traditional family structure. Traditional rural households lived under one roof, with the elderly members being looked after by the young, and as many as four generations living in one dwelling. Those of working age had their children looked after by the retired grandparents. But in the new, mobile China, this structure has started to break down. Often husbands or wives and in many cases both had to be away from home working as migrants in cities or areas in which they had yet to secure proper residency permits. Long-term separation has led to a rising trend in divorce levels. In the new China, the family was as much under attack by the disruptive forces of modernity as in any other industrialized society. This is not to romanticize the past – traditional China was as full of stories of unjust repression and stifling conservatism as anywhere else. But in a society which suddenly found itself with large numbers of elderly people, the issue of how to care for them as their health declined and they were unable to look after themselves, became a live one. By 2012, there were the first appearances of retirement homes well-known in some Western countries. In Shanghai in late 2012, a man was discovered in his apartment who had died several months before and simply decomposed. In old China, this sort of isolation would have been impossible. In new China, it became all too possible.

One of the great challenges for the government in the coming decade will be to deal with some of these issues through creating a stronger social welfare system. A nationwide level of social welfare has collapsed since the dismantling of the cradle-to-grave work unit system that prevailed for most of the first four decades of CCP rule. From the late 1990s, the Chinese people were often left to their own devices to find care. The older urban generation, with a sense of entitlement from the state born from years of listening to propaganda about how people would always be looked after, had a rude awakening from the early 2000s. While the new leaders talked of harmony and scientific development, many of the benefits of free health care, hospitals, schools and other public goods were eroding or had already disappeared. Hospitals in particular became places where payments needed to be made to get anything beyond the most basic treatment. Often, they were run as successful businesses on a far more ruthless model than even in the USA. The best of China's hospitals, in the coastal cities, were superb. But those that serviced the rural areas were often dirty, primitive and poorly run. Kick-backs from pharmaceutical companies and patients to doctors were common, though this became one of the targets of the anti-corruption campaign from 2013. Even worse was the spate of counterfeit medicines produced by unscrupulous businesses which resulted in injury and sometimes even death (Guo, 2010).

Schools and universities were also becoming as expensive as in the West. Once again, there were wide regional differences at the primary and secondary levels in the country, and between the cities and the countryside. The 12th Five Year Programme for the years 2011 to 2015 has set out an extensive programme to create more social welfare to reduce the anxiety of the middle class as they need to look after demanding children and ageing parents.

The Rise of Civil Society

In the Republican era China had a nascent civil society sector with church groups, trade lobby groups, trade unions and other smaller interest groups. The 1949 revolution changed this, with the assumption that the state could step in and provide everything. A single trade union was formed, patriotic church groups were established (under much duress) and any literary or cultural groups were kept under tight rein.

With the 1978 reforms came an increasing desire for less state direction in people's lives. In the 1980s and 1990s something approaching civil society started to appear, with organizations for protection of the environment, for support for marginalized groups, religious beliefs and cultural interests. One estimate from 2010 put such non-government organization (NGO) groups at over 200,000. The Ministry of Civil Affairs in 2011 only recognized about 3,000 such groups.

Civil society has a big role in contemporary China largely through the withdrawal of the central and local state from many of the services it once provided. Care for the elderly or disabled, for special-interest groups and for migrant children is now largely handled by such groups. There has also been support for volunteering, with over 100,000 deployed in disaster relief after the 2008 Wenchuan earthquake. Despite this, civil society lives under political uncertainty and suspicion in China, and is often seen either as masking foreign attempts to interfere in the country's internal affairs, or concealing local political ambitions to undermine the Party. Tibetan environmental groups were targeted in 2009–10 because of worries they were only promoting separatist messages under another guise. Gay and legal rights groups have also been attacked. The usual vulnerability for civil rights sector workers in China is a chronic lack of funding channels. Despite this, the government does recognize that these groups have a huge role to play in social cohesion and stability. So despite state ambiguity, they are thriving and multiplying and only likely to continue into the future.

The Networked Society: China and the Internet

The internet's political impact was discussed earlier in the book. Its impact on society and on how debates are conducted shows a great deal about how quickly and how radically China has changed. According to the Chinese author, Yu Hua, China at the beginning of the twenty-first century is a place where the internet has created its own reality, a reality that does not need to accord with the truth because it often has its own momentum. Those who could harness the internet for their own purposes were able to accrue immense power; but those who fell foul of noisy, blogging communities lived to rue the day that the World Wide Web had ever reached the country (Yu, 2011).

How the internet is impacting on people's privacy and intimacy is as delicate an issue as in other countries. Instances of Hong Kong or Taiwanese film stars or celebrities having their accounts hacked into and personal information being dragged out are common. The most striking internet phenomenon in China is the 'flesh searches', in which particular figures are selected, demonized, pursued and sometimes driven from their homes by a barrage of attacks. This can happen to officials who have angered people locally, or film stars who have 'humiliated China' by appearing to suck up to the West. Perhaps the most violent examples involve those who have said or done the wrong things regarding relations with Japan. On this issue, the indignation of the virtual community is seemingly inexhaustible.

One thing that the Chinese internet does help us to understand is the nature of public opinion in the modern PRC. This is despite the fact that, as anywhere else on the planet, an enormous amount of the material online is ephemeral, often focusing on celebrities and gossip. Until the 2000s, as more people have accessed the World Wide Web and been involved in the Chinese social media, trying to understand what Chinese public opinion is regarding domestic or international issues is often almost impossible. State newspapers or television, whether the mouth-piece of the CCP, the *People's Daily*, or the national network of state-directed TV stations, the Chinese Central Television (CCTV) channels have usually proclaimed that their content reflected the views of 'all 1.3 billion Chinese'. Noisy declarations by the government that its statements were representative of all Chinese people had figured in the past in, for example, condemnations of the UK over difficulties before the handing back of Hong Kong to the PRC in 1997 (the last governor, Chris Patten, was consistently accused of 'hurting the feelings of all Chinese' in this period), or attacks on Japan when in 2005 it tried to gain permanent membership of the United Nations Security Council. Elite leaders spoke on behalf of 'the mass of Chinese people', and because of the lack of meaningful surveys contradicting them, largely went unchallenged. Hearing what the Chinese people themselves might have actually thought, in the absence of a free press, elections and freedom of speech was simply not possible.

The internet has challenged this. It gives at least some insight into what is on the minds of large segments of the Chinese population. Issues such as food and housing costs, as everywhere else, came to the fore from late 2011. Anger at corruption is also high, with many complaints being levelled at official malfeasance. The state of the environment gets high levels of coverage, as does the kind of celebrity-driven trivia that takes up endless acres of virtual space in the West. Chinese public opinion is, unsurprisingly, as diverse and varied as it is in the West – with noisy extremes and then passionate debates on the more central ground about issues of public and foreign policy. Weibo, QQ, Weixin (We Chat) and Tencent offer a rich audit of how public views are evolving and changing in the modern PRC as it continues its rapid transformation and development. It is here, more than anywhere else, that one can see the radical and rapid changes that are taking place in a country which, only three decades before, barely had TV or radio coverage. In many cases, what first appears in blogs and online posts is then taken up by the mainstream media. This was the case with the fleeing of Wang Lijun, former deputy mayor of Chongqing, to the US consulate in Chengdu on 6 February 2012 (see Chapter 3), which surfaced as a story on Sina Weibo but then made it into the printed media later in the month.

The internet has become a wonderful symbol of the complexity of China, both in the battles between government censors and users over how to control, and how to circumvent controls, but also in the remarkable way in which it represents the sheer impossibility of blandly categorizing Chinese mass opinion. One way in which China now differs from the China of even a decade ago is in the relative lack of ease these days with which politicians in the country can grandly claim to be speaking on behalf of 'all Chinese'. As the internet shows vividly, such a concept, if it ever had much meaning, is now pretty empty. There are many times when the country seems not just one of 1.3 billion people, but of 1.3 billion contrary opinions and ideas. And this has had an impact not just on the country's economy and politics, but perhaps most profoundly, on its cultural identity. That will be the subject of Chapter 7.

7

Chinese Culture

In 2004, one of the country's main liberal magazines, *Southern Weekend,* issued a list of the 50 most influential people in China. It included scientists, writers, political thinkers, artists and business people. The list led to a storm of debate online, with many disagreeing with who were included in the list, the reasons they were included or proposing other people instead. Within a few days of the list appearing, it was effectively censored, and became unobtainable within China.

The question of who has the most profound influence in the PRC was not so easy to dismiss, however. Of course, the elite leadership of the CCP was in control on most levels, and yet, as previous chapters in this book have shown, there were whole areas of the key public agenda in this increasingly complex country where it no longer had such authority, and was, in all sorts of areas in life, simply not heeded. Bookshops in the major Chinese cities were often piled high with the latest political tracts, but the works that sold in great numbers were frequently imported and translated. For a time, *The World is Flat*, written by Thomas Friedman (Friedman, 2005), became hugely popular, even being studied by officials at the Party School in Chongqing. Works by Michel Foucault, Jürgen Habermas, Pierre Bourdieu and Noam Chomsky were all available in Mandarin. Even the complete works of the philosopher Ludwig Wittgenstein had been produced by an academic at Beijing University. And these works don't even start to touch on the traction of J. K. Rowling's *Harry Potter* series or the vast print runs done for American business gurus.

The CCP leadership, through figures like Hu Jintao and then Xi Jinping, consistently stated that it was in charge of delivering modernization in China, and that through it the key ideas of reform and change had come to a country which had been held back under the yoke of feudalism and imperial restraint. Even so, the CCP itself often appeared to be culturally out of step with a country brimming with diversity and a ferment of new ideas. Chinese bloggers complained bitterly that there were so few internationally recognized Chinese writers, public intellectuals and thinkers. This was best captured by the remarkable campaigns to acquire a Nobel Prize for China from the 1980s onwards, supported by the Ministry of Culture, and culminating in the award of the Prize for literature in 2000 to the émigré writer Gao Xingjian, and the award for peace to the imprisoned Chinese dissident Liu Xiaobo in 2010, neither individual being admired by the government. China's love affair with the Nobel Prize died when the Peace Prize committee announced Liu's name as the winner in late 2010, but it was partially revived by the award, in 2012, of the Literature Prize to Mo Yan, despite criticisms subsequently levelled at Mo by Xi Jinping in 2014.

A Mirror of Cynicism: Contemporary Chinese Painting

One area where products from China have had the greatest external impact since 1990 has been in paintings and art. Chinese works now fetch high prices on the international market, and a large number of international art galleries specialize in Chinese avant-garde works. The most prominent of contemporary China's artistic figures is Ai Wei Wei, a Beijing-based installation artist whose fame was sealed by two events – his involvement in the design of the 2008 'bird's nest' stadium used during the Olympics, and his detention for several months in 2011 at the height of a clampdown that year.

Ai Wei Wei is a highly symbolic figure in Chinese modern art. The son of an esteemed poet who had been imprisoned in the 1930s and exiled to Heilongjiang province during the anti-rightist campaign in 1957, Ai himself was brought up in the north-east after his family was sent to the countryside during the Cultural Revolution. This experience is typical of the urban youth of his generation, and shared by many members of the political elite. On his return to Beijing in 1978, he attended the art academy when universities reopened fully after Mao's death, counting film directors such as Zhang Yimou and Chen Kaige among his contemporaries. In the 1980s, he was in the USA, and only returned to China in 1993 to look after his elderly father. He has been based in Beijing ever since.

Ai's involvement in the 2008 Olympics perfectly captures the contradictions of this vast event. For the political elite it had been central to their project to capture international recognition and to present the acceptable face of their modernizing country to the world. They expended enormous effort to get the votes of the International Olympic Committee (IOC) to host the 2008 Summer Olympics, and reportedly spent more than US$45 billion on rebuilding large parts of the city and putting in place the infrastructure for Beijing to hold the games. That Ai was involved in this seemed strange. He had built up a reputation as a sharp critic of the regime over the previous few years. He also belonged to a significant, albeit small, group of public intellectuals who were highly pessimistic about the value of so-called traditional Chinese culture in the globalizing world of the twenty-first century, feeling that such elements had been recruited by self-serving elites to promote their own political objectives and had no links to any of the complex communities in China and their modes of expression. Ai's own attitude is best summed up by the photographic triptych of him holding, and then dropping, a 2,000-year-old Han Dynasty vase, letting it smash to pieces on the floor.

For figures like Ai, Chinese culture, especially the Confucian traditions, was a heavy burden. This had been an issue wrestled with by almost every artistic figure of the modern era, from the intellectual Hu Shi, who had been instrumental in arguing for language reform from the 1920s and in introducing modernist ideas via figures such as Albert Einstein, and philosophers William James and Bertrand Russell into intellectual life in Republican China, to the subversive and iconoclastic author Lu Xun (see below) over whose legacy the CCP fought from 1949 onwards. Writers such as the Taiwanese Bo Yang had expressed the mixture of hubris and self-disgust that lay at the heart of Chinese identity in the contemporary era, in his scathing book *The Ugly Chinaman*, written in 1985 in Chinese and published in English in 1988 (Bo, 1988). For Bo, as for Lu Xun, Chinese 'tradition' was a prison from which people had to find exit routes.

The great problem for many modern Chinese intellectuals up to the 2000s was the feeling that most of those exit routes were supplied from the West, raising all sorts of questions about the backwardness and lack of intellectual and artistic development of their country. He Qing, a prominent scholar from the 1990s, wrote an immense four-volume critique of China's modernity, in which he argued that the great contradiction was that, in modernizing, China was mainly equipped with tools from the West, and yet one of its great aspirations was to get away from the universalist environment of Western thought and create something modern and uniquely Chinese (Davies, 2009).

The response of artists such as Ai Wei Wei has been to adopt a form of biting satire, half embracing the detested forms of 'traditional' culture and art, and half subverting them. Involvement in the Beijing Olympics served to give Ai's criticisms even greater prominence, with his design for the 'bird's nest' stadium, implemented by a Swiss engineering firm, dominated the newly constructed central park; Ai appeared on television denouncing the whole event and what he called its moral and aesthetic bankruptcy.

As far as critics were concerned, this bankruptcy was available for all to see during the opening ceremony. Vast waves of performers trooped out after a 'shock and awe' beginning of electronically managed fireworks and frenetic dancing. More than 2,000 drummers hammered out tunes before a pageant of the 'great family' of the modern Chinese state marched past, watched by the eyes of the world via television. The whole vastly expensive event culminated in a highly representative 'run-through' of Chinese culture, with the key claim being an encoded celebration of the stability, length and duration of the great signifiers, from Confucian philosophy to the Ming Dynasty explorer Zheng He, to the Great Wall and the Terracotta Warriors.

For Ai Wei Wei, the central problem was that almost all of these symbols were backward-looking. For other critics, they were highly contested. The Great Wall was dealt with in Chapter 1. Its ambiguity as a national symbol, being an assertion of both China's limitations and its introspective nature, and its ineffectiveness as a defensive system, have long been discussed both inside and outside China. More striking was the complete absence of references to Mao Zedong from the great event, despite the fact that his portrait is still hanging on the Gate of Heavenly Peace in Tiananmen Square. This seemed highly contradictory. Was the Chinese government secretly ashamed of the great founder's record?

Ai's criticisms were tolerated, at least during the ceremony itself. But once the Olympics were over, the Beijing government's appetite to put up with public dissent quickly, and dramatically, declined. By 2011, with the Jasmine Revolution and others in the Middle East making the CCP even more nervous (something reinforced by protests in 2014 in Hong Kong and Taiwan) Ai was one of the key figures placed in a semi-legal form of detention, simply being removed from his home and kept in isolation for several weeks. International efforts might have played a part in securing his release, after he was accused of failing to pay tax bills. Whatever the value of his art, Ai's treatment was representative of a PRC in which limits to freedom of expression clashed with overt statements of the need to think freely and embrace modernity to improve the country. In such a highly politicized environment, could the CCP, with its rigid power structures, have a kind of pick-and-mix modernity, a modernity geared to its own narrow political purposes, with discordant and anarchic elements discarded? These are the questions that the case of Ai Wei Wei raised.

There were plenty of other artists who captured elements of this great contradiction in a powerful way. The invented characters of Xu Bing's *Tianshu* ('Book from the Sky') captured issues of the centrality of the written form of Chinese in its cultural self-expression. His forms of Chinese characters, half familiar and yet wholly imaginary, were both unsettling and beautiful. The more disturbed output of practitioners involved, in one case, living things hung on a metal grille, and, in another, an artist who reportedly filmed himself eating the foetus of an unborn child from a prostitute he had paid to make pregnant and then go through an abortion. The state's continuing power to judge between life and death through the one-child policy, and the numbers that were executed each year, were constant reference points. How could such power present itself as being in some way benign, friendly and loveable, especially when public art was contaminated by the political programme and circumscription of the state? Such issues were brought to the fore by figures like Guo Jian, born in China but an Australian citizen after living in Sydney from the late 1990s. Guo was unceremoniously detained ahead of the 25th anniversary of the Tiananmen Square massacre in 2014. On the other hand, Yue Minjun, producer of industrial amounts of portraits of leering faces which sold at increasingly high prices on the international market, largely stayed out of trouble. There seemed to be a compact: it was acceptable to make art that sold well, but becoming too pointed in political commentary was a dangerous track to go down. Perhaps one of the most fascinating contemporary uses of an art form tapping into Chinese ancient history but obliquely making points about the country's current situation was Cao Guoqiang's mesmerizing photos of explosions and fireworks. Their dynamism, texture and immediacy stood alongside the ways they referred to a history in which China claimed it had invented pyrotechnics, and their portrayal of violent events in a way which captured a moment of beauty distilled the almost constant complexity and ambiguity of contemporary China.

The Unacknowledged Legislators

Uniquely, the PRC was a regime brought to power by a poet. Mao Zedong's poetry, which he continued to write throughout his life, was distinctive, a mixture of classical forms and powerful imagery. According to experts on calligraphy, even his style of writing in Chinese was forceful, driven and unique to himself. His poems were quoted exhaustively in the latter part of his period in power, with one commentator stating that in the PRC, from the Cultural Revolution onwards, the language of Mao was unlike the language of anyone else, treated in a highly privileged way almost like the scriptures in Western contexts.

Mao had expressed himself as a king of artistic vision in his speeches in the revolutionary hideout in northern Shanxi in 1942. Prefiguring one of the most vicious purges against intellectuals, including writers such as Ding Ling and political figures such as Wang Meng, Mao had stated in his speech 'Yan'an Talks on Literature and Art' that the primary purpose of socialist literature and painting was to represent the life of the people and contribute to their struggle for emancipation. A clear line was drawn between what was acceptable and what was not, and while the line shifted a little over the decades after 1942, it remained a well policed one, with those such as the early great follower of Lu Xun, the Shanghai-based writer of Republican China, Hu Feng, being sent to jail for anti-rightist slander after 1956, and not released until 1980.

Lu Xun's was a particularly difficult case. It was true that he expressed sympathies, before his death in 1936, towards the Communists. But his biting satire would have been hard put to survive after 1949. Even Mao admitted that had Lu lived into the PRC era he would have either fallen silent or been put in prison. In Lu's most powerful works, such as *The True Story of Ah Q*, he dissected the weaknesses of the modern Chinese psyche in a world in which it had become sidelined. The great images of the hopelessly stranded Ah Q being humiliated, put down and bullied by the figures around him, and able only to speak in his defence in private when no one was about, represented the national condition, in which China seemed to have laid itself open to almost clinical weakness. After 1949, the CCP mounted an energetic campaign to recruit Lu Xun's reputation to its cause, and in the Cultural Revolution Lu Xun's works were, ironically, among the few still available, though presented as being profoundly supportive of the project the Cultural Revolution represented (Xun, 2009).

The Cultural Revolution was, in fact, at its heart a political campaign among elites where the battleground was the world of ideology, power structures and their accompanying language and symbols. This cultural aspect is frequently forgotten but, as Jiang Qing, one of the key protagonists, was to state during one of the hotter moments of this epic period, the whole idea was to fight with words not weapons, and to engage in what she called 'a battle for people's souls'. The cultural products of the Cultural Revolution deserve close attention today. The symbols of the period – Mao's profile rising into the sun, with his arm frequently stretched out over the brave new world he was bringing into being – are among the most famous images the country has ever produced. They continued to be reproduced long after the Cultural Revolution ended, sometimes admiringly, but more often than not, especially these days, with heavy irony. The Maoist Utopian dream has, in modern times, been held up in some quarters of China to sarcastic scrutiny, and used as a means for Chinese people to look at the fracturing of their earlier, more naïve dreams. But mingled with this there is an occasional note of nostalgia and loss. Mao's emotional appeal to Chinese people was authentic and powerful. His final betrayal of the trust vested in him is something it is hard to openly speak about even today. Mao truly was the God that failed, and this disappointment lurks behind the oblique criticisms made of him.

Feeding off Mao's legacy still carries good returns in domestic politics. 'Red songs' reminiscent of the Cultural Revolution era were dusted off and used again during Party secretary of Chongqing Bo Xilai's rule in Chongqing before his fall from power. But it is well to remember that in the Cultural Revolution period itself literature and music were restricted to a narrow range of approved works, with the work of Beethoven being banned and Lu Xun only tolerated as a searing critic of the old China rather than a supporter of free thought and liberalism (Yu, 2011). The creation of eight model 'red' operas and ballets with their pastiche of ballet forms and traditional northern Chinese peasant dancing, their cast of characters including imperialists, proletarian workers and exploiting landlords, are symptomatic of an era in which everyday life was invaded by political actions and intervention.

The true legacy of the Cultural Revolution in terms of art is probably not the works that were produced during this period, but those that appeared afterwards, which memorialized and commemorated its effect on the spirit and life of a nation recovering from the trauma of the Maoist era. Ba Jin, who died in 2005 at the age of 100, represents the ambiguity of this period – a writer from the 1930s whose fidelity to the CCP's cause was to be undermined by the treatment he and his wife received at the hands of zealous radicals in the late 1960s. Ba Jin's most searching work is a collection of short essays, *Random Thoughts*, produced from the 1980s onwards, in which he returns repeatedly to the question of why China had gone though this extended festival of grim self-attack and internal loathing (Ba, 1984). For Ba, the responsibility was to memorialize, to try to establish, physically and artistically, a museum of the Cultural Revolution period, so that some meaning could be made of it. In an essay criticizing Ba Jin in 2011, Yu Hua wondered aloud why it was that Ba Jin, for all his courage in demanding this in the 1980s, had never fully questioned his own support for anti-intellectual campaigns prior to 1966, nor been wholly candid about the real culpability for the Cultural Revolution and the suffering attached to it, when it was the CCP itself that remained in power and had in some way shifted blame for the event onto previous misguided leaders and their devious advisers who had perverted the course of the revolution (Yu, 2011).

From 1978, a genre of writing captured this confusion. 'Wounded literature' was an outpouring of anger, grief and pain at what had happened over the previous decade – a return to some forms of expressivity in a period of comparative openness, by writers such as Zhang Xianliang, whose work referred to life in the prison camps during the Cultural Revolution, or the Tianjin author, Sun Li, whose short accounts of a travelling life before and after the Cultural Revolution expressed as much through what they hid as what they explicitly stated. This tradition had deep roots in Chinese literature. Perhaps the finest novelist modern China has produced, Qian Zhongshu, with his wife, the writer and translator Yang Jiang, represented this well, through the eloquent brevity of their accounts of being sent down to Cadre Schools in the late 1960s, their language pared down to the minimum as they tried to convey the emptiness of a period in which fundamental human relations and the value of trust were undermined. Yang Jiang's *A Cadre Life in Six Chapters* (Yang, 1986) remains the finest, and the briefest, work remembering this period. The strategy of others, such as short-story writer Sheng Congwen, was simply to migrate to writing about non-contentious issues – in his case, the history of clothing. At least through this strategy he avoided the fate of the playwright Lao She, who was hounded to death in 1967.

After the 1980s, two forms of expression became dominant. Of the first, the best representative is Wang Shuo, whose irrelevant 'hooligan' literature captures the heady, energetic and anarchic atmosphere of post-reform China in its early days. Wang's burlesque humour spawned a number of popular films, and is typified by the belligerent remarks he puts into the mouth of one protagonist, who declares that 'The sole objective is to piss people off. If I am not pissing people off, then I have failed.' A little later, a new genre of Chinese 'chick lit' kicked off with *Shanghai Babe*, a steamy tale of cynical exploitation by Wen Hui, a highly photogenic female author from Shanghai. Wang Shuo and his chick lit colleagues captured the strain of tired cynicism that has prevailed in much of the PRC in the twenty-first century.

Perhaps most striking of all was the way in which the highly formulaic, rigid language of the elite leaders had become separated from the natural language used in daily life in the PRC. Relating the pompous, contorted formulations of a declaration such as Hu Jintao's at the 17th Party Congress in October 2007 to how people communicated with each other normally proved challenging. Elite leaders in the past (particularly Mao), had been earthier in the registers they used. Mao's words, however, were almost never conveyed publicly, and his speeches, when he deigned to give them, were in closed sessions, with variant versions being leaked out as time went on. His language was strewn with so many expletives that it needed sanitization by a team of ghostwriters. Some utterances still await clean-up work before publication. For Deng, his thick Sichuanese accent meant that when he did try to speak to an audience, most Chinese found him almost impossible to understand. Only with Jiang Zemin and Hu Jintao did the set public utterance make an appearance – and in Hu Jintao the PRC had its first key leader who was able to speak relatively standard Mandarin.

This distance between the language of the rulers and that of the ruled carried profound symbolic meaning. Yu Hua complained that, in modern China, the only thing that could not be slandered and lied about was the top leadership, who inhabit a zone of carefully protected sanctity. Anything else was fair game, with attacks being unleashed on almost every subject, public figure or institution. The search for a more convincing public register was one of the great tasks of the CCP leadership, but one it was appearing hard-pressed to achieve.

By the 2000s, contemporary Chinese literature began to have an impact internationally, with the sensational *Wolf Totem*, by Jiang Rong, which appealed to the memories of sent-down youths from the Cultural Revolution (Rong, 2009). For Jiang (the pseudonym for Lu Jiamin), the setting was Inner Mongolia during the 1960s, a place that had experienced a particularly vicious purge against CCP members, most of whom were of Mongolian ethnicity. The tragic events of this era left a deep mark on people's memories, with Beijing admitting in 1980 during the partial rehabilitations that over 22,000 people had died, and many tens of thousands more had been mistreated, tortured and wounded over the period 1966 to 1976, the bulk of the violence occurring in the first three years. The fact that this period was still sensitive mean that Jiang's book, when it appeared in Chinese, attracted close attention, selling over two million copies and being one of the first to have a major impact in the West when it was published in English. Critics of Jiang's book were struck by its highly contestable ethnic politics, with Mongolians equated to being noble savage wolves, and the Han as in some way enlightened, albeit invasive, outsiders. The decision to award Mo Yan the Nobel

Prize for Literature in 2012 went some way to reassuring Chinese writers they now had some global reach.

Literature did, however, give some voice to those who had largely been unheard during the chaos of the reform period when there had been change almost every day. Sheng Keyi, originally from Hunan province, is representative of this group – a woman from a rural area who worked in Shenzhen with migrant labourers before becoming an author. Her *Northern Girls* was written in the 2000s but published in English translation in 2011. It plots the lives of two women from the countryside surviving in the cut-throat world of urban China where jobs are lost and won in a single day, rape and abortion common, and police brutality a fact of life. Despite this, Sheng portrays the sense of solidarity amongst this vulnerable and rootless segment of modern Chinese society, and shows their humour, optimism and humanity.

Popular Culture: Music and Films

One area where China did have figures that achieved international recognition was in films, where they were commonly addressed as the fifth generation of film directors – ones that had come of age after 1980 – and began to attract critical attention. Pre-1949, China had a flourishing film industry, largely based in Shanghai, and it was indeed from this world that Mao's third and final wife, Jiang Qing, had emerged. Films immediately after 1949 were heavily propagandistic, culminating in works such as *The East is Red* from 1966, a lengthy filmic act of worship directed at Mao, and screened with clearly signalled epic aspirations but a highly limited aesthetic impact.

The works after 1980 were different. One of the most powerful, a multi-part series for television in 1987 called *Yellow River*, contained a powerful critique of the weight of Chinese culture in modern life, using the Yellow River as a symbol. After a very successful initial showing on the national TV station, it was banned, partly because it was blamed for creating the environment that, in the political elite's eyes, at any rate, was responsible for the outright defiance against the Party by key groups in 1989. The films of Chen Kaige and Zhang Yimou became the most celebrated, with Zhang's career in particular offering a vignette of the paths of Chinese artists in the 1990s and beyond.

Zhang was a graduate of the Beijing Film School, where he had studied at the same time as Ai Wei Wei. His first successful work was an adaptation of a novel by Mo Yan, *Yellow Earth*, set during the Sino-Japanese war. Zhang's productions in the 1990s won him a garland of international prizes – *Raise the Red Lantern* from 1993 in particular winning international recognition. It was based on a novel by Su Tong about female rivalry and suppression in the Qing Dynasty. Zhang's *Ju Dou* strayed into the sensitive territory of infidelity in China, and it was the banning of this film because of its ostensibly racy, unwholesome content (in the eyes of the authorities) that first indicated that Zhang had run foul of the authorities.

Zhang's powerful cinematography was what captured the attention of critics outside China – and his keen sense of drama. But for critics within the country, he simply represented a skewed view of China and its faults, which they felt pandered to Western preconceptions and prejudices. This was a criticism trotted out from many quarters on almost every Chinese product that had any measure of success outside the country. It also was

Box 7.1 The power of song

One of the great enigmas of the contemporary PRC has been its failure to produce a single internationally successful pop singer. In many ways, the PRC remained the key target market for Taiwanese and Hong Kong singers, but very few mainland Chinese made any kind of impact in return, even in Chinese-speaking communities. 'Cantopop' enjoyed huge success with figures such as Faye Wong (Wang Wei Fei) and Andy Lau gathering vast hordes of followers across China from the early 1990s. But the greatest pop singer of post-1980 greater China was Teresa Teng (Deng Lijun), a Taiwanese ballad singer whose soulful love songs had swept China in the 1980s, prompting jokes that in fact there were two Dengs who really ran the PRC – Deng Xiaoping who ran the country during the day, and the singer who ran it by night.

Teresa Teng's own life ended tragically early in 1995 when she died of a respiratory attack while in Thailand (she was a lifelong sufferer from asthma). But the sales of her records continue, and the sound of either her own versions of songs, or cadres or business people mimicking them, floats up from karaoke parlours and nightclubs to this day across the length and breadth of the PRC. One issue that Teng's career does highlight is the extraordinary success of Taiwanese soft power in the PRC. Even in 2012, Taiwanese pop singers and film stars and, in the case of Ang Lee, directors, are more influential and exportable than their PRC equivalents. The Taiwanese, after all (rather than the Japanese), were the inventors of karaoke, and their export has conquered the PRC in ways that eerily reciprocate the rather different kind of conquest of the CCP.

Illustration 7.1 An opera singer being photographed, Beijing

No society has ever developed on such a scale and so quickly as China. Many embrace this fact with excitement and enthusiasm, but for many there is a lingering nostalgia for the quieter, plainer past they have come to believe in, and icons of 'traditional' Chinese culture are appealed to for reassurance and a sense of identity.

used energetically against Gong Li, Zhang's leading lady and for a time his lover, whose huge success in the USA and Europe was attacked bitterly by some Chinese commentators, attacks compounded by her marrying a Singaporean and acquiring Singaporean nationality herself during the 2000s.

After his clash with the authorities, Zhang performed an abrupt turnaround, producing the commercially successful *Hero* in 2002, based on historic tales from the period of the First Emperor. The peak of Zhang's acceptance by the Party was his appointment to be artistic director of both the opening and closing ceremonies of the 2008 Olympic Games. He had come a long way since the 1992 *The Story of Qiu Ju*, which recounted the search for justice, by a character played by Gong Li, against a local official who had beaten up her husband. The more epic register of his latest works is shown in *Coming Home,* released in 2014, which tells the story of a Chinese returnee from the USA who ends up in a labour camp in Maoist China. Many felt that his immensely successful later films lacked the raw bite and energy of his simpler earlier ones. A more brutal view of contemporary China could be found in *Blind Shaft*, a 2003 production which plotted the careers of two conmen who murder miners and then claim their compensation. The portrayal of a China of cheap brothels, vicious mine owners and almost constant insecurity and hardship was evidently too close to the bone for Chinese authorities, who promptly banned it once it appeared. One of the most acclaimed of the most recent generation of directors, Jia Zhangke, has also enjoyed critical acclaim abroad for films like *Still Life* (2006) and *A Touch of Sin* (2013) but also experienced problems with the censors back home.

Free: Within a Cage

The issue of what is, and what is not, tolerated in the PRC of the twenty-first century is among the most vexed and the most confusing. On the one hand, Chinese people have probably never been freer in terms of how they conduct their lives, the role of the local and national forms of the state in their daily existence, and the ability to choose life directions. And yet bewildering levels of censorship exist, from the lists sent out to newspapers and journals from the Ministry of Propaganda about what can and cannot be covered, to restrictions on which books are available and which are banned, and directives about where state financial support for the arts can, and cannot, be given.

This is an important issue, as much for Chinese artists and public intellectuals working within this environment as for those on the outside who are trying to understand what is going on. For the Chinese authors who attract official displeasure, at best their works will not be publishable or performable – and at worst, they can find themselves detained, harassed or imprisoned. Yu Jie, author of a scathing 2009 biography of Wen Jiabao that attacked his benign public image as a charade masking sharp political ambition, was first banned from publishing in the PRC. Then he was subjected to violent attacks by state security agents before fleeing the country in 2012. In exile in the USA, he was to write a similarly damning work on Xi Jinping, calling him 'China's Godfather', comparing him to the boss of a mafia ring. Liao Yiwu, author of the powerful performance poem, *Scream*, about the 1989 massacres, and of a subsequent collection of real-life accounts of figures from contemporary Chinese society, *The Corpse Walker* (Liao, 2009), was also forced to flee the country, in this case to Germany after lengthy harassment in 2011. The usual attack point from the authorities has been that authors have engaged in subversive behaviour and offended public taste. The possibility that one of the functions of art and literature might be to question some of these boundaries has been discounted. Following the example of the Soviet Union, the artistic policies of the Beijing leadership have been conservative and risk averse. Cultural work has almost always been seen within a political framework.

Censorship, however, has proved an immense enterprise, because the CCP encouraged creativity and free thinking in some areas, and yet militated fiercely against it in others. The boundaries of the policed areas were constantly moving, accounting for books being publishable one day, then quickly withdrawn from circulation the next, after coming to the attention of powerful figures. On the internet there were many writers who were able to practise a new version of highly creative censorship evasion, by deploying heavily coded ways of speaking about sensitive issues. The dense talk from 2004 from the central leadership of the 'harmonious society', 'hexie shehui' in Chinese, was cleverly translated into discussions of 'water crabs', which happened to be a homonym of the word 'harmony'. The internet was full, therefore, of loaded conversations about the usefulness or not of water crabs, the ability of the government to promote them successfully or at least to preserve them, and the ways in which water crabs might be smashed or destroyed. Practised readers of this material knew well that the real objective was a critique of official discourse on the notion of a harmonious society. In these clever internet campaigns, activists were digging into an honourable tradition of sardonic wit and irony, one practised for centuries in eras in which to state something overtly was to risk being punished or even executed. The issue, however, for a society so laden with double meanings was where, and how, to locate the truth, and how to sort out what to believe, and what to see as something referring to something else. In more ways than one, therefore, the PRC became increasingly, to borrow the phrase of French philosopher, Roland Barthes, 'an empire of signs'. The battle was about how to interpret those signs, and who had the power to arbitrate between contested meanings.

The Ghost of Confucius

The comeback of Confucius has been one of the greatest turnarounds in modern Chinese history. The fact that the image of Confucius appeared during the 2008 Olympics opening ceremony while that of Mao did not was commented on in Chapter 1, as was the use of his name and image to spearhead the government's soft power campaign abroad through the opening of Confucius Institutes. Perhaps even more noteworthy is the invocation of his thought by intellectuals in the PRC, such as international relations expert Yan Xuetong and philosopher Jiang Qing. While some rail against the virus of Confucianism and the critical mission to finally root out his pernicious influence, others have reconstructed his image in a modern guise and appeal to it for support in their own arguments and programmes.

This has not been a wholly straightforward process, however. While attempts to erect a statue of him in Tiananmen Square in 2010 failed, this did not stop elite political leaders in the CCP, such as Hu Jintao, referring indirectly to ideas that were at least imputed by others to the Sage – the notions, for example, of harmony, and of a harmonious society to which the country's president referred from 2004, partly as a code to indicate that the CCP was taking the issues of rising inequality in Chinese society seriously and trying to do something about it.

By 2010, over 500 Confucian Institutes existed across the world, in places as far afield as Australia, the USA, Africa and across Europe. In some places, these managed to arouse virulent feelings. For some, they were simply examples of crude state-directed propaganda, embedded more often than not in reputable universities, which stood accused by some of the critics of taking the money from the Chinese state and then censoring themselves. This was perhaps a simplification. Some of these institutes ran events at which poets, writers and thinkers who were banned in China were able to speak. Others simply concentrated on language learning. Finding hard proof of the Chinese government dictating what centres might do proved difficult. But in terms of perception, the institutions highlighted the complexity with which China was viewed by much of the rest of the world. In the eyes of some, they were pushing a benign, rose-tinted view of a China of cuddly pandas, picturesque stretches of the Great Wall and wonderful cuisine. For many, they had no authenticity, and had no part to play in trying to discuss the less attractive aspects of a country beset by social, environmental and political issues.

And for a time at least, the Chinese government's interests in soft power were considerable. During President Hu Jintao's visit to the USA in January 2011, a film of different Chinese people speaking to the camera about their lives was played on one of the giant screens in Times Square. The Chinese Central Television station expanded abroad, and established a channel purely in English, featuring programmes such as *Dialogue*, where eminent Western thinkers were grilled about their views on the global economy or about China. Xinhua, the official news agency, began to expand its international presence, as well as setting up its own television station. And the English-language newspaper, *China Daily*, again owned by the Ministry of Propaganda, started to appear in international editions across Europe and North America, even managing to do a deal where it was available as a pullout from the *Washington Post* several times a month.

Surveys from 2009 onwards showed that the image of China had improved across the world, and that many in the West regarded it in a positive light. According to the Pew Research Center, from 2008 onwards, the Chinese population was increasingly satisfied with the government and the image presented of their country. But this sat uneasily with evidence from both inside and outside the country that there were areas of nuance and contention, and that questions about the outside world, when asked in China, produced wildly different responses depending on the way they were asked, and the same applied to those outside the country.

In the end, no single image or idea captured what China was becoming, and its impact on the world. Bloggers in 2009 within China furiously debated the Pixar blockbuster cartoon film from the USA, *Kung Fu Panda*, and why it was that a film full of Chinese themes and symbols, which had been hugely popular across the world including in China itself, was the product of people who were not Chinese. 'Why,' one irate netizen asked, 'can't we do this?' This undercurrent of lack of confidence was illustrated by the fact that the central government's Ministry of Culture allowed only 20 non-Chinese films to be put on general release from 2009 throughout the country's cinemas – this despite the fact that almost every major film, wherever it was from, was quickly copied and then distributed illegally despite several major clampdowns by the authorities. Yu Hua, the Beijing writer, complained that China was the land of the copycat, and, in fact, copying had become so endemic that the real thing was, in some ways, an anomaly.

By the second decade of the twenty-first century, politically and culturally at least, China had come almost full circle from a century before, when the young, protesting students during the 4 May 1919 movement had dreamed of an authentic Chinese version of modernity – something from them, from their lives and souls, and from their own soil. A refrain from intellectuals throughout the twentieth century, and repeated into the twenty-first, was that the template of modernity had come from outside the country, and that there was something unjust and inappropriate in this. The most candid authors, people such as Qian Zhongshu, admitted that the greatest crisis was the country's fight with its own history, with the victim mentality that had been born in it from its century of humiliation from 1839, and from the terrible suffering during its external and internal wars in the middle decades of the twentieth century. The hunt for an appropriate image of a modern, but authentically Chinese, self-identity continued, and looks set do so in the years ahead, as China's political, social and cultural values struggle to keep pace with its economy.

One of the figures who seemed best able to achieve this was the Shanghai-based racing driver who had become a popular online writer, Han Han. Han Han typified Generation Y in China, from his urban lifestyle to his nonchalant writing style in which he expressed a general cynicism, much of it directed at figures like Confucius and his great cultural comeback. His attitude to the strong expressions of patriotism in China and the worship of money have made him, like Ai Wei Wei, a popular moralist at least outside the country, and his style is accessible and direct. But even someone as fast-paced as Han had problems keeping up in a country almost permanently on the move. It was therefore not surprising that Xi Jinping, when addressing artistic figures in October 2014, talked nostalgically of the need for artists to address themes of real life, daily struggle and morally edifying messages. It was hard to know whether he too was not being deeply ironic, in view of the cultural maelstrom surrounding him.

8

China in the World

In the three decades since 1978, China's international role has become more important. As an importer, exporter, investor and geopolitical player, the PRC now ranks as one of the world's key countries. It has emerged from the era of Maoist isolation to become a potential superpower. Since the beginning of the twenty-first century, as its economy has grown, more and more pressure has been put on the country's leaders to speak out on the PRC's main international objectives. A number of government statements have attempted to define these, talking reassuringly of a country that is rising peacefully and seeking win–win outcomes, avoiding the kind of hegemony that the world experienced under European and, latterly, American, dominance. Xi Jinping in particular talks of the 'China Dream', something that should be positive and benign for everyone and which the world can share in. And yet the PRC has also been accused of having covert aims to exploit more of the world's international space for its own ends, seeking to assert itself in the Asia-Pacific region, and nursing historical grievances, in particular against Japan, but more widely against the old colonizing powers from Europe which, it feels, visited humiliation on it in the past. The vastness of China's economic impact means that its international role is no longer so easy to ignore. But the complexity of the country's internal situation is reflected in the lack of an easy framework in which the outside world can place it. On the one hand, it is a vibrant, free-market supporter that has signed up to most international agreements on trade, supporting free-trade concords and becoming a key player in the World Trade Organization. On the other hand, it is accused by some of concealing long-term aims to dominate the region, and then the wider world, for its own ends. Building a relationship with the country's leaders has become a key preoccupation of those who are running most major Western countries, and international organizations. And yet, in many ways, China, just by being one of the world's final countries with a Marxist party enjoying a monopoly on power, strikes a sometimes discordant note, accused of being purely self-interested in its international relations, and supporting some of the world's most egregious offenders on human rights. The foreign policy of key players such as the USA and the EU is often geared to trying to influence the behaviour of China. But there are frequent nasty shocks, like China's use of its veto alongside the Russians on the UN Security Council in February 2012 against condemnation of the Syrian government's suppression of internal demonstrations. Getting China right for external policy-makers will be a key challenge in the years ahead – and yet China itself seems less easy to second-guess as it becomes a major international player.

The Five Principles of Peaceful Coexistence

After the revolution in 1949, the newly established PRC entered an initial phase where it was a member of the Communist bloc, and regarded itself as being closely aligned with countries allied with the USSR. After its falling out with these countries, the PRC entered a period of isolation. During the Cultural Revolution, China's friends were few and far between. It enjoyed cordial relations with Albania, because of their unorthodox attitude to the international Communist movement, and regarded itself as the leader of revolutionary movements in much of the developing world. But this posture often antagonized other countries, with China being accused of funding anti-government forces and creating instability beyond its borders.

This was ironic, because the principles that the PRC had enunciated, through Premier Zhou En-lai at the Bandung Conference in 1955, were very firmly against interfering in the affairs of other countries, and for respecting the sovereignty of fellow states (see Table 8.1). These principles had originated in discussions between the PRC and India over the status of Tibet in the 1950s.

The newly founded PRC's moral stance on this was clearly based on its own historical experience of suffering from interference by other powers in its internal situation, through war, aggression and colonial

Table 8.1 The Five Principles of Peaceful Coexistence, 1955

- Mutual respect for each other's territorial integrity and sovereignty
- Mutual non-aggression
- Mutual non-interference in each other's internal affairs
- Equality and mutual benefit
- Peaceful coexistence

exploitation. So the Five Principles were based on bitter experience, and were at the heart of Chinese foreign policy for the next six decades.

In the years of isolation, it was easy enough for the PRC to avoid involvement in international issues. It had no seat in the United Nations until 1971, when, through the support of a two-thirds majority of UN members, it was allowed to replace the Republic of China, but was not formally recognized by the USA until 1978. But, as Richard Nixon noted in 1968, before becoming president, having a nation of over 800 million people outside the international system, especially one that now had the atomic bomb, made no sense. The 1970s mark a period during which China began to become, through its involvement in the UN, and through its rapprochement with the USA, more deeply embedded in the international system. But until 1979 it was a relatively isolated and largely misunderstood player, and one seen as being introspective, cut off and impenetrable.

China's economic changes also transformed its international role. As it became a larger participant in manufacturing, it also started to attract overseas investors, and embedded itself in international supply chains that led its interests directly into the affairs of others. Chinese peacekeeping troops began to appear in international UN-led operations, and it began to be a key part of international agreements on non-proliferation of weapons and conventions on human rights or security issues. By 2001, with the country's entry to the WTO, China had already effectively reversed the policy of remaining outside international treaties and organizations. It was now, more often than not, at their centre; and as globalization continued into the 2000s, its role through the G20, and even talk of a G2, became more central.

The Five Principles of Peaceful Co-existence sit beside another key statement on China's international role, one supposedly enunciated by paramount leader Deng Xiaoping in the 1980s. This is the '24-Character Statement': remain cool-headed to observe; be ready to react; stand firmly; hide your capabilities and bide your time; never try to take the lead; and be able to accomplish something. There remains controversy over when, where or even *if* Deng made such a statement, but it has gained an almost canonical status in the last few years, as an indication of how China wishes to keep to sorting out its own problems and not be dragged into becoming something of a global policeman, like the USA. A more sceptical look at the statement, however, sees in it the latent promise that one day, once its capacity has been built up, the PRC will seek to dominate the world, but until then it is biding its time.

The Peaceful Rise

Attempts to modernize China's international aspect have been led by the senior Party School official in Beijing, Zheng Bijian, who was at the forefront from 2004 of the 'Peaceful Rise' doctrine, first spelt out in the US magazine *Foreign Affairs* and subsequently in a number of speeches. The Peaceful Rise doctrine was an attempt to reassure those unnerved by the country's rapid economic growth, and those who feared it was harbouring ambitions to be more dominant in the international system. Fractious relations with the USA, in particular during 2000 and 2001, and fears about China's intent towards Taiwan and the potential use of full-on military force there were the more tangible signs of this unease. But there were plenty of other clues, for the PRC's critics, that it was becoming a disruptive new major player in the international order. It was close to unpopular regimes, for example that of the Democratic People's Republic of Korea (DPRK), of the Sudan during the vicious civil war there, and of Zimbabwe, where it was accused in 2007 of shipping arms to support the reviled dictator Robert Mugabe. China's maintenance of its non-intervention stance was seen as hypocritical when it was often providing infrastructure and making investments to support its own investment interests. The most worrying aspect of China's rise, however, was the element of strong nationalism that many saw in public opinion in the country. Sometimes, over-excited generals in the PLA were accused of expressing this. One in particular, Xiong Guangkai, bragged that the USA might want to choose between poking its nose into China–Taiwan affairs and having some of its western-edge cities wiped out by a nuclear attack. Such bellicosity was not, thankfully, reflected in the elite politicians, who steered clear of picking fights with the rest of the world. But China's attempts to clear up its border disputes, to source its burgeoning needs for energy in the outside world and to find markets for its goods meant its presence was felt in almost every part of the globe, stable and unstable, and its international exposure has increased by the year.

The doctrine of China's Peaceful Rise was designed partly to reassure the outside world, and partly to explain what China's international stance might be, especially as its leaders were, on the whole, stiff and awkward before the media, and avoided confrontations with interviewers asking sharp questions about China's internal affairs. Hu Jintao, in particular, gave no one-to-one interviews with any Western media during his period in power, and was only once faced by a media pack while at the White House during his final visit to the USA in January 2011. Chinese Ministry of Foreign Affairs spokespeople often use the language of respect for the affairs of other countries, international equality, and seeking win–win situations. But from 2009, as the global economic crisis ate into the resources of the developed world, many accused China of being assertive and bullying. Some examples of this will be dealt with later in this chapter. As the 2000s wore on, the idea of Peaceful Rise was married to that of China offering an alternative model of development to Western capitalism. The Beijing model was touted in parts of Africa, Latin America and elsewhere in Asia – being seen as giving state direction a stronger say in the running of the economy and in seeking ways to hunt out new technologies that were not reliant on the developed world. Chinese officials themselves were, however, loath to admit publicly that they had such ambitions, and said more often than not that they felt the Chinese way to development had, in many respects, been unique and would be hard for other countries to emulate. This was particularly underlined by the fact that Wen Jiabao himself simply said that the Chinese model was 'unsustainable.' In that case, why ask others to follow it?

The nationalist argument in China, according to Liu Xiaobo, was driven by the idea that the country was so great that it existed at the centre of the world, and that in becoming a rich, strong nation again it needed to seek recompense from those who had laid it low in the past. The CCP had worked up a narrative since 1949 of returning the country to proud, strong unity, and changing it from being a victim at the hands of external aggressors and imperialists. They claimed a history of peaceful unity on which the current China was founded, something interrupted by the century of humiliation after the first Opium War of 1839. In fact, as I argued earlier in this book, Chinese dynasties before the rise of the CCP had fought land battles to extend the western and northern borders of the country. But the statement that China was never an aggressor from 1949 was not correct, even though, on some counts, there were plenty of wars in which the PRC was involved, from the unwilling fighting of over a million of its soldiers in the Korean War from 1950 to 1953 to the more willing attacks on India in 1962, Russia in 1969, and Vietnam in 1979. Maoist China was often a fractious power. With economic strength, would this feature return, only this time with far larger ambitions? Ultra-nationalists in China, as anywhere, are keen to pick fights with anyone who slightly questions what they regard as their inalienable rights. But the question is: would China, in the end, get involved in battles when a peaceful, stable international environment had served it so well in terms of helping its economy grow and bringing it prosperity?

In order to placate at least some of the nervous critics outside the country, the government used the language of 'peaceful development' from the mid-2000s onwards. For many, though, the question of what China, and the Chinese themselves, wanted now they were growing wealthier, became an important one to answer. For the elite, from the late Qing, through the Republican era, into the Maoist and reform periods, the dream was always to create a 'rich, strong country'. But in the late 2000s, this became tougher. Should China see itself as an emerging superpower, trying first to aim for regional dominance, then to compete with the USA globally? Should it think even more boldly, and see itself as presenting not just a new economic and developmental model, but a new way of conducting diplomacy, offering different, more pragmatic values to a West that had become mired in the war against Islamic extremism and terrorism in Iraq from 2003, and Afghanistan since 2001? Many outside China, disillusioned with what the traditional great powers offered, wanted to see if China was able to offer something different – less morally hectoring, and more respectful of the values and integrity of other countries and their right to determine their own affairs. Yan Xuetong, a professor of international relations at the elite Qinghua University in Beijing, stated that China needed to look at its ancient history and the philosophers from over two and a half millennia before, living in or soon after the time of Confucius, who etched out, he felt, a relevant model of states respecting, listening and understanding each other, which the contemporary world could use. For Yan, the aim was for China to offer the same kinds of ideas, beliefs and role model that the USA had, until the Bush presidency. But even within China, this ambition was fiercely disputed, with some arguing that China barely had enough time to deal with its own immense internal issues without setting itself up as a model for others, and some wondering how it might offer a moral vision that might be attractive beyond its borders. The simple fact was that, since 1978, China had become more integrated, not just economically but also politically in the world system; it had become involved in most international decision-making forums; it had established a global network of diplomatic partners; and had, more often than not, co-operated with the system, at least on issues that did not impact on it directly. Since it took up its seat in the UN in 1971, it had only used its veto seven times, against the dozens of times that the USA had deployed vetoes (most of them on resolutions that condemned Israel's behaviour). China's relations with key partners were at the heart of its diplomatic challenges, and this chapter will look at those in the Asian region, the USA, Russia, Africa, the EU, and the developing world generally (Yan, 2011).

China in the Asian Region

Whatever kind of power China is, it is an Asian one. It shares borders with 14 other countries, and is in dispute with several over maritime border issues. It has one outstanding dispute with India still running on its land borders, something that has caused immense fractiousness between the two. China's Asian role is a key one, as are its relations with countries around it in the area where it is most likely to have problems, as their issues impinge on it far more directly than powers geographically more distant.

China's key relationship in Asia, in terms of trade at least, is with Japan, but it is also one of its most difficult relationships. Their shared history is a dark one, with war, aggression and conflict at its heart. From 1937 to 1945, as many as 20 million died in the Sino-Japanese War (known in China as the War of Resistance to Japan), one of the worst in history in terms of levels of violence and numbers of casualties. When victory came, it did so at the cost not only of so many lives, but also of the country's infrastructure and its political integrity. Events such as the Rape of Nanjing in 1937, where, as noted earlier, as many as 300,000 died in a massacre by rampaging Japanese troops, still linger powerfully in the collective memory, with a major museum to commemorate the dead being established in the city, and, from the 1990s, a number of memorial days and events to ensure that the Chinese never forget the suffering from this event. This has not been helped by the denial by some prominent Japanese, including, most recently, the mayor of Nagoya, a city in Japan twinned with Nanjing, who told a visiting Chinese delegation in February 2012 that he doubted that civilians had in fact died in the event (Mitter, 2013).

Japan's relations with China over the Reform period have, despite this tragic history, been strong. Japan was one of the first, and the largest, to give aid and finance to China as it began its economic reforms, after signing a friendship agreement with China in 1978. Companies such as Toyota, Sony and Mitsubishi were major investors in the country. Many see strong elements of the Japanese restarting of their economy in the 1950s and 1960s in what the Chinese have done. Many Chinese respect the way in which Japan became the world's second-largest economy through modernizing successfully, though China supplanted it in 2010. The Chinese also admire Japan's ability to create globally successful brands. But the political links between the two countries are always at the mercy of nationalist sentiment in China, and of the constant need, expressed with increasing intensity since 1990, for Japan to give a stronger apology for what happened in the past. The most difficult period in recent times was between 2001 and 2006, when the then prime minister of Japan, Junichiro Koizumi, insisted on visiting the Yasukuni Shrine in Tokyo to commemorate Japanese war dead, despite the fact that it has grade one listed war criminals buried there. Over this period, no senior Chinese leader visited Japan, as a sign of anger at this public lack of contrition. In 2005, Japanese lobbying to gain a seat among the UN Security Council permanent members was blocked energetically by China. Even worse were the riots that broke out in the same year in Beijing, when the Japanese football team was victorious in a match against the Chinese national team in a leg of the Asian Cup.

Diplomatic effort cooled this period down, but in 2010 there was another dangerous moment when a drunken Chinese sea captain allowed the ship he was in charge of to ram a Japanese coastguard vessel near one of the disputed maritime borders in the East China Sea. The detention of the captain created national outrage in China, with bloggers growing increasingly bellicose and demanding that their government get tough. A delegation of Japanese schoolchildren intending to visit the Shanghai Expo being held that summer had their invitations withdrawn. The Chinese government spokesperson expressed anger at the 'illegal detention' on behalf of all Chinese. Matters were only resolved when the Japanese authorities ordered the release of the captain.

The events of 2010 only reminded the rest of the region, and the world, how deep was some of the animosity between these two major powers. The change in the power dynamics between them was symbolized best by the moment when, late in 2010, China overtook Japan, at least in gross terms, as the world's second-largest economy. With the return of Shinzo Abe as Prime Minister in 2013, however, the relations entered perhaps their longest downward period in recent history, with Abe visiting the Yasukuni Shrine in December 2013 despite advice from Japan's key ally, the USA, not to do so. In 2014, with the creation by the Chinese of a special Air Defence Zone that came close to Japanese territory, and clashes between aircraft and ships, many started to talk about an imminent military conflict in the area. Abe seemed to articulate a more aggressive response back to what was interpreted as China's pushiness in the region, and was receiving plaudits at home for it – the one audience that mattered to him.

With North Korea, China had a different attitude, with officials over the age of 50 often joking that this country reminded them of how China had been in the late Mao period. The challenges posed by the DPRK's nuclear programme, made public in 2007, were no joke, however. China was the isolated North Korea's last substantial ally. Senior leaders crossed the borders between the two with great regularity, with the late Kim Jong-il, 'dear leader' of the North Koreans, visiting China no fewer than three times within 18 months during 2010–11 to cement the succession of his third son, Kim Jong-un, who replaced him in December 2011.

Most Chinese people were disdainful of the poverty of people living in the DPRK. But their links were deep historic ones. The founder of the regime, Kim Il-sung, had lived in China, and fought on the side of the Chinese Communists in the Sino-Japanese War. This closeness was termed officially as being more intimate 'than lips and teeth'. Visiting Chinese leaders were accorded the highest possible accolades and treatment when they went to Pyongyang. This was underlined by the simple fact that over half of the country's trade, and more than 90 per cent of its energy, came from the PRC. In 2007, rumours circulated that, to express its anger over the nuclear programme, the PRC had simply turned off the DPRK's energy supply for three days.

Of all contemporary China's international relations, the one with the DPRK falls most easily into that which on the surface looks like a vassal-state relationship. The PRC has been accused of trying to emulate the imperial habit of regarding foreign powers as having asymmetrical relations with it, recalling an ancient period when countries such as Vietnam were supposedly obliged to bring yearly tributes to Beijing to express good-neighbourliness. The interpretation of this custom has become a hot topic in recent years, with some simply dismissing it as an ancient custom maintained long after it had any meaning, and others saying it indicated something profound about the Chinese world view. That Chinese officials sometimes talked with patronizing disdain about the DPRK was true, even stating in the popular press and in blogs that the country is China's 'little brother'. A Chinese vice-minister of foreign affairs, according to one of the leaked cables publicized in Wikileaks in 2009, complained of how the DPRK was often akin to a spoilt child, demanding much more attention than it merited. But the DPRK's strategy of unleashing surprising and unwelcome events on the world was best shown in its launch of another nuclear test on the eve of the G20 summit held in London in April 2009. When the world accused China of being the only party with any real influence over the secretive DPRK leadership, many in the Chinese government protested that they had as little idea as any other country about what was truly going on in North Korea. With the collapse of the Six Party Talks involving the USA, South Korea, Japan, Russia, China and the DPRK in 2007, it seemed that only through Beijing putting pressure on the Pyongyang regime would there be any meaningful change.

This was not to underplay the mutual distrust between the two, despite this unique relationship. In many ways, the DPRK seemed trapped with its vast neighbour, though it wanted most of all to talk directly to the USA. Attempts to resurrect the Six Party Talks are going nowhere however, with the leadership in Pyongyang prone to capricious moves such as inviting US basketball player Denis Rodman to undertake demonstration games under the eyes of the new young leader. Not so amusing was the execution of one of the people believed to be Kim's key advisor, his uncle, who was shown on state television being physically removed from a Korean Workers Party meeting. That the executed uncle was one of those regarded as closest to the Chinese and most in sympathy with adopting some of the elements of the reform programme to see if it worked at home was also ominous. Chinese policy-makers admitted that they felt little connection with their neighbour and very little sympathy with it. The only certainty was that they did not want another US ally in the form of a unified Korea on their border.

The situation is less harmonious with the PRC's other Communist neighbour in the Asia region. Vietnam, unlike the DPRK, is a regime that has been reforming and expanding its economy in ways that bear some resemblance to China's activities. The country has, however, a fractious relationship with the PRC, and the two saw all-out war as recently as 1979, with further skirmishes in 1984. Deng Xiaoping's declaration that he would teach the Vietnamese a lesson was, in fact, to deliver only a Pyrrhic victory. The Sino-Vietnamese War of 1979 ended with huge casualties for the PLA and a general loss of face, with their army sucked into a bloody contest and making a quick retreat after declaring symbolic victory. That China had been irritated by the Vietnamese invasion of Cambodia in January 1979, when they had felled the brief but bloody regime led by Pol Pot, was only one of the reasons for their strike on Vietnam. The conflict continues in different ways to this day, feeding on centuries of mutual distrust and strategic competition. The greatest impediment to wholly smooth relations in the years since 2000 has been the ongoing dispute over maritime borders in the South China Sea, some of which cover areas with rich natural oil and gas deposits. Chinese encroachment with an oil exploration platform into waters claimed by Vietnam led to major riots against Chinese interests and investments in Hanoi and Saigon in 2014.

Mutual distrust also dominates relations with India, a country that in many ways has aspirations to be a rival economic superpower to the PRC. To Indians, the memory of the humiliating defeat in a battle over one of the border disputes in 1962 remains fresh. This is the sole land border dispute that China has yet to resolve with a neighbour – one with Russia, involving far more land, was sorted out peacefully in the late 1990s, with the agreement that many thousands of square kilometres of land would be ceded to Russia to ensure a secure, undisputed border. While many Indians look with admiration on what the PRC has achieved, and attempt to emulate at least some of the country's success, they also guard their international status jealously, with efforts being made during the presidency of George W. Bush between 2000 and 2008 to court the Americans into having India as one of their best partners in the region (Emmott, 2008). This was partly helped by the fact that India is a democracy, and has a more benign international image. However, the most telling facts are that India's economy remains only a third the size of the PRC's, despite India excelling at the kinds of hi-tech industries China aspires to, and the country looks set to have a greater population than the PRC by 2024. One issue that impacts on relations between China and India is the very close link that exists between Pakistan and the PRC, a relationship that has pushed some leaders to talk of the two being all-weather friends. China's most immediate interest in Pakistan, however, is the border they share with the Xinjiang region, and the ways in which these two powers have to work together to counter terrorism. A particular issue for the PRC is the hosting by India of the Dalai Lama, who fled across the border in 1959. The election of Narendra Modi as Prime Minister of India in 2014 with a huge popular mandate to energize the economy of his country seemed to supply new impetus, however. Despite reported skirmishes across the Indian–Chinese border at the time, Xi Jinping went on a formal visit to China's vast western neighbour in September 2014 and signed deals reportedly worth US$20 billion. But China also looked on nervously as Modi undertook trips to Japan and the USA in search of new economic partners and allies.

The final significant relationship in the Asian region is with the ten members of the Association of Southeast Asian Nations (ASEAN), a body that includes Vietnam, but also embraces Laos, Indonesia, Thailand, Burma, the Philippines, Malaysia, Singapore, Cambodia and Brunei. China has specific links with these powers through the mechanism called 'ASEAN plus one'. With some of these nations, China has outstanding maritime border disputes, with others it shares a political model, and with all of them it is enjoying rising investment and trade levels, something symbolized best by the signing in 2010 of a free-trade agreement with the whole group. It also shares with them a belief in the utter importance of sovereignty.

China and the USA

The relationship between China and the USA has been called the most important in the world in the twenty-first century Some were even prompted to talk in 2008 and 2009 of a 'G2' grouping, rather than a G20, or G8, if only because, without the USA and China being involved in international agreements, they had no real force. The USA has been accused, by some Chinese, of pursuing a strategy that mixes containment with engagement. On the other hand, influential constituencies in the USA see China as the greatest threat of the modern era. It was this strain that emerged in the campaigns of some of the contenders for the Republican nomination during the US presidential elections in 2012. China's political differences from the USA – it not being a democracy, its failure to spell out its intentions clearly for the future, and the ways in which it seems to compete with US interests for resources, both in the Asian region and increasingly further afield – have pushed some to describe it as a worse threat than the USSR during the Cold War.

This is strange, if only because the USSR set itself up as an ideological and political competitor of the USA, and many times stated its intention of seeking to thwart the USA's ambitions overseas. Does China really present a similar kind of threat, in the form of an opponent harbouring in its heart the desire to see the USA simply disappear from the world? There might be extremists in the PRC who see the world in this way, but the most striking thing over the decades since the great rapprochement under Mao Zedong and President Richard Nixon has been the ways in which China has seen keeping close to the USA as being its best bet for a peaceful environment and the space in which to continue developing and growing more prosperous.

When Deng Xiaoping visited the USA in 1979, as part of a series of visits to developed countries to better understand the nature of their economies and see what might be transferable to conditions in China, there was growing excitement that the world was looking on a reformist who might change not just the way China made money, but how it ran its own affairs. Deng was made *Time* magazine's 'Man of the Year' twice. His pragmatic approach in the 1980s convinced many that they were seeing the gradual conversion of China to capitalism. When reforms began in the USSR under Gorbachev, these ideas became even stronger. The impact of the massacre of students in June 1989 at Tiananmen Square was all the greater because Deng had been misinterpreted by many in the USA. His military background, and the fact that he remained a hard-line Communist, had been forgotten.

The events of 1989 could have made the USA and China opponents for the long term – but two things avoided this. The first was the efforts of the George H. W. Bush presidency to hold back, and ensure that the Chinese regime did not become too isolated. While nauseated by the bloodshed they had seen in Tiananmen Square, Bush and his senior advisers echoed Nixon's words of over a decade before – a country that constituted a fifth of humanity could not be left out in the cold, no matter what it had done. Attempts to communicate with and influence it had to continue. Bush was able to pursue this tack with even more conviction because he had been the US representative in Beijing in 1974–5 and understood the country well. The second help was Deng's own re-energizing of the reforms in 1992. Fears that a new cold war would begin, and China would return to isolation, passed. With the unsuccessful bid in 1994 for the 2000 Olympics, the gesture at least showed the PRC was not going into deep seclusion.

This did not prevent some steep ups and downs in the bilateral relationship over the ensuing decade, however. The start of each presidency seemed to see a sharp deterioration in relations, as though the Chinese were testing out the new incumbent. Successive US election campaigns also saw tough language used against China by candidates. Again, all of these were later to prove to be merely phases, with each side eventually realizing they had no choice but to deal with each other. President Clinton famously promised to get tough on China during his campaign in 1993, but when he came to office he was forced to change tack. The debates over granting China 'most favoured nation' (MFN) status from the 1990s within the USA are usually seen as the start of attempts to influence China's internal human rights issues through external trade pressures. But with China's entry to the WTO in 2001, these became irrelevant, because the agreement in effect granted China permanent favoured status in terms of tariffs and other trade benefits. What was not so easy to ignore were the strong feelings of antagonism towards the USA within some groups in the PRC. These came to the fore in 1999, when a US plane bombed the Chinese embassy in Belgrade during a NATO-led attack. The excuse given by the USA was that the hit had been an accident, and the wrong coordinates had been given to the pilot. Others, however, were suspicious. China had publicly maintained neutrality during the conflict, abstaining during UN votes, but there were claims that it was sympathetic to Slobodan Milos̆ ević, leader of the Serbs. To people in China, the bombing was deliberate, and demonstrations were held outside the US and UK embassies in Beijing, with both being attacked and bombarded with stones.

For the USA and China, one of the key things has been the need to build personal chemistry between their respective leaders. The Belgrade bombing showed the problems arising from not having easy and direct links with key decision-makers in China, as the elite leadership in Beijing were completely unavailable for a day or two, unreachable by anxious diplomats and their leaders. For Jiang Zemin, the serving president and Party Secretary at that time, the issue reawakened criticisms that he was soft on the USA, a complaint that stemmed in part from his reining in of the PLA over the Taiwanese presidential elections in 1996.

The issue of Taiwan was the most vexatious topic for US–China relations. When the USA shifted its diplomatic recognition from Taipei to Beijing in 1978, it passed an act of congress – the Taiwan Relations Act – to reassure the Taiwanese government. This committed the US executive to seek the views of Congress and to come to the aid of the island in the event of any attack from across the Taiwan Strait. The act, in effect, guaranteed Taiwan a security blanket. For many congressmen and senators, the support for Taiwan was like an act of faith. President Clinton visited Taiwan four times before he was elected. The lobbying effort of the Taiwanese in Washington was formidable. But as China's economy grew, this compact became more complex, especially once Taiwan became a fully functioning democracy with universal suffrage for its presidential and legislative elections from 1996.

For George W. Bush, when he came to office in 2001, there was a similar initial testing period to the one that Clinton had endured. The trigger incident here was the collision between an American spy plane and a PLA air force plane over the southern island province of Hainan. The Chinese pilot died in the crash, but the American ones survived and were taken into custody. This incident, in April 2001, was accompanied by strong words from President Bush about the need to protect and defend Taiwan. This whole landscape was changed, however, with the 11 September 2001 (9/11) terrorist attacks in the USA. As in many other areas of foreign policy, these attacks reconfigured the international landscape, causing the USA to focus on its struggle against terrorists at the expense of almost everything else. China proved to be an ally in this, and in the process secured admission to the international list of recognized terrorist organizations of two Xinjiang groups. Support from the Chinese for the various UN resolutions on Iraq, and over the invasion of Afghanistan, was also important. Over the remaining period of Bush's presidency, while the USA and China had occasional spats, there was a sense that the priorities for the Americans lay elsewhere. And in many ways this suited the Chinese very well.

US Presidents in China

US presidential visits to the PRC are now increasingly important. However, such visits have been beset by protocol and logistic issues – and sometimes by examples of the 'lost in translation' syndrome. Richard Nixon evidently found his ground-breaking visit to the PRC in 1972 engaging enough to return many times in the years in which he was out of office. Ronald Reagan's visits to China were during one of the easier periods in the relationship, when the USA was viewed as a key partner in helping China achieve the changes it needed to reform its economy. Bill Clinton, however, was to arrive in 1998 at a more delicate time, soon after the Taiwanese elections that had seen shrill anger between China and Taiwan, and military exercises off the coast of the PRC. For domestic constituents in the USA who felt the country was being too friendly with a country that had such serious human rights issues, Clinton had insisted on a walkabout in central Beijing, and being able to talk to students when he lectured at Beijing University. At the insistence of the USA too, during the press conference between President Clinton and President Jiang, the broadcast went out live, no censorship was allowed, and Clinton was able to refer to the need for respect for universal human rights. As part of the ritual of a high-level visit, a number of Chinese dissidents were released from prison, the most prominent being Wei Jingsheng, author of the 1979 tract on the Fifth Modernization during the Democracy Wall movement, who had been imprisoned for consecutive 11-year terms by the government. Clinton was also able to visit the ancient former capital of Xian and see the Terracotta Warriors.

George W. Bush's visits were guided by his twin preoccupations of getting further Chinese support for his global war on terror, and also doing as much as he could to promote the freedom of religion in the PRC. For Barack Obama, however, the visit in November 2009 was perhaps the most contentious of any since rapprochement in 1972. Before the visit, all the indications were good: no US president had come to power with more public support from the Chinese, and the first few months of Obama's time in office were remarkably free from the teething problems of previous presidents' early stages. In addition, Obama was the first US president to visit China within a year of being sworn in, something interpreted as testifying to how important China now was diplomatically. The actual conduct of the visit, however, turned out to be a public relations and diplomatic disaster for the Chinese leadership. Obama was allowed hardly any contact with ordinary Chinese people, his sole public event being a talk to university students in what to many looked like conditions of a security lockdown on the outskirts of Shanghai. No questions were allowed at the press conference held in Beijing before Obama left, and Hu Jintao was at his most formal and stiff. Despite the signing of a lengthy joint statement during the visit, another staple of high-level meetings, the November trip was largely seen as a missed opportunity by an inept and nervous Chinese leadership whose behaviour became even more uneasy during subsequent months.

For the visits of Chinese leaders to the USA, matters have been even more fraught. In 2001, during Hu Jintao's last visit to the USA before he became state leader and Party boss, a Falun Gong supporter was able to infiltrate a closed group of reporters and begin to harangue the president-to-be. Hu's final visit to the USA as president in January 2011 was much more controlled, though his mishearing a question during the press conference he had finally agreed to give at the White House caused some nerves to rise. Hu was unable to emulate the previous president, Jiang, who had a fondness for singing karaoke and quoting poetry to visiting dignitaries, and who, when on visits abroad, liked to show off his foreign language skills.

China and the USA since 2009

For Chinese, the single largest change in relations with the USA since 2009 has been the joint impact of the global economic crisis on the US financial sector, and the winding down of the conflicts in Iraq and Afghanistan, with a re-concentration of forces on the Asian region. The USA, as President Obama stated during his visit to the region in November 2011, is a Pacific power. From 2010, Secretary of State Hillary Clinton described the South and East China Seas as key strategic areas for the USA. Over this period, many talked of a US pivot back to Asia, where so many of its key strategic interests and alliances remain. And to the Chinese, the USA often seemed to be ubiquitous. Wang Hui, a Beijing-based professor of literature, complained that, in the twenty-first century, the borders of the USA came right up to those of China through US troops being based in South Korea and Japan, and its alliances with almost all of the countries around China's edges. The strength of the USA as a sea power also was critical – with its 15 aircraft carriers compared to China's single one (and that was a Ukraine-bought refit). In the eyes of the Chinese, the strength of the US shield of alliances was a constant source of frustration, though this was to some extent a mixed reaction: some more sanguine voices recognized that at least this gave a stable security blanket to key players in the region and maintained balance there.

Chinese views of the USA have always been ambiguous. On the one hand, there is admiration for the dynamism and openness of the USA. Liu Xiaobo wrote of the morning when the news came through that Obama had been elected president, and the feeling that it was a great thing for a country that had experienced so many bitter and tragic fights over race to finally see a black man voted in as its president. But, for many others, the USA is a zealous promoter of its own values, trying to push the rest of the world towards the model of governance that it has. Chinese people often refer to the rates of murders and gun crime in the USA. In the official Chinese annual human rights report on the USA (prepared as a riposte to the US State Department's hard-hitting report on China) it often dwells on the dysfunctionality of some aspects of modern American life, of the high number of people in prison, and the number of people raped, mugged and shot. The moral sheen of the USA had plummeted during the Bush presidency, when photos of abused prisoners in Iraqi jails were broadcast across the world. Many Chinese who have visited the USA return home with contradictory feelings. Some embrace the values that the USA espouses, but many others find the country an unsettling opponent, crowding and circumscribing China's room for action in the Asian region and the world. In recent years, the greatest fear for the Chinese has been of containment. For many Chinese policy-makers, the USA being active in Myanmar once again since 2011, making links with the Vietnamese, selling arms to Taiwan, and maintaining troops in Japan and South Korea, are all linked by the strategic intent to hem in China. Those who look forward to a world where China stands a chance of being number one are mindful of the sobering statistics of the USA's involvement beyond its borders in 125 countries, with over 650 military installations, and US$700 billion a year spent on its defence, seven times more than the amount that China itself officially states that it spends (however, real numbers might be much higher) (Cumings, 2009, p. 393).

Despite all this, the options for both countries are limited. Conflict would be unthinkable. What has occurred are more attritional battles over issues such as US demands that China revalue its currency to be more driven by market rates rather than set by the government, or claims that China in particular is at the forefront of internet espionage. On climate change and non-proliferation, China and the USA have, after serious arguments, found a common cause. And many would argue that, in embracing the rules of a US-dominated world, the Chinese leadership has been able to forge ahead with internal reforms. It was the threat of international competition in the finance sector that disciplined Chinese banks during a particularly difficult period in the late 1990s, and the opening of the Chinese market in 2001 on entry to the WTO that led to an explosion of growth that is still going on at the time of writing. While the USA may sometimes wish to see a change of political structure in China, since the heady days of the 1980s when anything seemed possible, a more pragmatic view now reigns. In this, the two countries accept each other's differences, and look for more carefully defined areas in which to pursue their interests. For China, these have been summed up by talk of 'core interests' since 2008 – though these appear to be more a work in progress, and at the time of writing focus more on maintaining China's claims over its disputed maritime and land borders, and, most critically, over Taiwan.

An accumulation of misunderstandings and issues led to Xi Jinping breaking with protocol and visiting the West coast of the USA only a few months after coming to power. Xi spent over nine hours in discussion with President Obama at the Sunnylands resort in California in mid-2013, and attempted to articulate the USA and China within the framework of 'great power relations'. He stated at the press conference held after the talks that China believed 'the Pacific was big enough for both powers'. This indicated some of the frustration that China felt – one of the world's most important economies, but still feeling that its strategic space was being encroached on by a USA which shared treaty alliances with countries from Japan down to New Zealand. The search for space where the USA would not cramp China's hand seemed to be on the minds of the leadership, with them protesting noisily when Australia, one of their largest suppliers of resources, agreed with the USA to station marines in Darwin, northern Australia, for the first time.

But the US–China relationship is never one to be complacent about. In mid-2014, the Federal Bureau of Investigation took the unprecedented step of issuing warrants for the arrest of five PLA officers accused of being involved with industrial espionage against US companies. This effectively put paid to the first convening of the US–China cyber committee which had just been established to discuss mutual concerns about cyber security. The Edward Snowden revelations which began in 2013 of vast US electronic surveillance of domestic email accounts and foreign leaders only added to China's feeling that it had been hard done by in being so regularly accused of being a violator of international norms in this space. The US claim, however, that its companies and interests were being targeted on a huge scale by Chinese actors, whether from the PLA or elsewhere, was probably correct. The chances of an international agreement to try to regulate this area, while sound in principle, became less likely as the main players, the USA and China, continued to try to score points against each other. Similar things could be said of two other key issues where cooperation was often tripped up by domestic political reservations: climate change and terrorism. The latter in particular intensified in 2013 and into 2014 with a spate of unpleasant attacks in China against civilians for groups linked in particular with Xinjiang. The failure of the US press to label the Kunming Station attack in early 2014 as clearly terrorist caused great offence in China.

China and the European Union

During the 1990s, the Chinese foreign policy mantra was to aim for a multipolar world, away from one in which, since the collapse of the Soviet Union in 1991, the USA had been the sole superpower and enjoyed its moment of 'unipolarity'. To the Chinese, this created disharmony, by breaking the delicate power equilibrium between continents and nations. The talk of multipolarity lessened in the Hu Jintao era, possibly because the USA seemed to become more, rather than less, dominant. Part of this may have been inspired by the failure of the European Union (EU) to live up to its political promise for the Chinese.

The Chinese and the European Economic Community (EEC) had established relations in 1975, with the signing of a trade accord. A decade later they had promoted this through a more comprehensive strategic agreement, but the emphasis was still on trade. As trading partners, the relationship between the two flourished. The EEC developed into the EU and, during the 1990s and 2000s, acquired new members until it stood at 27 member states in 2011. It also acquired a constitution, a diplomatic service, and, with the euro from 2000, a currency for the majority of its members. The EU, as an ideal of multilaterality and co-operation between states, intrigued the Chinese. Many came to look at how it worked. But they were less keen on the more vociferous attitude that the EU took on values and human rights. What had begun as a relationship only about trade and market access gradually began to acquire new dimensions around governance and legal values. This in part was motivated by the EU's own evolving definition of what common political values membership of it entailed. But logically that extended to what sort of relations it wanted from those who were its main economic and political partners. While being less aggressive in its assertion of these values, they were stated through numerous position papers, démarches and declarations on the human rights situation in the PRC.

While China may have felt it had little choice but to take this sort of criticism from the USA, the sole remaining superpower in the world, they were less keen on being given lectures by an entity such as the EU, which was neither a sovereign state, nor, for that matter, particularly unified in the way it spoke. Many member states within the EU pursued their own interests despite the collective position of the EU itself on specific issues. This aroused accusations of hypocrisy and disunity from the Chinese side. With China's entry to the WTO, however, the trade relationship between them expanded to such an extent that by the end of the decade they were the world's largest trading partners. Their interdependence here, however, meant that arguments in other areas became more noticeable.

There have been three particular issues between China and the EU since 2001 that have proved challenging and have defined the relationship. The first has been the failure of the EU to lift the arms embargo on China imposed after the massacre of 1989. This was reviewed by the member states in 2004, in the hope that its lifting would be a powerful symbol, though carrying no real practical impact, because the export of sensitive dual-use technology to the PRC would already be covered under separate legislation. The EU leaders, however, were reckoning without the views of the US government, which was adamant that the embargo should stay in place. Despite lobbying at the highest level, the attempt to cancel the embargo failed. The Chinese interpreted this episode as showing that the EU had very limited political will when faced with the might of the USA. The second issue has been the failure of the EU to grant China market-economy status, arguing that the state's role in the economy is too great at the present time. China's response has been that the same situation applies to other countries, such as Russia, and yet these countries were granted this status many years ago. Once again, while granting it would have little impact, as a symbolic move it would be powerful and useful. Even so, this is still an action that, at the time of writing, the EU has failed to take. Finally, on the EU side, there have been ongoing arguments regarding the securing of greater market access to China for EU companies, as the trade deficit between the two has increased massively in China's favour since the early 2000s. Again, progress here has been very limited. While Germany, alone in the EU in 2011, enjoyed a surplus in its favour from trade with China because of Chinese hunger for its cars, the other member states have no similar advantage.

In terms of soft power, and as an ideal, the EU has a good image in the PRC. It attracts increasing numbers of tourists, and a large number of students (mainly to the UK, because of the English language). But in terms of political reality, the EU fails to rate for the Chinese in a multi-polar world, because they well understand that it is still constituted by member states, and many of these have contrasting and sometimes conflicting interests. Since the Eurozone crisis, which began in 2009, the Chinese have been pushed into the strange position of frequently stating publicly that they wish to see the euro succeed, and that they believe in the ability of European leaders to solve these problems – even with little evidence that the EU main leaders are able to live up to this expectation despite the many crisis meetings and their outcomes throughout 2010 and 2011.

With the Xi leadership, there seemed to be a slight new calibration. Xi visited Brussels in March 2014, the first ever Chinese head of state to go to a place regarded as the headquarters of the EU. While there, he made a speech in which he called the two not so much strategic partners as 'civilisational' ones. This accorded great status to the EU, but meant that China would not get dragged into trying to define which particular member states it felt it had the best relations with and who it felt most understood it. After the previous decade's disappointments with the EU, this represented a more pragmatic approach.

China and Africa

In the 1960s, Mao Zedong's zealously revolutionary China saw African nations as potential allies in the global struggle to free developing countries from the yoke of colonial oppression, and in opposition to the Soviet Union. Over 6 per cent of China's GDP went to support Marxist parties in countries across the world, many of them in Africa, in their struggle for power and revolution in the early 1970s. By the 1980s, however, interest had shifted towards the USA, Europe and Japan. The aid projects China had supported in countries such as Tanzania in the late 1960s, building railways and roads, stalled. It was only in the 1990s, driven by the PRC's need to look for energy resources outside its borders, that Africa was once again interesting. By 2005, China had established relations with all but four of the nations in the African continent (these four tiny states, however, still recognized the Republic of China), establishing a Forum on China–Africa Cooperation (FOCAC) in 2000 which has met five times since then, the most recent meeting being in Beijing in July 2012.

Beyond the rhetoric of friendly relations between China and the African countries with which it has links there lies a complex network of different interests and dynamics, some of which have been heavily criticized. The PRC's investments in the region have increased dramatically in recent years, rising from US$800 million in 2004 to more than US$13 billion by the end of 2010. Such huge increases, however, mask the complexity of what China is doing in Africa, and how uneven its progress has been. In countries such as South Africa and Botswana, which have relatively sophisticated economies, Chinese investment has been regarded positively. In environments like Zimbabwe, Sudan and Ethiopia, however, things have been less straightforward, with accusations that China has been one of the few sources of funding for internationally shunned regimes. Sudan, in particular, has caused problems, with China trading with the discredited regime of President Omar al-Bashir when he stood accused of supporting genocidal campaigns in the Darfur region of his country. The appointment of a senior retired diplomat, Liu Guijin, as special rapporteur for the region was an attempt to show the world that China was trying to play a constructive role, as was the decision to contribute a large number of peacekeepers to the UN forces sent to the conflict zone in 2008. Even so, the accusation of pursuing commercial and energy interests at the expense of all others was hard to deflect. There were also fractious noises within Africa, where some countries stated that the sole interest of China was to create infrastructure and manufacturing jobs for its own people. As many as a million Chinese were reportedly living in Africa by 2010. Many were part of small businesses working in the import and export sectors. But the state-owned energy companies were also there in force, bringing in many workers, who were accused of taking jobs from local people. In the 2008 presidential election in Zambia, China figured as a country against which, in the opinion of the opposition, the government needed to take tougher action because of the easy terms given to it when setting up businesses that were contrary to Zambia's national interest. A Human Rights Watch report from 2011 showed that Chinese investors were often ignorant of local environmental and labour laws, and stood accused of exploiting and sometimes bullying staff. Lurking in the background were accusations that had been made elsewhere (most powerfully by a British journalist, Martin Jacques), that many Chinese had a superior attitude towards black Africans, and this affected their treatment of black workers (Human Rights Watch, 2011). The Chinese responded that it was not going to take lectures from Western countries about how to operate in Africa in view of the tragic outcomes of some of their own colonial projects there. And heads of state, such as a president of Senegal, were vociferous fans of the speed and ease of working with Chinese employers compared to Europeans or Americans.

China and Russia

China and Russia share the world's longest border, extending for 4,300 kilometres (2,700 miles), interrupted by the vast bulk of the Republic of Mongolia. This is an indication of the two countries' historic importance to each other. It was the 1917 Russian Revolution that inspired Chinese Marxists and led to the creation of the Chinese Communist Party in its very early days in Shanghai, and it was with financial and technical help from Russia that the CCP had been able to survive and grow, before it became the Maoist fighting force of the 1930s and 1940s that won the Civil War and established the PRC. This modern historical link, however, conceals a great deal of mutual distrust. As Henry Kissinger, and later Richard Nixon, were to discover in their talks with the Chinese in 1972, while the USA appeared as the ultimate imperialists, they were regarded with more trust than were the Russians, from whom the Maoist leadership felt they faced a real threat of nuclear attack. The border clashes that left hundreds dead in 1969 caused further tension, and by the early 1970s the two countries were embroiled in one of the frostiest periods they had experienced, and were barely able to communicate with each other.

The contemporary view of the collapse of the Soviet Union differs markedly in China from that in the West. While the CCP distrusted and disliked the Soviet Union and the alliances it had built around it, the fact that so much of China's political model had been borrowed from Moscow meant that the fall of the Communist regime in the USSR in 1991 was not viewed as a good thing in Beijing. Soul-searching began almost immediately, and to some extent it has continued to the present day. The mistakes imputed to the leadership around Mikhail Gorbachev are that political reforms were started before economic ones; that they did not deal firmly enough with dissension when it erupted; and that they abandoned Communist ideology too quickly. That the USSR split up in the 1990s, and the economy collapsed, along with male mortality rates and other human development markers, only confirms to most Chinese, at least within the CCP, that the demise of the Soviet Union was a bad thing.

The leadership of Vladimir Putin in Russia has at least restored more structure to elite Russian politics, in Chinese eyes – and he is more admired, both amongst the Beijing CCP elite and the blogging community, than his predecessor, Boris Yeltsin. Xi Jinping has even reportedly referred to him as a leader he would like to emulate, at least in terms of reputation for toughness. The Russian annexation of the Crimea from Ukraine in 2014 isolated Russia from the USA and the EU, but it also supplied Putin with an opportunity to grow closer to China. Xi Jinping, after all, following the lead of Hu Jintao, had undertaken his first overseas visit as President to Russia. The country mattered to China. One of the biggest opportunities was the huge gas reserves in Siberia, and it was these that China had in its sights when Putin came to Shanghai in mid-2014 and signed a huge deal for their exploitation with Chinese investment and sale into the PRC market.

Despite this recent warmth, while China's relations with Russia in the twenty-first century are hardly those of two close allies, they have devised a way of working with each other to their mutual benefit; one commentator has labelled this 'an axis of convenience' (Lo, 2008).

China and the Middle East

Since 1993, the PRC has been a net importer of oil, its own easily accessible reserves being limited. The main partners in this have been, and remain, countries in the Middle East, and in particular its largest supplier, Saudi Arabia, and one of the countries in which it briefly placed much of its investment for the region, Iran. China uniquely preserves good relations with countries across the Middle East, and manages to balance the interests of having good relations with Israel with recognition of the Palestinian authorities. In many ways, China's key priority has been to avoid being sucked into the treacherous and endless political problems of the region. It abstained during the UN vote authorizing the first Iraq War in 1990, and maintained the same studied neutrality during the negotiations over support for the second war, under George W. Bush, a decade later. Over the 2000s, it succeeded in putting sizeable investments into construction, manufacturing and energy production in such countries as Libya and Saudi Arabia, and perhaps most significantly and contentiously, Iran.

With the arrival of the Arab Spring in early 2011, however, things have become much more difficult. The initial response in Beijing was nervousness, and speculation that the same kind of backlash against the elites might be coming to them. That the first uprising, in Tunisia, happened because an aggrieved market stall-holder set himself alight in protest at official bullying in late 2010 only heightened the nervousness in Beijing. A Maoist phrase that had been popular in the past was that 'a single spark can light a prairie fire'. Any one of the thousands of incidents that took place across the PRC in the course of a year had the potential to expand and become unmanageable. For this reason, the government mandated the security services to become even more repressive after February 2011, spending US$92 billion on internal security, a billion more than on national defence. There were fewer parallels than dissimilarities between the situation in the Middle East and that in China, however. Countries such as Egypt or Libya had been led for decades by the same person, whereas in China there had been a turnover in leadership. While the CCP had maintained itself in power, the figures at the top at least had changed. As the Arab Spring spread, however, it caused China deeper diplomatic problems, with Libya and Syria being the most difficult to handle.

China had more than 35,000 workers in Libya, who needed to be evacuated swiftly when the troubles grew more intense within the country in April 2011. When the UN mandated NATO-led action to protect citizens from military attack, however, China abstained at the Security Council, invoking its long-held principle of non-intervention in the affairs of other states. Part of China's neutrality came from a long-term dislike of Colonel Qaddafi, the dictator of Libya who had been in power since 1969, and who had in the past courted Taiwan, and made provocative statements as the unrest grew in his own country that he would treat the rebels in the same way that the Beijing leadership had treated the students in 1989 – sentiments unlikely to please the CCP elite of 2011, who wanted to put this period behind them. When the regime finally collapsed in September 2011, China was the last of the major countries to recognize the transitional authority. Its leaders were also appalled by the sight of the undignified treatment of Qaddafi after his fall, with the beatings being filmed and put on the internet, and his bloodied face held up before his death.

With Syria, China was emboldened by the opposition of Russia to join it in vetoing action in February 2012. Unlike Russia, though, it had no deep security or economic links with the country, but it had been worried by the 'mission creep' in the action on Libya, feeling that NATO military activity had gone far beyond UN Resolution 1973 which had mandated a 'duty to protect' response, but not the full-out attacks on the Qaddafi loyalist forces that China believed it had seen. In addition, Chinese analysts felt that Syria was a far more significant and complicated country with which to deal, and that external involvement might well spark a civil war. The escalating violence in Syria was, the Chinese thought, unlikely to be calmed down by external action and up to 2014 they have resisted all attempts at external intervention.

With Iran, China's diplomatic skills had been tested over several years from 2006 when it took the opportunity to build closer links with the

Iranian leadership, and invest in several of its gas fields. Iran became an observer with the Shanghai Cooperation Organization (one of the few global bodies from which the USA was excluded), which China had established alongside Russia and other central Asian players in the late 1990s. Iran's continuing nuclear programme, however, caused further sanctions to be imposed by the UN. China observed these despite the entreaties of the Iranians themselves. With the escalation of tension from 2011 over claims that Iran was coming closer to creating facilities to make enriched weapons-grade uranium, China played the same game, observing the international consensus and ensuring that it was not dragged into a situation where it might be brought directly into conflict with the USA's strategic aims. China was one of the rare actors in the Middle East that was able both to have its cake and eat it, balancing sometimes wholly contradictory demands across the region to in some way maintain its hard-earned neutrality.

China as Leader of the Developing World?

In view of its geographical, economic and population size, China has often presented itself as the leader of the developing world, both during and after the Maoist period. Grouped with other fast-developing markets, from 2005 it was seen increasingly as a great stabilizer for the world, an exemplar for the development policies other countries might wish to use, and at the head of the G77 group of developing nations. Chinese leaders were uniquely able to present themselves as being at the head of a country that was both rich in aggregate terms, but also poor per capita. Even so, the overwhelming drive of Chinese foreign policy was to serve what its elites defined as being in its national interest: to maintain the CCP in power; to ensure continuing rapid and strong economic growth; and to pursue the dream of creating a 'rich, strong nation' that would never again be exposed to the bullying and humiliation that had happened in the past. The PRC had embraced multilateralism since the 1960s, and placed itself at the centre of most multilateral organizations, from the UN to the World Bank and the International Monetary Fund (IMF). While it embraced these, believing that they helped to create a more stable world, and one in which China could continue its progress towards economic strength, it often aggravated other powers by what they considered was the assertion of its national needs over all others.

The parameters of Chinese foreign policy in the twenty-first century were contradictory, because they seemed to be more suited to a middle-sized country, still finding its way, rather than one of the most powerful nations of the modern world. On the one hand, China acted as though it was a regional power, wanting its demands to be taken seriously. And yet it often responded to counter-demands on its diplomatic attention and time by stating that it was still a developing country and therefore had to focus on its own internal issues rather than become stretched by dealing with issues far beyond its borders.

The two issues of the status of Taiwan's and China's resource needs were the most likely areas where the country might see conflict with others. China was also being approached by countries wishing to gain its support, such as Pakistan, Iran or the DPRK, thus putting great pressure on its diplomacy. Foreign policy making structures in the PRC were far from optimal, with the Ministry of Foreign Affairs being weak (its foreign minister was only ranked at number 250 in the CCP hierarchy), and real decision-making taking place in the Small Leading Group on Foreign Affairs, chaired by the Party Secretary and President. Foreign policy involved a complex body of decision-makers, from state-owned enterprises to the PLA, the Ministry of Trade and the Ministry of Finance. Obtaining a consensus on complex issues from all of these was never easy. Even more difficult was the input of public opinion into foreign affairs, especially over issues such as relations with Japan.

Outsiders categorize China either as a fragile superpower, unsure and ill at ease with its new prominence, or as a country harbouring a real strategic threat to the West, and to the USA in particular, being ideologically and politically opposed to it. And while few doubt that engagement is the correct policy and should be pursued, in some areas this is becoming increasingly challenging.

Conclusion

The stated aim of the CCP is that it wants the country to become a middle-income economy by 2020. By this time, if all goes to plan, it will attain a per capita GDP of US$13,000–14,000. On projections at the time of writing, the plans are well on track. Per capita GDP in 2014 in PPP was US$8,000, but with a growth rate of 7.5 per cent a year predicted at least until 2015, achieving a doubling of per capita levels within less than a decade appears, at the current time, under- rather than over-ambitious. If things continue smoothly, China may well hit these targets earlier than it, or the rest of the world, expects. This continues a trend established since the 1970s, whereby the pace of some fundamental changes has exceeded the expectations of outside experts.

Even so, the challenges the country faces as it nears its target cannot be underestimated. Two of these challenges are easy to predict. In the next decade, the population of China will start to age rapidly, and at some point, a little beyond this timeframe, the population will peak and then start to fall. In the next decade too, the balance of males to females will worsen. These imbalances in themselves are enough of a headache to the government, but the more complex issues will be around how the CCP, in its guidance of the political life of the nation, moves from governing a country where the priority is simply being a factory of GDP growth to producing better-quality growth, clearing up some of its huge environmental problems, and addressing the issues of inequality and lack of a social infrastructure.

The environmental problems are particularly grave. China's addiction to fossil fuel has wrecked havoc on its air and water quality. Ice caps in its largest source of water, Tibet, are reportedly thawing fast. A China whose future is blighted by floods, and by disease caused by poor air quality is becoming likelier. And while the country is investing huge amounts into new technologies to try to remedy this, at the moment it is clearly a race against time.

These problems are all set out clearly in speeches by Chinese leaders, in analysis by outside and inside experts, and in papers from think tanks. China's challenges, in the transition to becoming a middle-income country, are also the challenges of how to deal with social and political rather than purely economic issues. And building consensus around these between the conservatives and reformers, within a realistic timeframe, will be tough.

The scenarios for the short to medium term of the country can be distilled to three broad options: gradualism; crisis; and big bang.

Gradualism is the option favoured by the largest number in the CCP, at least according to what can be gleaned from their public statements. In a well-sequenced way, over the coming three to four decades, China will tackle its development issues in stages, ensuring that, at each step of the way, it will have the right levels of economic development and per capita GDP to take society to the next stage of development without experiencing instability or crisis. In this way, by about 2050, China will be ready for democracy with Chinese characteristics – it will have built a proper social basis on which to achieve this, maintaining the unity of the country and ensuring that the issues of balance and inequality can be dealt with in a manageable timeframe. By the end of this period, the country will have achieved its goal, stated since the Qing dynasty, of being a 'rich, strong country'. It will do so in a world that will remain largely conflict free and benign towards China, and which will make space for the political and resource needs of the new great power.

The second option, of crisis-led change, is, of course, the worst. But it has a pedigree in Chinese dynastic history. For over 2,000 years, dynasties in the various states (sometimes there were multiple contending states at the same time) that preceded the PRC each thrived only for a time before collapsing, usually with a colossal loss of life and great destruction. The Yuan in 1368, the Ming in 1644, and the Qing Dynasties in 1911–12 all went through lengthy periods of decline, and were swept away by changes, with varying levels of violence, but all devastating, which reconfigured the political nature of the country. A collapse along these lines by the PRC, while it is unlikely, is enough to haunt the words of some of the leaders, who talk in worried tones about the internal threats and challenges they face, and wave the spectre of this sort of collapse before the people with the implicit message that the CCP, for all its faults, is at least the best bulwark against this kind of failure. The sometimes almost obsessive talk by the fourth generation of leaders of the need for stability feeds into this almost visceral fear of 'chaos', with the Cultural Revolution as an event evincing the most distaste because it came very close to tipping China back into the internecine rivalries and deadly internal divisions that had so damaged it in the 1920s, 1930s and 1940s. For the rest of the world, too, collapse would be a disaster, causing untold economic damage, creating instability in one of the crucial, if not the most crucial, areas of the world, and destroying major supply chains. China's collapse would be a nightmare not only for China, but also for everyone else.

A third option would be the 'big bang' – a sudden, unexpected change, started by the leadership, but leading to a radical but controllable transformation of areas of China's current political configuration. An example would be moves similar to those used by Taiwan in the 1980s as it lifted martial law, which had been in place since 1949, and the Chinese Nationalist Party (KMT) first tolerated, and then legally enfranchised oppositional political parties. This model is one that some Chinese think tanks and academics have examined. It has the attraction of combining control with potentially radical change. What makes 'big bang' possible is that in many ways it has a precedent in the radical changes the leadership made in 1978, even when, for many both in the rest of the world and in China, it seemed that such deep change was unlikely. With hindsight, of course, what happened in 1978 – the start of the embrace of market reforms, further integration into the global economy, the acceptance of a non-state sector, and reforms of the agricultural sector – seemed wise and rational. According to the memoirs of leaders such as Li Lanqing, who was an official in the city of Tianjin at the time and then ended his career on the CCP Politburo Standing Committee, the flow of the reform was largely straightforward, based on observations of what other countries had done, and an understanding of what would work in China. But more candid memoirs by leaders such as Zhao Ziyang, who was Party Secretary from 1987 to 1989 before being ousted over Tiananmen, showed that there was sometimes fierce opposition to the reforms as they proceeded. Their final success was less certain than many at the time (and subsequently) realized (Li, 2010).

The one major difference between the 'big bang' changes heralded in the economy from 1978 and the changes occurring in 2012 is the different kind of leadership that runs China these days. The 1978 leaders were veterans of revolutionary struggle, most of whom had been in the Party as it fought its many battles to come to power. They enjoyed considerable support within the Party, and they had immense political goodwill and capital. Current leaders operate in a different terrain. They have to demonstrate their abilities in a wholly changed world, a world in which the key battles are not for regime survival against foreign aggressors, but for producing sustainable, balanced growth and continuing to raise people from poverty and deliver the CCP's vision of 'a rich, strong country'.

For the leaders of the PRC in the twenty-first century, therefore, the political tasks are similar to those of Western politicians – to communicate and convince a sometimes deeply sceptical public of the merits of concentrating on some areas of reform, while sacrificing or postponing others. There have been many winners in the reform process since 1978, but also a huge number who see their lives stagnating or, in many cases, regressing as society speeds ahead around them. It is people like this who set off bombs, as one aggrieved farmer did in 2011, in front of a police station, when his petitions were ignored, killing himself and bystanders; or arm themselves with knives and start killing officials, as another did in north-east China in the same year, when his land problems with a neighbour became unbearable. According to one report in late 2011, China now has that most dreadful of Western inflictions, serial killers, one of whom may have murdered as many as 50 sex workers over the previous 15 years. For a society constantly on the move, crafting a message from politicians that shows they are on the side of the people, and are able to keep up, is proving to be increasingly tough. The current leadership around Xi Jinping still adopt a lofty, wise, almost scholarly air as they proceed around the country, demonstrating the Party's solicitude and care, but always with the understanding that the Party is unified, and that anyone who crosses it will be dealt with swiftly. The Party's tolerance of violence as the final card to deal with dissent has been there since it was founded. But in the era of Weibo, QQ, Weixin and Tencent (all Chinese versions of Twitter), just smashing opponents down becomes riskier, as people tire of the CCP's proclivity to tolerate argument up to a point, then pull out a gun or a hammer and smash people into allegiance. In the twenty-first century, the Party has to find a way to win people's hearts and minds in order to confront the immense reform issues that lie ahead in the realm of politics and society.

From 1949, one of the great achievements of the Mao leadership was to craft a message that did have mass appeal, and carried itself across China's vast territories and its complex society. The propaganda achievements under Mao were impressive – the creation of a national narrative of liberation in 1949; the demonization of the old 'dog eat dog' society from before 1949; and the sense that the Party was carrying people to a brighter, better future. As the Maoist period went on, however, this vision darkened. The optimistic language of the propagandists jarred with the social turbulence that was happening around people. The vision of the 'big family of China' had to be held against a family in which all too many members were rejected, bullied or suppressed. The Maoist imprint on language, on the ways in which the landscape developed (Mao was famously keen to wage war on nature in order to win human victories), on the symbols which held people together in society and the narratives and stories they believed, in the management of the news and the restructuring of society, was very profound. Mao casts a long shadow over China almost four decades after his death, and attempts made most bravely by

Illustration C.1 Bicycles in Beijing

The greatest irony of modern China is that as it industrializes and becomes richer, so many of the former national habits such as bicycle riding and sustainable farming may well be solutions to the country's immense environmental and resource problems.

amateur and unofficial historians such as Yang Jisheng, author of the epic *Tombstone*, recording the deaths during the great famine of the 1960s, testify to the return from what historian Ralph Thaxton has called 'a whispered history', where things were known but not publicly recognized, to a spoken one, where the trauma of the past is finally confronted (Thaxton, 2008).

This element of trauma seems contradictory, when one looks at the thriving dynamism of modern China now. But the many contradictions at the heart of what China has become cause some of the confusion about where it wants to go. Historians such as William A. Callahan talk of

China's odd mixture of optimism and pessimism – its bold declarations of success and energy which face off against constant reminders of historical grievances. Actresses daring to appear in films that feed into this denigration of China before its historical enemies, at least for the vast armies of bloggers and netizens in China, run the risk of being humiliated and slandered both in public and online. The prurience of many of these commentators was illustrated by the rage many showed when Zhang Ziyi, one of the most internationally successful of modern Chinese stars, was violently attacked for appearing semi-naked in one film and being seen in pictures taken on the beach elsewhere abroad. These are only the most superficial and visible of the jarring self-images that modern China has. More deeply felt is the sense that China is a country overwhelmed by change, in which, every day since 1978, it has experienced things becoming different, in which the appearance of the world, the ways in which people relate to each other, the economy, and almost every other aspect of life is constantly on the move. For this society, being still or at peace is a distant aspiration.

Within China, among intellectual and other elites, there is a vibrant debate about what China is, in what direction it might go, and what sort of power it should become. For figures such as Wang Hui, one of the so-called new leftists, China offers a distinctive trajectory not just on modernization, but on modernity itself, one in which it is finally nearing a long-standing aspiration to be a country with a strong cultural identity, but one that is forward-looking, and has intellectual and moral integrity. The Chinese rejection of what they see as widespread cultural hegemony from the West sometimes takes on a nationalist slant. But since the 2008 economic crisis in the developed world, many more feel emboldened to say that they can now develop more indigenous models of governance and organization, and intellectual activity, and need not always seek these in the West. There are others, however, who are far more scathing about the country's continuing inability to resolve its ambiguity over, on the one hand, aspiring to be like the West, and on the other, becoming in some way more 'Chinese'. Once more in this debate we arrive back at the question of what, finally, it means to be 'Chinese' at all, with a claim by some figures that in many ways the term goes far beyond nationhood and ethnicity, and relates to a specific vision of the human condition itself.

The energy of modern China is something that is visible and powerful on even the briefest visit. It is a society that is developing more rapidly than perhaps any other society ever has down the centuries. The immense energy of this process is, of course, something that impacts on the rest of the world. The issue of where, internally, the Chinese – from the leaders to other elites, to business people and those who work either in the countryside or the new cities – wish to take this vast project will have a global impact, whether it succeeds or not. The vision in 1949 of a reconstructed, unified and powerful China is, in 2014, coming clearer by the day. But just as the leaders then had to struggle with the problems of failure, breakdown and collapse, so those of the twenty-first century have to fight with the problems of rapid development, and success. That is a remarkable journey for a country to have taken in just over half a century. It is almost impossible, therefore, to think of the kinds of changes this society might see in the next half century, and what these will mean for a world that, more than ever before, is dependent on the stability, success and coherence of the PRC.

Recommended Reading

1 What Is China?

On the issue of ethnicity in China, and its historic roots, Dikötter (1992) gives a good overview. Lovell (2006) is a highly readable questioning of what exactly the term 'China' means, and the role the Great Wall has played as a symbol of the country. Bulag (2002) looks at the issue of ethnicity through the case of the Mongolians in Northern China, and their sometimes tragic history. Millward (2007) does a similar job for the vast north-western region. Wolin (2010) offers a readable account of the impact that China had, during its most enclosed phase in the late 1960s and early 1970s, on those from elites in the West who were able either to visit or to claim inspiration from it. For Richard Nixon and Henry Kissinger's meetings with Mao, the transcripts can be found in Burr (1999). A book which in a remarkable way combines visual and written material that captures something of the dynamism, complexity and contradictions of modern China is Koolhaas and Leong (2001). For the best overview of Chinese history from earliest times to the present in an accessible form, then Brook (2011), Kuhn (2009), Rowe (2009) and Lewis (2007, 2009, 2011) offer wonderful insights. Brown (ed.) (2014) offers a biographical overview of over 100 of the key figures throughout the imperial past as another entry point into a sometimes intimidatingly long and complex history.

2 The Making of Modern China

The most comprehensive histories are in Immanuel Hsu (2000) and Fenby (2009). Spence (1999) is excellent on the intellectual roots of the attempts to modernize China from the late Qing onwards. Westrad (2012) gives a magisterial overview of China's interaction with the world from the Qing onwards, and the formation of national identity through this process. The most accessible modern history of the Opium Wars is in Lovell (2011). Spence (1996) tells the story of the epic Taiping Rebellion through the life and viewpoint of the movement's founder; Mitter (2004) gives a moving account of the decades following the 4th May Movement in 1919; and Eastman (1984) gives a vivid account of the reasons why the KMT was to fail after the Sino-Japanese and Civil Wars. Mitter (2013) gives a fine account of the sources and course of the Sino-Japanese war, and explains why it is such a raw subject to this day. Callahan (2009) covers the issue of the manipulation by the CCP of the modern history of what it labels its 'humiliation' at the hands of other nations. There is an enormous corpus of biographical and analytic material on Mao Zedong, from collections of his works issued in

Beijing, to biographies of him, going into exhaustive detail about the manifold controversies of his career. The most negative is Chang and Halliday (2005). More sanguine accounts are in Spence (2002) and Short (1999). Chiang Kai-shek is covered by Fenby (2003) and Taylor (2011). On the very earliest years of the PRC, see the essays in Brown and Pickowicz (2007). The harrowing era of the Great Leap Forward and the subsequent famines are covered in Becker (1996), Thaxton (2008) and Dikötter (2010). Overviews of the Cultural Revolution from 1966 ran from the epic title of MacFarquhar and Schoenhals (2007) to Clark (2008), which is focused more on the cultural aspects of the movement. J. Brown (2012) looks at the issue of de-urbanization in the Maoist period particularly around the time of the Cultural Revolution. The Tiananmen Square uprising is best covered by Brook (1992) and the internal papers reportedly leaked from China in Nathan *et al.* (2001), the publication of which effectively caused the US authors to be banned from the PRC. Zhao (2010) is an account of his time as Party Secretary in the two years leading up to 1989 and was sensationally smuggled out of China to Hong Kong in the form of recordings and published after his death. The era of Hu Jintao is covered in Lam (2006) and K. Brown (2012). For excellent overviews of aspects of Tibet, see Yeh (2013), Tuttle and Schaeffer (2013) and Ma (2011).

3 The Communist Party and Politics

For the Party as it operates generally, see Brown (2009), Callick (2013) and McGregor (2010). Shambaugh (2009) describes and analyses many of the internal debates within the CCP in the two decades since the fall of the Soviet Union in 1991. For analysis of its current operations and functions, the excellent updates by Millar and Cheng on the China Leadership Monitor, run by the Hoover Institute in Stanford, USA, are worth looking at, as is Fewsmith (2008). Anything by Yongnian Zheng is also worth reading. For the composition of the elite, with immense detail on different segments and networks which make up the top membership of the CCP, see Bo (2010) – though the chapters on the elite involvement in the Olympics and the issue of Taiwan are perhaps less compelling. Cheng (2001) contains the most closely argued case for the existence of specific factions within the CCP and how these impact on the interaction between elite leaders. Li (2007) covers the history and functions of the People's Liberation Army. Pieke (2009), on cadre training in the twenty-first century, looks in particular at Party schools in Beijing and the south-west. Yu Keping, an official at the Compilation and Translation Department of the Central Committee of the CCP, has had his essays on democratization in the PRC translated in Yu (2009). Fravel (2008) covers the issues of why, and how, China has dealt with its sea and land border disputes since 1949. Taylor (2009) covers China's new and expanding interests in Africa well. Henry Kissinger's book (2011), barely readable and full of irrelevant historical material, is useful when he discusses his role in the rapprochement between the USA and China. For China–Russia relations, Lo (2008) offers a good overview. The Chinese thought apparatus structure is covered most comprehensively in Brady (2008). For an overview of the Chinese fifth-generation leaders under Xi Jinping, Brown (2014) contains details of their backgrounds and what can be divined so far of their political strategy.

4 How China is Governed

The structures of the Chinese government are spelt out clearly in Saich (2014), and highly stimulating essays on various aspects of state–society relations can be found in Shue (1988). Brown (2011) looks at the attempts to create carefully guided grassroots elections since 1987. Peerenboom (2007) covers well the issue of rule of law in the PRC.

5 The Chinese Economy

The best comprehensive overview of the Chinese economy since 1949 is in Naughton (2006) which explains the dynamics behind the early reforms, the challenges in changing the old state-planned economic structure under Mao to the market-led one under Deng, and some of the impacts of this. The works of Peter Nolan on aspects of Chinese economic globalization, and in particular Nolan (2001 and 2003) help in understanding the immense challenges Chinese corporations have had to undergo to truly enter the global marketplace. On the red capitalists, and private enterprise in China, Dickson (2003) and his subsequent study, Chen and Dickson (2010), explains who China's main private sector actors are, and why they are not, at the present time, a political problem for the CCP. Nee and Opper (2012) also explains, in great detail, the seemingly contradictory presence of capitalism and state guidance in modern China, particularly in provincial-level and below forms of government. On the imbalances within China, among its different provinces, and between the state and the non-state sectors, the two works by Huang (2005 and 2008) give an excellent, often witty, and data-stacked overview. Crabbe (2014) offers a salutary lesson on the vagaries of dealing with Chinese economic statistics. On the impact of China's rise on the rest of the world and the global economic order, see Kynge (2006). Clissold (2005) on the perils of foreign investment in China, Midler (2011) on manufacturing and Gerth (2010) on Chinese consumers introduce different aspects of the immense complexity of modern China's economy. Studwell (2002) is similarly sobering about the experience, just before and during Chinese entry into the WTO, of foreign companies and how they fared in the country. Economy (2005) spells out starkly the environmental costs of China's development over the three decades since the 1970s, and its current policy response. Elvin (2006) sets all this in context, covering the last two and a half millennia.

Watts (2011), Geall (2013) and Shapiro (2012) bring the story up to date, with particular emphasis on the different kinds of environmental problems across China's various provinces and geographies.

6 Chinese Society

Two works by Chinese authors capture much of the dynamism and complexity of modern Chinese society. The first, by Anhui journalists Chen and Wu (2006) is a powerful complaint about the huge tax and economic burdens on Chinese farmers, and their suffering at the hands of local officials. The second, by the respected sociologist Cao Jingqing (Cao, 2006), is the English translation of the account of life in the heartlands of modern China. For overall context, the most powerful works have been by the UK-educated sociologist Fei Xiaotong, whose concise account (Fei, 1992) remains as provocative now as when it was written in 1947. Wright (2010) looks at the class structure of Chinese society post-WTO, and wrestles with the issue of just how much modern business people will be involved in political change in the PRC. With reference to the internet, Yang (2009) gets to grips with an issue that has only really figured in analysis of China in the decade of the 2000s. A scholarly overview of the role of civil society, putting it in good historic context, can be found in Ma (2005). French and Crabbe (2010) provide copious data and analysis of the increasing phenomenon of obesity in modern China. Guo (2010) has useful chapters on the current situation in the health care and education sectors in China, setting out some of the key challenges. Loyalka (2012) gives a highly accessible account of contemporary society in a region of Xian.

7 Chinese Culture

Barmé (2000) offers, though dated only to 2000, a good and energetically written overview of the key cultural movements and issues in China since 1978. Davies (2009) analyses, with copious reference to key Chinese and Western postmodernist texts, the vexed history of the interface between Western and Chinese intellectual habits and movements. One of the authors cited, Wang Hui, has had several works translated well into English, the one giving the best overview being Wang (2011). Lovell has provided an excellent translation of the works of Lu Xun (Xun, 2009), presenting in a single volume the key essays and short stories of the man widely regarded as modern China's greatest writer. Sheng (2013) and Wang (2012) are two highly readable, well translated contemporary novels about female migrant labourers and corrupt officials respectively.

8 China in the World

Shirk (2008), Shambaugh (2013) and Gill (2007) offer good, and relatively up-to-date, overviews of China's internal views of its global role, and how this sometimes conveys itself in contradictory ways to the world outside. Shirk is particularly useful on China and Japan relations. Jakobson and Knox (2010), an excellent paper for the Stockholm International Peace Research Institute (SIPRI) about how Chinese foreign policy is made, is also extremely helpful, mapping out the complex vested interests and institutional complexities. Ross (2008) looks at the frameworks within which China has operated from the early 1970s to the 2000s, with excellent chapters on the falling-out between China and the rest of the world after the Tiananmen Square massacre in 1989. Foot and Walter (2010) offer an elegant treatment of the most important bilateral relationship of the twenty-first century, with excellent chapters not just on political and security relations but also the deepening economic co-dependency between China and the USA. Yan Xuetong, of Qinghua University, has been one of the most prominent commentators on international affairs from within China in recent years. Yan (2011) seeks to combine the philosophies and moral thinking of Confucius, Mencius and pre-Qin Dynasty figures from 2,500 years ago with the modern global order and China's role within it. The book also has interesting contributions from other Beijing-based academics. On the complex nexus between China, India and Japan, see Emmott (2008), and for the impossibilities of the DPRK, one of the best recent accounts has been in Lankov (2013). On China in Africa, French (2014) is an accessible account by a journalist who has served time both in China and in parts of Africa, along with Chan (2013). For the role of the EU, see in particular Kinzelbach (2014) and Men and Wei (2014).

Internet Resources

The main database of living Chinese elite leaders is available at: www.chinavitae.org.

The papers found on the *China Leadership Monitor*, available at http://www.hoover.org/publications/china-leadership-monitor, are always stimulating and useful, if a little US-centric.

The Jamestown Foundation also offers regular political updates with its *China Brief*, available at http://www.jamestown.org/programs/chinabrief/.

Chinese village elections and other matters related to society and governance, especially the NGO sector, are well covered by the Carter Center's http://chinaelectionsblog.net/.

A rich digest of online material relating to current events within the PRC, from the bizarre to the sobering, is run by the China Digital News network and available at: http://chinaelectionsblog.net/; also at China Smack, http://www.chinasmack.com/.

On the whole, Chinese government websites are the last to update, even though they contain the most authoritative information on data, personnel moves within the CCP and the government and so on. Government White Papers can be found at: http://english.peopledaily.com.cn/whitepaper/home.html.

The websites of Xinhua, the *People's Daily* Online, and *China Daily* are all worth looking over, at least for the official view of domestic and international events. China's environmental problems are covered in the bilingual website, China Dialogue, available at: www.chinadialogue.net.

Bibliography

Ba, Jin (1984) *Random Thoughts,* trans. Geremie Barmé (Hong Kong: Joint Publishing Co.).

Barmé, Geremie and John Minford (eds) (1989) *Seeds of Fire: Chinese Voices of Conscience* (Newcastle: Bloodaxe Books).

Barmé, Geremie (2000) *In the Red: On Contemporary Chinese Culture* (New York: Columbia University Press).

Barr, Michael (2011) *Who's Afraid of China? The Challenge of Chinese Soft Power* (London: Zed Books).

Barthes, Roland (2011) *Travels to China* (Cambridge: Polity Press).

Baum, Richard (1996) *Burying Mao: Chinese Politics in the Age of Deng Xiaoping* (Princeton, NJ: Princeton University Press).

BBC website (2011) 'China Overtakes Japan as World's Second-biggest Economy', 14 February. Available at: http://www.bbc.co.uk/news/business12427321; accessed 5 August 2012.

BBC website (2012), 'China's Military Budget Tops USD 100 Billion', 4 March. Available at: http://www.bbc.co.uk/news/world-asia-china-17249476; accessed 5 August 2012.

Becker, Jasper (1996) *Hungry Ghosts: China's Secret Famine* (London: John Murray).

Bloomberg (2012) 'China's Urban Population Exceeds Countryside for the First Time', 17 January. Available at: http://www.bloomberg.com/news/2012-01-17/chinaurban-population-exceeds-rural.html; accessed 5 August 2012.

Bo, Yang (1988) *The Ugly Chinaman and the Crisis of Chinese Culture* (New York: Hill and Wang).

Bo, Zhiyue (2010) *China's Elite Politics: Governance and Democratization* (Singapore: World Scientific).

Bongiorni, Sara (2007) *A Year Without 'Made in China' – One Family's True Life Adventure in the Global Economy* (New York: Wiley).

Brady, Anne-Marie (2008) *Marketing Dictatorship: Propaganda and Thought Work in Contemporary China* (Lanham, MD: Rowman & Littlefield).

Branigan, Tania (2011) 'China's Great Gender Crisis', *Guardian*, 2 November. Available at: http://www.guardian.co.uk/world/2011/nov/02/chinas-greatgender-crisis; accessed 10 July 2012.

Brødsgaard, Kjeld Erik and Yongnian Zheng (2006) *The Chinese Communist Party in Reform* (London: Routledge).

Brook, Timothy (1992) *Quelling the People: The Military Suppression of the Beijing Democracy Movement* (New York: Oxford University Press).

Brook, Timothy (2010) *The Troubled Empire: China in the Yuan and Ming Dynasties* (Cambridge, MA: Harvard University Press).

Brown, Jeremy and Paul Pickowicz (2007) *Dilemmas of Victory: The Early Years of the People's Republic of China* (Cambridge, MA: Harvard University Press).

Brown, Jeremy (2012) *City Versus Countryside in Mao's China: Negotiating the Divide* (Cambridge: Cambridge University Press).

Brown, Kerry (2007) *Struggling Giant: China in the 21st Century* (London: Anthem Press).

Brown, Kerry (2008) *The Rise of the Dragon: Chinese Inward and Outward Investment in the Reform Era 1978–2007* (Oxford: Chandos).

Brown, Kerry (2009) *Friends and Enemies: The Past, Present and Future of the Communist Party of China* (London: Anthem Press).

Brown, Kerry (2011) *Ballot Box China* (London: Zed Books).

Brown, Kerry (2012) *Hu Jintao: China's Silent Ruler* (Singapore: World Scientific).

Brown, Kerry (2014) *The New Emperors: Power and the Princelings in China* (London and New York: I B Tauris).

Brown, Kerry (ed.) (2014) *Berkshire Dictionary of Chinese Biography* Volumes 1–3 (Great Barrington, MA: Berkshire).

Bulag, Uradny (2002) *The Mongols at China's Edge: History and the Politics of National Unity* (Lanham, MD/Oxford: Rowman & Littlefield).

Burr, William (1999) *The Kissinger Transcripts: The Top Secret Talks with Beijing and Moscow* (Darby, PA: Diane Publishing Co.).

Callahan, William (2009) *China: The Pessoptimist Nation* (Oxford: Oxford University Press).

Callick, Rowan (2013) *Party Time: Who Runs China and How* (Collingwood, Ontario: Black Inc.).

Cao, Jingqing (2006) *China Along the Yellow River: Reflections on Rural Society* (Abingdon/New York: RoutledgeCurzon).

Chang, Jung and Jon Halliday (2005) *Mao: The Unknown Story* (New York: Vintage).

Chang, Leslie T. (2010) *Factory Girls: Voices from the Heart of Modern China*, 2nd edn (London/New York: Picador).

Chen, Guidi and Wu Chuntao (2006) *Will the Boat Sink the Water? The Life of China's Peasants*, trans. Zhu Hong (New York: Public Affairs).

Chan, Stephen (2013) *The Morality of China in Africa: The Middle Kingdom and the Dark Continent* (London: Zed Books).

Ch'en, Jerome (1967) *Mao and the Chinese Revolution* (Oxford: Oxford University Press).

Chen, Jie and Bruce J. Dickson (2010) *Allies of the State: China's Private Entrepreneurs and Democratic Change* (Cambridge, MA: Harvard University Press).

Cheng, Li (2001) *China's Leaders: The New Generation* (Lanham, MD: Rowman & Littlefield).

China Daily (2011) 'China's Communist Party Exceeds 80 Million', 24 June. Available at: http://www.chinadaily.com.cn/china/2011-06/24/content_12768094.htm; accessed 10 July 2011.

Chinese National Bureau of Statistics Data on List of Per Capita GDP by Province (2011) quoted in Wikipedia, http://en.wikipedia.org/wiki/List_of_Chinese_administrative_divisions_by_GDP_per_capita; accessed 5 August 2012.

CIA, *World Factbook, China* (2014) https://www.cia.gov/library/publications/the-world-factbook/geos/ch.html; accessed 24 September 2014.

Clark, Paul (2008) *The Chinese Cultural Revolution: A History* (Cambridge: Cambridge University Press).

Clissold, Tim (2005) *Mr China* (London: Robinson).

Crabbe, Matthew (2014) *Myth-Busting China's Numbers: Understanding and Using China's Statistics* (Basingstoke: Palgrave Macmillan).

Cumings, Bruce (2009) *Dominion from Sea to Sea: Pacific Ascendancy and American Power* (New Haven, CT: Yale University Press).

Davies, Gloria (2009) *Worrying About China: The Language of Chinese Critical Enquiry* (Cambridge, MA: Harvard University Press).

Dickson, Bruce J. (2003) *Red Capitalists in China: The Party, Private Entrepreneurs and Prospects for Political Change* (Cambridge: Cambridge University Press).

Dikötter, Frank (1992) *The Discourse of Race in Modern China* (London: Hurst).

Dikötter, Frank (2010) *Mao's Great Famine: The History of China's Most Devastating Famine 1958–1962* (London: Bloomsbury).

Dittmer, Lowell (1997) *Liu Shaoqi and the Cultural Revolution*, 2nd edn (London: M. E. Sharpe).

Eastman, Lloyd (1984) *Seeds of Destruction: Nationalist China in War and Revolution 1937–1949* (Palo Alto, CA: Stanford University Press).

Ebray, Patricia Buckley (2014) *Emperor Huizong* (Cambridge, MA: Harvard University Press).

Economist, The (2012) 'Streaks of Red', 30 June. Available at: http://www.economist.com/node/18895430; accessed 5 August 2012.

Economist, The (2013) 'The Death Penalty: Strike Less Hard', 3 August. Available at http://www.economist.com/news/china/21582557-most-worlds-sharp-decline-executions-can-be-credited-china-strike-less-hard; accessed 24 December 2014

Economy, Elizabeth (2005) *The River Runs Black: The Environmental Challenges to China's Future* (Ithaca, NY: Cornell University Press).

Elvin, Mark (2006) *The Retreat of the Elephants: An Environmental History of China* (London: Yale University Press).

Emmott, Bill (2008) *Rival: How the Power Struggle Between China, India and Japan will Shape Our Next Decade* (London and New York: Viking).

Ernst & Young (2011) 'All Renewables Index 2011'. Available at: http://www.ey.com/GL/en/Industries/Power—Utilities/RECAI—All-renewables-index, London.

Fairbank, John King (1986) *The Great Chinese Revolution 1800–1985* (New York: Harper & Row).

Fei, Xiaotong (1992) *From the Soil: The Foundations of Chinese Society*. A translation by Gart G. Hamilton and Wang Zheng (Berkeley, CA: University of California Press).

Fenby, Jonathan (2003) *Chiang Kai-shek: China's Generalissimo and the Nation He Lost* (New York: Carroll & Graf).

Fenby, Jonathan (2009) *The Penguin History of Modern China* (London: Penguin).

Fewsmith, Joseph (2008) *China Since Tiananmen*, 2nd edn (Cambridge: Cambridge University Press).

Foot, Rosemary and Andrew Walter (2010) *China, the United States and Global Order* (Cambridge: Cambridge University Press).

Forbes (2012) 'The World's Biggest Companies', http://www.forbes.com/global2000/; accessed 5 August 2012.

Fravel, M. Taylor (2008) *Strong Borders, Secure Nation: Cooperation and Conflict in China's Territorial Disputes* (Princeton, NJ: Princeton University Press).

Frazier, Mark M. (2010) *Socialist Insecurity: Pensions and the Politics of Uneven Development in China* (New York: Cornell University Press).

French, Howard (2014) *China's Second Continent: How a Million Migrants are Building a New Empire in Africa* (New York: Knopf).

French, Paul and Matthew Crabbe (2010) *Fat China: How Expanding Waistlines are Changing a Nation* (London: Anthem Press).

Friedman, Thomas L. (2005) *The World Is Flat: A Brief History of the Twenty-first Century* (New York: Farrar, Strauss & Giroux).

Gao, Mobo (2008) *The Battle for China's Past: Mao and the Cultural Revolution* (London: Pluto Press).

Gao, Wenqian (2008) *Zhou Enlai: The Last Perfect Revolutionary* (New York, Public Affairs).

Gardam, Tim (2011) 'Christians in China: Is the Country in Spiritual Crisis?' BBC Radio 4, 12 September. Available at: http://www.bbc.co.uk/news/magazine-14838749; accessed 29 July 2012.

Garnaut, John (2013) *The Rise and Fall of the House of Bo* (Harmondsworth: Penguin).

Geall, Sam (2013) *China and the Environment: The Green Revolution* (London: Zed Books).

Gerth, Karl (2010) *As China Goes, So Goes the World: How Chinese Consumers are Transforming Everything* (New York: Hill & Wang).

Gifford, Rob (2008) *China Road: One Man's Journey into the Heart of Modern China* (London: Bloomsbury).

Gill, Bates (2007) *Rising Star: China's New Security Diplomacy* (Washington, DC: Brookings Institution).

Goodman, David S. G. (1981) *Beijing Street Voices: The Poetry and Politics of China's Democracy Movement* (London: Boyars).

Goodman, David S. G. (1994) *Deng Xiaoping and the Chinese Revolution: A Political Biography* (London/New York: Routledge).

Guo, Baogang (2010) China's Quest for Political Legitimacy: The New Equity-Enhancing Politics (Lanham, MD: Lexington Books).

Guo, Xiajuan and Yongnian Zheng (2008) 'Women's Political Participation in China', University of Nottingham China Policy Institute Briefing, Issue 34.

Hewitt, Duncan (2008) *Getting Rich First: Life in a Changing China* (London: Vintage).

Hing, Xia (2006) 'The Communist Party of China and the Party State', *New York Times*. Available at: http://www.nytimes.com/ref/college/coll-china-politics 002.html; accessed 10 July 2012.

Hsu, Immanuel C. Y. (2000) *The Rise of Modern China*, 6th edn (Oxford,: Oxford University Press).

Huang, Bao (2011) 'Principle of Three Cautions in Police Response to Mass Incidents', *Asian Social Science*, 7(2), February.

Huang, Ray (1982) *1587, A Year of No Significance: The Ming Dynasty in Decline* (New Haven, CT: Yale University Press).

Huang, Yasheng (2005) *Selling China: Foreign Direct Investment During the Reform Era* (Cambridge, Cambridge University Press).

Huang, Yasheng (2008) *Capitalism with Chinese Characteristics: Entrepreneurship and the State* (Cambridge: Cambridge University Press).

Huc, Evariste Regis (1859) *A Journey through Tartary, Thibet and China during the Years 1844, 1845 and 1846,* 2 volumes, trans. D. Appleton (London: Longman).

Human Rights Watch (2009) *An Alleyway in Hell: China's Abusive Black Jails* (New York: Human Rights Watch).

Human Rights Watch (2011) *You'll Be Fired if you Refuse: Labour Abuses in China's State-Owned Copper Mines* http://www.hrw.org/reports/2011/11/04/you-ll-be-fired-if-you-refuse; accessed 5 August 2012.

Hutton, Will (2007) *The Writing on the Wall: China and the West in the 21st Century* (London: Little, Brown).

Jacques, Martin (2008) *When China Rules the World* (London: Allen Lane).

Jakobson, Linda and David Knox (2010) *New Foreign Policy Actors in China*, SIPRI Policy Paper 26 (Stockholm: SIPRI).

Jenner, W. F. (1992) *The Tyranny of History: The Roots of China's Crisis* (London: Allen Lane).

Jiang, Rong (2009) *Wolf Totem,* trans. Howard Goldblatt (Harmondsworth: Penguin).

Jiang Yang (1988) *A Cadre Life in Six Chapters,* trans. Geremie Barmé (Hong Kong: Joint Publishing Co.).

Kinzelbach, Katrin (2014) *The EU's Human Rights Dialogue with China: Quiet Diplomacy and Its Limits* (London: Routledge).

Kissinger, Henry (2011) *On China* (New York: Penguin).

Koolhaas, Rem and Sze Tsung Leong (eds) (2001) *Great Leap Forward: Harvard Design School Project on the City* (Cologne: Taschen).

Kuhn, Dieter (2011) *The Age of Confucian Rule* (Cambridge, MA: Belknap Press).

Kynge, James (2006) *China Shakes the World: The Rise of a Hungry Nation* (London: Weidenfeld & Nicolson).

Lai, Hairong (2004) 'Semi-Competitive Elections at Township Level in Sichuan Province', *China Perspectives*, January/February. Available at: http://chinaperspectives.revues.org/document787.html; accessed 5 August 2012.

Lam, Willy Wo-Lap (1999) *The Era of Jiang Zemin* (New York/Singapore: Prentice Hall).

Lam, Willy Wo-Lap (2006) *Chinese Politics in the Hu Jintao Era: New Leaders, New Challenges* (New York: M. E. Sharpe).

Lankov, Andrei (2013) *The Real North Korea: Life and Politics in the Failed Stalinist Utopia* (Oxford: Oxford University Press).

Lewis, Mark Edward (2007) *The Early Chinese Empires: Qin and Han* (Cambridge, MA: Belknap Press).

Lewis, Mark Edward (2009) *China's Cosmopolitan Empire: The Tang Dynasty* (Cambridge, MA: Belknap Press).

Lewis, Mark Edward (2011) *China Between Empires: The Northern and Southern Dynasties* (Cambridge, MA: Belknap Press).

Leys, Simon (1988) *The Burning Forest: Essays on Chinese Culture and Politics* (London: Paladin, 1988).

Leys, Simon (1991) *The Death of Napoleon* (London: Quartet Books).

Li, Lanqing (2010) *Breaking Through: The Birth of China's Opening Up Policy* (Oxford: Oxford University Press).

Li, Xiaobing (2007) *A History of the Modern Chinese Army* (Lexington, KY: University Press of Kentucky).

Li, Zhisui (1996) *The Private Life of Chairman Mao: The Memoirs of Mao's Personal Physician* (London: Arrow Press).

Liao, Yiwu (2009) *The Corpse Walker: Real Life Stories, China from the Bottom Up,* trans. by Wen Huang (New York: Anchor Books).

Lin, Shuanglin (2009) 'The Rise and Fall of China's Government Revenue', EAI Working Paper No. 150.

Liu, Xiaobo (2012) *No Enemies, No Hatred: Selected Essays and Poems* (Cambridge, MA: Harvard University Press).

Lo, Bobo (2008) *Axis of Convenience: Moscow, Beijing and the New Geopolitics* (London: Chatham House).

Lovell, Julia (2006a) *The Politics of Cultural Capital: China's Quest for a Nobel Prize in Literature* (Honolulu, HI: University of Honolulu Press).

Lovell, Julia (2006b) *The Great Wall: China Against the World, 1000 BC–AD 2000* (London: Atlantic Books).

Lovell, Julia (2011) *The Opium War: Drugs, Dreams and the Making of China* (London: Picador).

Loyalka, Michelle Dammon (2012) *Eating Bitterness: Stories from the Front Lines of China's Great Urban Migration* (Berkeley, CA: University of California Press).

Ma, Qiusha (2005) *Non-Governmental Organisations in Contemporary China: Paving the Way to Civil Society* (London: Routledge).

Ma, Rong (2011) *Population and Society in Contemporary Tibet* (Hong Kong: Hong Kong University Press).

MacFarquhar, Roderick and Michael Schoenhals (2007) *Mao's Last Revolution* (Cambridge, MA: Harvard University Press).

MacMillan, Margaret (2006) *Seize the Hour: When Nixon Met Mao* (London: John Murray).

McGregor, Richard (2010) *The Party: The Secret World of China's Communist Party* (London/New York: HarperCollins).

Men, Jing and Wei Shen (2014) *The EU, the US and China – Towards a New International Order?* (Cheltenham: Edward Elgar).

Midler, Paul (2011) *Poorly Made in China: An Insider's Account of the China Production Game*, 2nd edn (Hoboken, NJ: John Wiley).

Millward, James (2007) *Eurasian Crossroads: A History of Xinjiang* (New York: Columbia University Press).

Mitter, Rana (2004) *A Bitter Revolution: China's Struggle with the Modern World* (Oxford: Oxford University Press).

Mitter, Rana (2013) *China's War with Japan, 1937-1945: The Struggle for Survival* (Harmondsworth: Penguin).

Moore, Michael (2011) 'China's Billionaires Double in Number', *Daily Telegraph*, 7 September 2011.

Nathan, Andrew J. (1986) *Chinese Democracy* (Berkeley, CA: University of California Press).

Nathan, Andrew J., Perry Link and Zhang Liang (2001) *The Tiananmen Papers* (New York: Public Affairs).

Naughton, Barry (2006) *The Chinese Economy: Transition and Growth* (Cambridge, MA: MIT Press).

Nee, Victor and Sonja Oppen (2012) *Capitalism from Below: Markets and Institutional Change in China* (Cambridge MA: Harvard University Press).

Ng, Wei-Shiuen, Lee Schipper and Yang Chen (2010) 'China Motorization Trends: New Directions for Crowded Cities', *Journal of Transport and Land Use*, 3(3), Winter.

Nolan, Peter (2001) *China and the Global Economy: National Champions, Industrial Policy and Big Business Revolution* (Basingstoke: Palgrave Macmillan).

Nolan, Randall (2003) *China at the Crossroads* (London: Polity Press).

OECD (2005) China: Economic Survey 2005 (Paris: OECD). Available at: http://www.oecd.org/eco/surveys/economicsurveyofchina2005.htm; accessed 5 August 2012.

Oi, Jean C. (ed.) (2011) *Going Private in China: The Politics of Corporate Restructuring and System Reform in the People's Republic of China* (Stanford, CA: Asia Pacific Research Center).

Orlik, Tom (2011) 'Unrest Grows as Economy Booms', *Wall Street Journal*, 26 September.

Osborne, Alistair (2011) 'Chinese Are the New Big Spenders in Town', *Daily Telegraph*, 31 December.

Palmer, James (2012) *The Death of Mao: The Tangshan Earthquake and the Birth of New China* (London: Faber & Faber).

Pascoe, Michael (2011) 'Barbienomics: The Reality of Manufacturing' in The Sydney Morning Herald, 31 August 2011. Available at http://www.smh.com.au/business/barbienomics-the-reality-of-manufacturing-20110831-1jl6y.html; accessed 24 December 2014.

Peerenboom, Randall (2007) *China Modernizes: Threat to the West or Model for the Rest* (Oxford: Oxford University Press).

People's Daily Online (2010) 'China Rural Migrants Number Nearly 230 Million', 24 March. Available at: http://en.people.cn/90001/90776/90882/6929156.html; accessed 10 July 2012.

Pieke, Frank (2009) *The Good Communist: Elite Training and State Building in Today's China* (Cambridge: Cambridge University Press).

Purdy, Mark (2013) 'The Chinese Economy, in Six Charts', in Harvard Business Review, 29 November 2013. Available at https://hbr.org/2013/11/chinas-economy-in-six-charts/

Reuters (2012) 'China Mobile Subscribers up 1.07% in May to 1.03 Billion', 20 June 2012. Available at: http://www.reuters.com/article/2012/06/20/china-mobile-idUSL4E8GL61F20120620; accessed 10 July 2012.

Ross, Robert S. (2008) *China's Security Policy: Structure, Power and Politics* (London: Routledge).

Rowe, William T. (2009) *China's Last Empire: The Great Qing* (Cambridge, MA: Belknap).

Saich, Tony (2015) *Governance and Politics of China*, 4th edn (Basingstoke: Palgrave Macmillan).

Scheidel, Walter (ed.) (2009) *Rome and China: Comparative Perspectives on Ancient World Empires* (Oxford: Oxford University Press).

Shambaugh, David (2009) *The Communist Party of China: Atrophy and Adaptation* (Berkeley, CA: University of California Press).

Shambaugh, David (2013) *China Goes Global: The Partial Superpower* (Oxford: Oxford University Press).

Shapiro, Judith (2001) *Mao's War Against Nature: Politics and Environment in Revolutionary China* (Cambridge: Cambridge University Press).

Shapiro, Judith (2012) *China's Environmental Challenges* (London: Polity).

Shirk, Susan L. (2008) *China: Fragile Superpower* (New York: Oxford University Press).

Short, Philip (1999) *Mao: A Life* (London: Hodder & Stoughton).

Shue, Vivienne (1988) *The Reach of the State: Sketches of the Chinese Body Politic* (Palo Alto, CA: Stanford University Press).

Snow, Edgar (1962) *The Other Side of the River: Red China Today* (New York: Random House).

Snow, Edgar (1968) *Red Star Over China* (revd edn) (New York: Grove).

Snow, Edgar (1972) *The Long Revolution* (New York: Random House).

Spence, Jonathan D. (1983) *The Gate of Heavenly Peace: The Chinese and Their Revolution 1895–1980* (Harmondsworth: Penguin).

Spence, Jonathan D. (1996) *God's Chinese Son: The Taiping Heavenly Kingdom of Hong Xiuquan* (London: HarperCollins).

Spence, Jonathan D. (1999) *The Search for Modern China: A Documentary Collection*, 2nd edn (New York: W. W. Norton).

Spence, Jonathan D. (2002) *Mao Zedong: Penguin Lives Biographies* (Harmondsworth: Penguin).

Studwell, Joe (2002) *The China Dream: The Elusive Quest for the Last Great Untapped Market on the Earth* (London: Profile Books).

Taylor, Ian (2009) *China's New Role in Africa* (Boulder, CO: Lynne Rienner).

Taylor, Jay (2011) *The Generalissimo: Chiang Kai-shek and the Struggle for Modern China* (Cambridge, MA: Harvard University Press).

Thaxton, Ralph A., Jr. (2008) *Catastrophe and Contention in Rural China: Mao's Great Leap Forward Famine and the Origins of Righteous Resistance in Da Fo Village* (Cambridge: Cambridge University Press).

Tuttle, Gray and Kurtis R. Schaeffer (2013) *The Tibetan History Reader* (New York: Columbia University Press).

Tverberg, Gail (2012) OurFiniteWorld.com, http://ourfiniteworld.com/2012/09/17/the-close-tie-between-energy-consumption-employment-and-recession/; accessed 29 January 2015.

Ven, Hans van de (1991) *From Friend to Comrade* (Berkeley, CA: University of California Press).

Vogel, Ezra F. (2011) *Deng Xiaoping and the Transformation of China* (Cambridge, MA: Harvard University Press).

Wagner, Daniel (2010) 'The Enigma of China's Middle Class', China.org.cn, 25 December. Available at: http://china.org.cn/opinion/2010-12/25/content_21611938.htm; accessed 10 July 2012.

Wang, Changjiang, Zhou Tianyong,Wang Anling (eds) (2007), *Gong Jian, Zhongguo Zhengzhi Tizhi Gaige Yanjiu Bao Gao, Shi Qi Da Hou*, (Storm the Fortress: A report on the Reform of China's Political System after the 17th Party Congress), (Xinjiang: Xinjiang Production Corps Publication House).

Wang, Hui (2011) *The End of the Revolution: China and the Limits of Modernity* (London: Verso).

Wang, Xiaofang (2012) *The Civil Servant's Notebook* (New York: Viking).

Watts, Jonathan (2011) *When a Billion Chinese Jump: Voices from the Frontline of Climate Change* (London: Faber & Faber).

Weatherley, Robert (2010) *Mao's Forgotten Successor: The Political Career of Hua Guofeng* (Basingstoke: Palgrave Macmillan).

Wei, Jingsheng (1998) *The Courage to Stand Alone: Letters from Prison and Other Writings* (Harmondsworth: Penguin).

Westad, Odd Arne (2012) *Restless Empire: China and the World Since 1750* (London: Bodley Head).

Wolin, Richard (2010) *The Wind from The East: French Intellectuals, The Cultural Revolution and the Legacy of the 1960s* (Princeton, NJ: Princeton University Press).

World Bank (2010) Gross Domestic Product 2010. Available at: http://siteresources.worldbank.org/DATASTATISTICS/Resources/GDP.pdf; accessed 5 August 2012.

World Bank (2012) *China 2030: Building a Modern, Harmonious and Creative High Income Society* (Washington/Beijing: The World Bank/Development and Research Council of the State Council, PRC).

World Bank (2015) *World Development Indicators* (GDP, current US$). Available at: http://data.worldbank.org/indicator/NY.GDP.MKTP.CD; accessed February 2015.

Wright, Teresa (2010) *Accepting Authoritarianism: State–Society Relations in China's Reform Era* (Palo Alto, CA: Stanford University Press).

Xie, Chuntao (2011) *How and Why the CCP Works in China* (Beijing: New World Press).

Xinhua, 'China to be World's Biggest Importer Soon', 18 March 2012. Available at: http://news.xinhuanet.com/english/business/2012-03/18/c_131474352.htm; accessed 5 August 2012.

Xun, Lu (2009) *The Real Story of Ah Q and Other Tales of China: The Complete Fiction of Lu Xun,* trans. Julia Lovell (Harmondsworth: Penguin).

Yan, Xuetong (2011) *Ancient Chinese Thought, Modern Chinese Power* (Princeton, NJ: Princeton University Press).

Yang, Chen (2012) 'Number of China's Billionaires Shrinks', *Global Times*, 9 March. Available at: http://www.globaltimes.cn/NEWS/tabid/99/ID/699335/Number-of-Chinas-billionaires-shrinks.aspx; accessed 30 July 2012.

Yang, Guobin (2009) *The Power of the Internet in China: Citizen Activism Online* (New York: Columbia University Press).

Yang, Jisheng (2012) *Tombstone* (Harmondsworth: Penguin).

Yeh, Amy (2012) *Taming Tibet* (New York: Cornell University Press).

Yu, Hua (2011) *China in Ten Words* (New York: Pantheon Books).

Yu, Jianrong (2010) 'Maintaining a Baseline of Social Stability' (Speech, 26 December 2009, Beijing Ministry of Finance Assembly Hall), *China Digital Times*, 20 February 2010. Available at: http://chinadigitaltimes.net/2010/03/yu-jianrong-maintaining-a-baseline-of-social-stability-part-i; accessed 5 August 2012.

Yu, Keping (2009) *Democracy is a Good Thing* (Washington, DC: Brookings Institution Press).

Zha, Jianying (2011) *Tide Players: The Movers and Shakers of a Rising China* (New York: The New Press).

Zhao, Ziyang (2010) *Prisoner of the State: The Secret Journal of Chinese Premier Zhao Ziyang*, ed. and trans. Bao Pu, Renee Chiang and Adi Ignatius (London/New York: Simon & Schuster).

Zheng, Yongnian (2010) *The Chinese Communist Party as Organizational Emperor: Culture, Reproduction and Transformation* (London: Routledge).

Index